REPORT FORM

FOR PRE-PURCHASE
HOME AND BUILDING
INSPECTIONS

Sweet Rain Press Regional Office: Los Angeles, California

Library of Congress Catalog Card Number: 2013922353

ISBN-13: 978-0615929958
Printed in the United States of America
Published by Sweet Rain Press
Los Angeles, California

DISCLAIMER: This book is not a substitute for a thorough home inspection or a professional consultation by a licensed engineer or architect, or by a qualified home inspection consultant. It merely furnishes homebuyers with insight and helpful information as to what such mentioned professionals look for while they conduct pre-purchase home and building inspections.

Terms and Conditions of Use:

Note that because building code requirements and construction details vary from locality to locality, and from year to year, this collection is intended to highlight a limited amount of information as a general guide book only. While some material presented herein might be appropriate for certain situations, nonetheless, it is recommended that readers consult with their local building department officials, architects, or engineers upon seeking specific advice concerning building inspection matters or other home construction matters for their particular needs. Indeed, some information may become outdated with changes and practice and conflict with specific code regulations in your area. Lastly, remember, home inspection work is inherently dangerous and can cause permanent injury or even death. Do not attempt to perform inspection work duties which are not safe and which you are not qualified to do. Both the author and the publisher are not responsible for any loss, or risk, personal harm, injury, damage or otherwise either directly or indirectly resulting from or arising out of the information, contents and use of this book.

REPORT FORM
FOR PRE-PURCHASE
HOME AND BUILDING
INSPECTIONS

Jeffrey I. Charloff, P.E., F.ASCE
Consulting Engineer

This book is dedicated to my family.

Sweet Rain Press
Los Angeles

Preface

This book was written to educate a home or building buyer about the process of assessing the condition of a property before purchase. It is a book containing a tutorial form as well as a stand-alone form for home inspection professionals to conduct thorough building inspections. Homebuyers will learn from this text what professionals look for while they conduct their inspections. The information in it will aid people to prepare themselves with a useful knowledge base so that home and building buyers can be proactive and well-informed to find the right home or building suitable for their lifestyle and needs.

From my collection of experiences in performing pre-purchase home and building inspections, I recommend this book to engineers, architects, homebuyers, homeowners, real estate personnel, builders as well as to attorneys as an aid to determine the physical condition of a home and building. The book includes commonly encountered problems of plumbing, electrical, roofing, heating, foundation and structure when conducting a home or building inspection. I have additionally presented building code and safety items herein as well. Realize that some of these problems have resulted from either poor or negligent workmanship. Indeed, the lack of good construction practice involves errors, omissions or even using inadequate or defective materials. Some other issues which I have encountered stemmed from mere aging. Many of these scenarios could have been avoided if only they were spotted early on enough before they had caused damage or, if only home and building owners had just known how to identify certain conditions which later turned into serious conundrums.

Note that because building code requirements and construction details vary from locality to locality, and from year to year, this collection is intended to highlight a limited amount of information as a general guide form book only. Although some material discussed herein may be appropriate for certain situations, nonetheless, it is recommended that readers consult with their local building department officials, architects or engineers upon seeking specific advice about building inspection or home construction matters for their particular needs.

Jeffrey I. Charloff, P.E.

Los Angeles, California

January, 2014

Contents

Introduction

Performing thorough pre-purchase home and building inspections allows one to learn about problems and conditions that a home or building has had, presently has, and problems and conditions the building may have in the future. In Report Form for Pre-Purchase Home and Building Inspections, it is my aim to simplify this journey of discovery for you by outlining the essential information which needs gathering. From *Starter Information* to *Part I's Advisory Concepts*, then on to *Part II Highlights* (which is loaded with common building problems), to building *Systems* all help enable the reader to be comprehensive in the assessment rating of a particular home or building. I have included numerous illustrations and tutorials for assisting the reader to recognize what is needed to look for as an apprised real estate buyer. As such, most of this book is a tutorial inspection report form. It is the last portion of the book, *Part III*, where the stand-alone *Report Form* is found.

In the beginning of each of my inspections, I take a cursory look at the exterior of the building premises first, and the interior second. That way, I get an idea of the magnitude and nature of the building inspection project. What's more is that I often meet with sellers and ask them questions regarding the history and various aspects of their property (which is especially helpful in completing *Part I* of this form). The rest of the inspection procedure calls for my inspection of the exterior of the building, the roof, and addressing items to be completed for the *Building Envelope*. I then proceed to conduct my inspection to the interior of the premise - starting from the underfloor location, while working my way up to the attic space. Of course, at that time, that is when I detail *Levels*.

No matter where I am located on the premise I utilize the form to address *Part II's* discovery problems. It's possible that there are problems which will be encountered that are not included in *Highlights*. And that's the reason why I have hereby included several pages for the reader's own particular discoveries other than the commonly found problems listed in this book. Be sure to complete the 'key elements' or *Systems* of the building and the page on *Items in Working Order*, too.

Report Form for Pre-Purchase Home and Building Inspections compliments my other book, Practical Guide to Home Inspection, well. You will find that these two books will definitely assist you in the decision-making process of purchasing a home or a building.

Fill in the following. Realize, of course, that you may need to interchange the word 'building' for either 'home' or 'house' in this book.

Date(s) of Inspection _____

Street Address of Property _____

Town or City _____

Purchaser(s) _____

Age of Home or Building _____

Style of Home or Building _____

Building shall be considered to be **located** (on) (off) (a corner lot)

    Side of Street □ northerly □ southerly □ easterly □ westerly

Lot Size _____ front feet by _____ feet or _____ acre(s) in size

    Shape of Lot □ regular or rectangular □ irregular □ pie-shaped

(concrete) (_____) **sidewalk**:
- ☐ partially uprooted
- ☐ cracked
- ☐ lacks the use of expansion joints
- ☐ poorly pitched
- ☐ in good condition
- ☐ _____

(concrete) (_____) **street curb**:
- ☐ juts outwardly
- ☐ cracked
- ☐ curves
- ☐ tall
- ☐ in good condition
- ☐ _____

(blacktop) (concrete) (concrete paver) (brick) **driveway**:
- ☐ poorly pitched
- ☐ cracked
- ☐ narrow
- ☐ in good condition
- ☐ _____

(attached) (detached) ____ **-car garage**:
- ☐ fundamentally sound
- ☐ okay, except as noted
- ☐ in good condition
- ☐ _____

(brick) (wood) (stone) (wrought iron) (_____) **mailbox post**:
- ☐ leans
- ☐ in good condition
- ☐ _____

wooden (_____) **decorative shutters**:
- ☐ old
- ☐ worn
- ☐ need painting
- ☐ in good condition
- ☐ _____

(concrete) (brick) (_____) **pathway** to (front) (main) (stoop) (porch):
- ☐ worn
- ☐ cracked
- ☐ in good condition
- ☐ _____

(front) (main) (concrete) (_____) **stoop**:
- ☐ poorly pitched
- ☐ need painting
- ☐ in good condition
- ☐ _____

(front) (main) (concrete) (_____) **porch**:
- ☐ poorly pitched
- ☐ need painting
- ☐ in good condition
- ☐ _____

(wooden) (_____) **raised back porch**:
- ☐ worn
- ☐ needs painting
- ☐ in good condition
- ☐ _____

(concrete) (brick) (wooden) (_____) **steps**:
- ☐ worn
- ☐ poorly pitched
- ☐ cracked
- ☐ in good condition
- ☐ _____

(wooden) (_____) **stairs**:
- ☐ needs reinforcement
- ☐ worn
- ☐ cracked
- ☐ in good condition
- ☐ _____

(concrete) (brick) (_____) **patio**:
- ☐ poorly pitched
- ☐ cracked
- ☐ in good condition
- ☐ _____

(wooden) (_____) **patio cover**:
- ☐ leans
- ☐ worn
- ☐ needs painting
- ☐ in good condition
- ☐ _____

(above-ground) (in-ground) **swimming pool**:
- □ no visible problems detected from the outside
- □ no evidence of significant differential settlement observed
- □ in good condition
- □ _____

spa: _____

(concrete) (brick) (_____) **decking surrounding pool**: _____

(concrete) (brick) (_____) **decking surrounding spa**: _____

additionally, the

_____

_____

_____

_____

_____

_____

_____

_____

_____

_____

_____

outdoor grading:

- ☐ allows water to pond next to (N) (S) (E) (W) side of the structure
- ☐ acceptable
- ☐ _____

landscaping:

- ☐ sparse
- ☐ mixes with other neighborhood landscaping
- ☐ _____

underfloor areaway wells:

- ☐ short
- ☐ normal
- ☐ _____

screened wall vent openings at underfloor area:

- ☐ missing
- ☐ torn
- ☐ missing
- ☐ are in good condition
- ☐ _____

hose bibbs:

- ☐ _____ didn't work
- ☐ _____ were counted
- ☐ _____

outdoor electrical outlets:

- ☐ none
- ☐ _____ were counted
- ☐ _____ is / are not of the ground fault interrupter variety
- ☐ are in good condition
- ☐ _____

caulking/sealing work:

- ☐ for example, around window and door frames, between the interfaces of the siding/trim, where needed, including sealing off any exterior areas of the house or building open to the elements should be routinely attended to
- ☐ in satisfactory condition
- ☐ _____

wood trim:

☐ weathered
☐ distressed in areas
☐ requires painting work
☐ does not need immediate painting
☐ is in generally good condition
☐ _____

(brick) (stucco) (stone) (wood) (_____) **exterior siding**:

☐ worn
☐ cracked in areas
☐ brick needs pointing work
☐ is in generally good condition
☐ _____

Note: there could be the possibility of damprotted wood inside building walls which does not display outward evidence of any structural damage. Until the development of such a sign, or if the walls are probed or removed, dryrot will remain undetected (should dryrot, in fact, exist).

broken or cracked windowpanes:

☐ (1) (2) (__) window panes were detected broken
☐ (1) (2) (__) window panes were detected cracked
☐ none were detected

window screens:

☐ not present
☐ _____ missing
☐ those that were present appear to be in _____ condition

rain gutters and downspouts (gutters and leaders):

☐ the building lacks their use
☐ old, could soon stand replacement
☐ holes were detected in the _____
☐ no holes detected
☐ in good condition
☐ _____

(asphaltic shingle) (_____ tile) (wood shingle) (wood shake)
(built-up gravel membrane) (mineral roll) (_____) **roof**:

☐ old, could soon stand replacement
☐ leaks at _____
☐ no evidence of leakage noted
☐ in generally good condition
☐ _____

roof flashing:

- ☐ in poor condition
- ☐ some flashing was lifted and is in need of attention
- ☐ was partly patched
- ☐ in good condition
- ☐ _____

observed metal flues above roof line:

- ☐ generally old and rusted
- ☐ aging
- ☐ in good condition
- ☐ _____

(brick) (stuccoed-over) (_____) **chimney**:

- ☐ leans
- ☐ separated from building
- ☐ fundamentally sound
- ☐ _____

Note: realize that the stack may not be safe during some periods of seismic activity.

attic ventilation:

- ☐ attic ventilation is absent
- ☐ attic ventilation is restricted
- ☐ acceptable

strange odors:

- ☐ an odor was detected in the _____
- ☐ no odors detected

ventilation of garage:

- ☐ low vents are absent
- ☐ the garage's low vent(s) were closed
- ☐ the garage's low vent(s) were blocked
- ☐ acceptable

(concrete) (blacktop) **garage floor**:

- ☐ incorrectly pitched
- ☐ poorly pitched
- ☐ is badly cracked and poses tripping hazards
- ☐ is cracked, but is functional
- ☐ minor cracking was noted
- ☐ is in good condition

Here is a place to detail the building level(s):

SLAB-ON-GRADE (or slab-on-ground) **HOUSE**:
- ☐ has only one level
- ☐ has two principal levels
- ☐ contains three principal levels
- ☐ _____

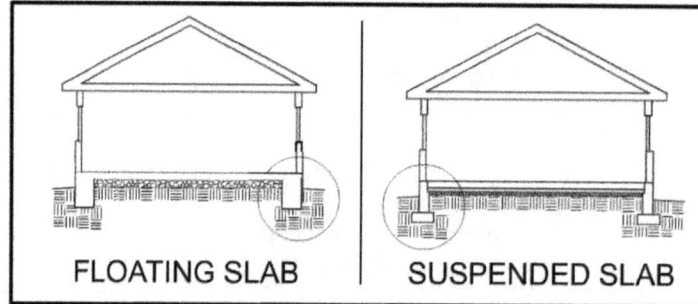

FLOATING SLAB   SUSPENDED SLAB

RAISED FOUNDATION HOUSE:
- ☐ has only two principal levels
- ☐ has three principal levels
- ☐ _____

There are three types of low levels defined in this form. These are as follows:

1. The CRAWL SPACE level consists of (one) (two) or (__) **crawl space(s). It runs beneath**:
- ☐ the entire building.
- ☐ the majority of the building.
- ☐ a large portion of the building.
- ☐ a portion of the building.

The crawl space is accessible:
- ☐ through (_____) hatch opening(s) on the (N) (S) (E) (W) side(s) of the building.
- ☐ through (_____) hatch opening(s) in the (N) (S) (E) (W) foundation wall(s).

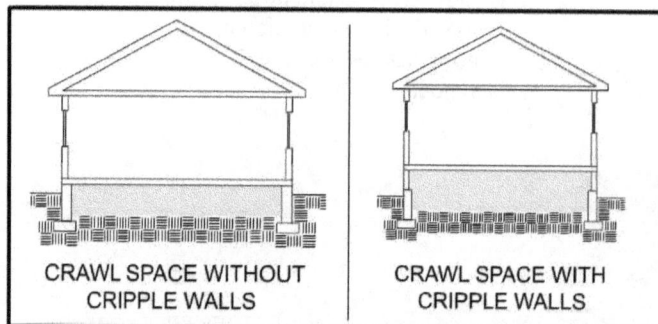

CRAWL SPACE WITHOUT CRIPPLE WALLS   CRAWL SPACE WITH CRIPPLE WALLS

2. The BASEMENT [and CRAWL SPACE] level.
      The basement is located:
            □ off the _____ .
            □ through a hatch in the _____ floor.
      [Access to the crawl space can be obtained:
            □ through _____ hatch opening(s) in the (N) (S) (E) (W)
              foundational wall(s).]
            □ from off the basement location.]

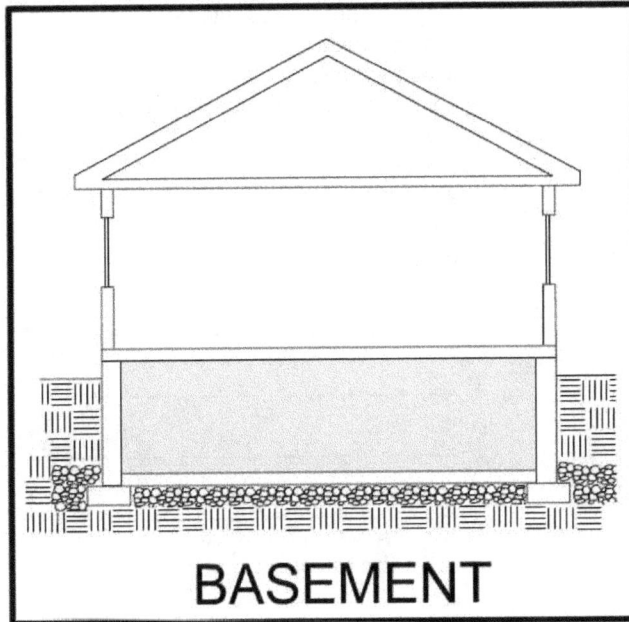

BASEMENT

3. The LOWER level which has been partitioned into:
            □ a _____ ,
            □ a _____ ,
            □ _____ ,
            □ _____ ,
            □ and the crawl space. The crawl space is accessible:
              □ through (____) hatch opening(s) on the (N) (S) (E) (W)
                side(s) of the building.
              □ through (____) hatch opening(s) in the (N) (S) (E) (W)
                foundation wall(s).

On this level are located

- ☐ the _____ furnace(s),
- ☐ the _____ boiler(s),
- ☐ the gas main,
- ☐ the water main,
- ☐ the circuit breaker panel(s),
- ☐ the fuse box(es),
- ☐ the electric meter(s),
- ☐ the main plumbing lines and drain lines,
- ☐ _____ hot water heater(s),
- ☐ a water pump,
- ☐ a sump pump,
- ☐ a washing machine and a clothes dryer,
- ☐ the slop sink,
- ☐ a refrigerator,
- ☐ a freezer,
- ☐ a bathroom sink,
- ☐ toilet,
- ☐ stall shower,
- ☐ _____,

- ☐ _____,

- ☐ _____,

- ☐ _____,

- ☐ and a fire safety detector.

Realize that

- ☐ the water meter,
- ☐ the electric meter and circuit breaker panel,
- ☐ the electric meter and fuse box,
- ☐ the electric meter and electrical service panel,
- ☐ and the gas meter

are situated outside the house [as well as (is) (are)
- ☐ the (covered) hot water heater and
- ☐ the _____ central air conditioning condenser unit(s)].

The MAIN FLOOR (or the AT-GRADE LEVEL) contains:

_____

_____

_____

_____

_____

_____

_____

_____.

The SECOND FLOOR (or the UPPER LEVEL) comprises:

_____

_____

_____

_____

_____

_____

_____.

[The THIRD FLOOR (or the UPPERMOST LEVEL) has been partitioned into:

_____

_____

_____

_____

_____

_____

_____.]

The ATTIC LEVEL (or the AIR PLENA LEVEL).

☐ **The (crawl) (standup) attic level was not accessible during our inspection.**

☐ **The (crawl) (standup) attic wasn't readily accessible during our inspection.**

☐ **Access to the (crawl) (stand-up) attic can be gained**
         ☐ through a hatch in the ceiling of the bedroom connecting hallway.
         ☐ through a hatch in the master bedroom closet ceiling.
         ☐ through a hatch in the _____ bedroom closet ceiling.
         ☐ via a pull-down ladder in the ceiling of the bedroom connecting hall.
         ☐ via a pull-down ladder in the ceiling of the _____.
         ☐ via a flight of steps leading from the (_____) floor connecting hall.
         ☐ via a flight of steps that are located in the _____.
         ☐_____.

It is (fully) (partially) (uninsulated) insulated:
         ☐ but has no catwalk or subfloor.
         ☐ and contains some planking across the ceiling joists.
         ☐ and contains a temporary catwalk.
         ☐ and contains a partial catwalk.
         ☐ and partially subfloored.
         ☐ (and) (but) fully subfloored.

PART I.

Advisory Concepts for

Homebuyers

Circle the pertaining item numbers which apply and check off or fill in the item accordingly.

1. Learn whether a **Certificate of Occupancy** (or **Final Approval**) exists for:
    - □ for the entire home as it is comprised at the present time;
    - □ for the building's present usage;
    - □ for the home or building following a significant fire;
    - □ for the home or building following an explosion;
    - □ for a revised interior layout;
    - □ for added rooms;
    - □ for extended room(s);
    - □ for a structurally remodeled (kitchen) (bathroom);
    - □ for an enclosed porch
    - □ for the new construction
    - □ for _____.

Form 123

DEPARTMENT OF BUILDINGS
CITY OF USA

No. **1554**
Date 5/14/74

CERTIFICATE OF OCCUPANCY

(Standard form adopted by the Board of Standards and Appeals and issued pursuant to Section 127 of the USA Charter, and Sections C.33-189.8 to C34-144.0 inclusive Administrative Code 3.4.3.8. to 8.9.3.1. Building Code.)

This certificate supersedes C. O. No.
To the owner or owners of the building or premises:
THIS CERTIFIES that the new-xxxxxxxxxxxx-building-premises located at
456 Hoover St., CITY OF USA

Block 1520   Lot 3

, conforms substantially to the approved plans and specifications, and to the requirements of the building code and all other laws and ordinances, and of the rules and regulations of the Board of Standards and Appeals, applicable to a building of its class and kind and at the time the permit was issued; and CERTIFIES FURTHER that, any provisions of Section 253 of the City of USA have been complied with.

> The document should be available for viewing at the local building department.

---

2. Check if **Grading Permits and Approvals** are in order for:
    - □ the (later) significant movement of soil material;
    - □ the (later) significant retaining work done;
    - □ the (later) drainage work done.

3. Learn whether **Building Permits and Approvals** exist for:
    - □ the building or the re-building of the (_____) chimney;
    - □ the building of a raised deck;
    - □ the construction of a patio cover;
    - □ the later roofing cover installation;
    - □ perhaps the later aperture work;
    - □ the swimming pool;
    - □ the spa;
    - □ and the newer structural/addition work done.

4. **Electrical Permits** should have been provided for:
   - ☐ the newer electrical wiring;
   - ☐ the 220 volt (electrical service) (circuit breaker) panel installation;
   - ☐ the 220 volt room air conditioner hookup(s);
   - ☐ the central air conditioning hookup;
   - ☐ the electric range hookup;
   - ☐ the 220 volt outlet provided for the electric dryer;
   - ☐ the hookup(s) of the _____ ;
   - ☐ as well as for (the) (some) newer construction.

5. **Plumbing Permits and Approvals** are required for:
   - ☐ the installation of the exterior underground lawn sprinkler system;
   - ☐ the installation of the (later) hot water heater(s);
   - ☐ the relocation of the new water heater;
   - ☐ the new water main;
   - ☐ the addition of copper piping;
   - ☐ the dishwasher hookup;
   - ☐ the hookup of the laundry equipment;
   - ☐ the later plumbing fixture work;
   - ☐ as well as for some later construction.

6. **Mechanical Permits and Approvals** are required for:
   - ☐ the installation of the new (furnace) (boiler);
   - ☐ the installation of the central air conditioning system;
   - ☐ the (later) climate ducting work done.

Remember, permits
need approvals.
Approved permits
should be on file
with the local
building department.

7. Check whether there are any unsettled **building violations** or **citations** against the property.

8. Check whether there are any unsettled **fire department violations** or **citations** against the property.

> If there are violations or citations against the property, be certain that they are removed or satisfied before Closing.

9. Learn from the **building department**:
   - □ whether there has been any known occurrence of neighborhood area flooding;
   - □ the flood levels of any nearby streams and waterways;
   - □ and if there is any known active landslides, falling rock zones or other pertinent geological conditions which exist in the neighborhood.

10. Call the local **fire department** to learn if there ever was a fire in this building.

11. **Fire evidence** was observed _____.

> The occurrence and evidence of a past fire can negatively affect the home or building's re-sale value.

> Should you notice evidence indicating the possibility of a fire, ask the fire department of its magnitude, its nature and if it affected the Certificate of Occupancy.

12. Determine the **exact property size** and the **boundary** locations.

> Realize that sometimes property lines don't follow perimeter fences. Perhaps a land survey was made for the property.

13. Learn of any **special zoning restrictions** in the event that future construction additions or changes be desired.

14. Ask the seller for a complete **approved set of plans** in addition to **building specifications**.

> Ask, too, for any possible later addition and remodeling plans.

15. Determine your **legal rights** and your **obligations** relative to the following conditions:

- ☐ any possible **utility company** or other (company) **easements** which might exist for the right of way along this site;
- ☐ **water drainage run-off** conditions with respect to prospective neighboring properties;
- ☐ **utility lines** which **cross** this site to service the (_____) neighboring house;
- ☐ the **community alley** that is located behind the site;
- ☐ the **tree branch** and **root growth** that cross neighboring sites;
- ☐ the **common driveway**, including learning who is responsible to clean, repair, or repave it;
- ☐ the **lack of** the existence of a **front sidewalk**;
- ☐ the presence of **utility pole(s)** being in the _____ ;
- ☐ the existence of **utility lines** which appear to **run** (a) (an) (N)(S)(E)(W) direction (partially) above the _____ most section of this site ;
- ☐ the possibility that the _____ **driveway entrance apron** partly encroaches the neighbor's property;
- ☐ **light encroachment(s)** from neighboring site(s);
- ☐ any **other** possible **encroachment(s)**;
- ☐ the **setback distance(s)** of the _____ with respect to the _____ property line;
- ☐ **other setback distances**;
- ☐ and _____ .

> It is recommended to seek advice from an attorney regarding this.

16. Ask who owns all the **perimeter fences (or walls)** in the event that maintenance is needed in the future:
    - ☐ (N) (S) (E) (W) _____
    - ☐ (N) (S) (E) (W) _____
    - ☐ (N) (S) (E) (W) _____
    - ☐ (N) (S) (E) (W) _____ .

17. Determine whether a **town's boundary line** crosses this property

18. **Survey** the **surrounding area** to learn whether the property is located within sound range **of** any outstanding **noises** such as from:
    - ☐ a schoolyard where children play
    - ☐ a major thoroughfare
    - ☐ a closeby railroad (which could produce vibrational effects from a passing train as well)
    - ☐ a mixed use street
    - ☐ _____

19. **Survey** the **surrounding area** to learn whether the property is located closeby an airport or below a flight pattern of low flying aircraft having disturbing sounds.

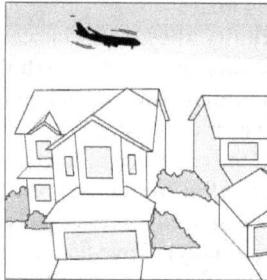

20. The **street lacks** adequate **lighting provision** which is not favorable by many from the standpoint of security.

21. Request the **termite control guarantee** for a posted sign exists in the
_____ indicating that a control job has been recently conducted.

Realize that possible
termite damage
inside wall sections
often doesn't get
corrected during
termite proofing or
fumigating the
building.

22. Obtain all **home service contracts** which the seller might have such as from
   □ a heating & air conditioning contractor
   □ appliance retailer(s)
   □ a pest control service
   □ a homeowner's warranty program

Learn whether the contracts are
transferable to you.

23. Examine the past **(gas) (oil) (electric) heating bills** because:
   □ the attic space is not insulated
   □ the attic has only minimal insulation
   □ in this old house the exterior walls have not been insulated
   □ the house doesn't utilize storm windows
   □ the house utilizes generally drafty old casement windows
   □ the house utilizes old drafty jalousie windows
   □ electric heat can be expensive

24. Recognize that this home uses **(aluminum) (steel) windows** which transmit
heat through them more than wood windows.

25. Ask for a list of all **window screens** which are being **stored** in the
_____ and have the owner provide you with a **directory**
indicating their placement locations on the house.

26. Find out where all **stored door(s)** being stored in the _____ come from.

Should they still serve a useful
purpose, you may want to have the
owner re-install them before Closing.

27. Realize that the house is in a **limited state of renovation**. Because problems with completing a renovation project are many, consider:
    - ☐ the use of on-site general contracting management supervision;
    - ☐ _____.

> "Ultimately, this should save you from getting "stressed out."

28. Ask the seller to **remove** all **debris and material** either being stored or observed to be lying about in such locations as:
    - ☐ outside the building
    - ☐ in the garage
    - ☐ in the attic

29. Have all **automatic garage door transmitters conveyed** to you.

30. Request that all **built-in blender or food center attachment(s)** be **conveyed** to you at the time of close.

31. Determine where the **closest fire hydrant** is located in relationship to this property for none was viewed in the immediate sight.

> Some localities provide reflective blue diamond-like markers in their streets as an aid to finding fire hydrants.

32. Realize that the **closest fire hydrant** observed is located _____.

33. Realize that all the **vegetative growth** on this premise should be **maintained cropped** as necessary to provide for a good margin of fire safety.

34. Recognize that there (is) (are) (one) (some) **tall tree(s)** nearby the house.

NOTICE THAT THIS NEARBY TREE ADVERSELY AFFECTS THE HOME'S FOUNDATION, EXTERIOR WALL AND SIDE PATHWAY.

> Check whether your homeowner's insurance policy would compensate you for losses due to nearby tall trees.

35. All **exterior drainage devices,** including the (leaders and gutters of the roof drainage system) (the _____ area drain) (the street curb drainage opening) (the concrete swale) (_____) should be **maintained free** of leaves, gravel, snow, ice, dirt and debris to prevent flooding or water backup action taking place at them.

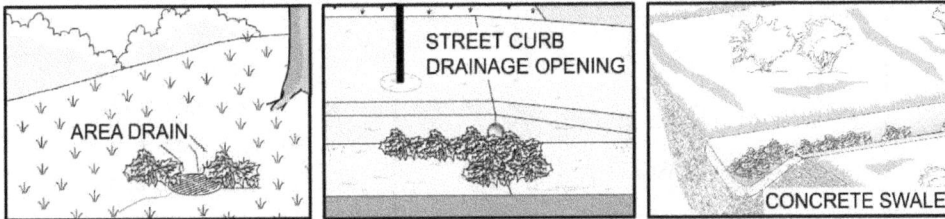

AREA DRAIN

STREET CURB DRAINAGE OPENING

CONCRETE SWALE

36. Recognize that this home's **driveway** is a (comparatively **steep**) (steep) and, as such, driving along it can be both difficult and dangerous.

37. Recognize that the **building uses exterior plaster cement** for (section[s] of) its siding which can be a maintenance headache.

EXTERIOR PLASTERER IS PATCHING STRESS CONCENTRATION CRACKS TYPICALLY FOUND AROUND WINDOWS AND DOORS.

Care must be exercised to patch and repair cracks and holes in stucco walls to help stop developed distress growth and to help obstruct the possibility of insect and moisture penetration into the building.

38. Request to **review** which **rooms** each **thermostat control activates** heating or air conditioning to.

39. Recognize that the _____ **room(s)** (is) (are) **unheated**. And recognize that this home's central **air conditioning** system **cools only** _____.

40. Realize that there is **no air conditioning** associated with this home.

41. Recognize that this home, having one central heating plant and which is activated and controlled by one thermostat, is considered to be a **'one-zone' heated home**.

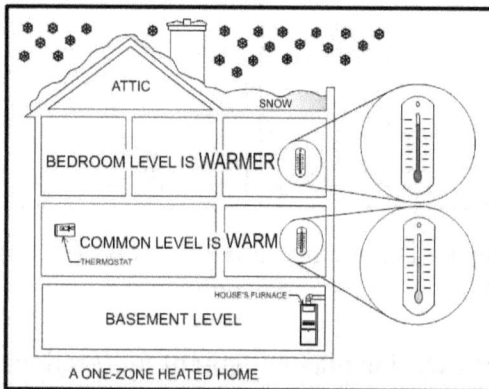

A ONE-ZONE HEATED HOME

Don't be surprised to learn that there's typically higher temperatures upstairs than downstairs in one-zone heated homes.

42. Recognize that the forced **hot-air ducts** in the _____ have been installed **close to** or at the **ceilings** which is an ineffective scheme for heat because hot air rises.

Hence, the floors in these rooms will tend to be somewhat cool. But the locations of the duct registers would be satisfactory for air conditioning.

43. Realize that the central **air conditioning duct registers** in the _____ have been installed at or **near the floors** which is not an efficient arrangement for cooling.

COOLING SUPPLY REGISTER

Simply, cold air does not tend to rise. On those hot summer days, cooler air is really needed near or at the ceilings.

44. Realize that the house utilizes
    - ☐ electrical resistance heat cables contained inside the ceilings
    - ☐ warmed water through copper tube coils buried in the concrete floor slab
    - ☐ warmed water circulating through tube coils which run in the ceilings

    for **radiant heat** as the source of heating system of this home.

Note that radiant heat is known to spread evenly throughout rooms without producing significant drafty convention currents, but the system heats slowly. What's more, should leakage develop from the heating pipes, the floor or ceilings must be generally opened to fix the leakage.

COPPER TUBE COILS WHICH ARE BURIED IN THIS HOME'S CONCRETE SLAB MAKE FOR A NICE AND WARM FLOOR.

45. Realize that the house utilizes an **electric heat pump** as the source of heating system of this home.

Electric heat pumps are more economical to operate where climates are warm and temperatures seldom go down very low.

46. Recognize that
    - ☐ every convenience electrical outlet
    - ☐ most electrical outlets
    - ☐ only some electrical outlets

    throughout the house don't have the third hole or **U-ground** that is normally found in today's **outlets** and, as such, should a 3-prong plug be used, one will need an adapter.

47. Recognize that there are **fewer electrical** convenience **outlets**
    - □ throughout the building
    - □ in some rooms of the building
    than are typically encountered in homes of today.

> As such, you will probably want to budget for the cost of more general purpose electrical outlets. Note that there is typically one outlet required for every 12 feet of long wall space. There are additional electrical code minimum requirements for spacing for different wall lengths.

48. Recognize that the building still (wholly) (partially) utilizes some old **knob and tube wiring**.

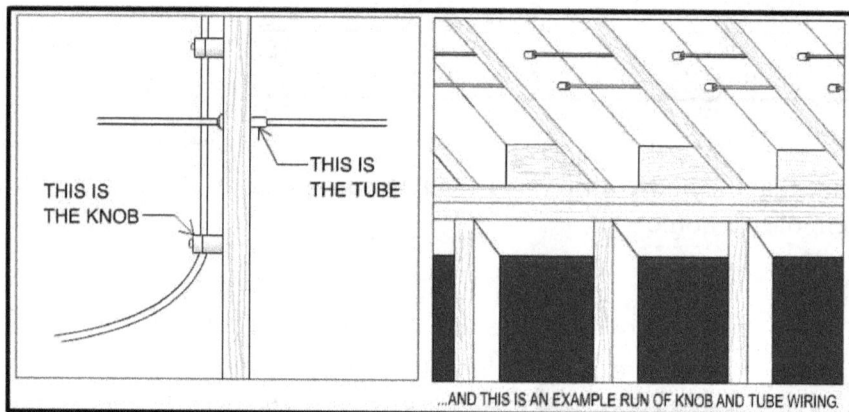

THIS IS THE TUBE

THIS IS THE KNOB

...AND THIS IS AN EXAMPLE RUN OF KNOB AND TUBE WIRING.

> The early system of house electrical wiring was comprised of two individual strands of wire that run parallel and closeby one another. It should be examined for brittle, torn or missing insulation along the cables, and for possible broken strands so as to prevent fire hazards from taking place or possible shock. Normally, one doesn't have to change out old, undamaged knob and tube wiring just because it exists.

49. Have the (balcony) (_____) **tested for its strength**, especially at its connections because you might have to budget for weak or adjustment connection repair.

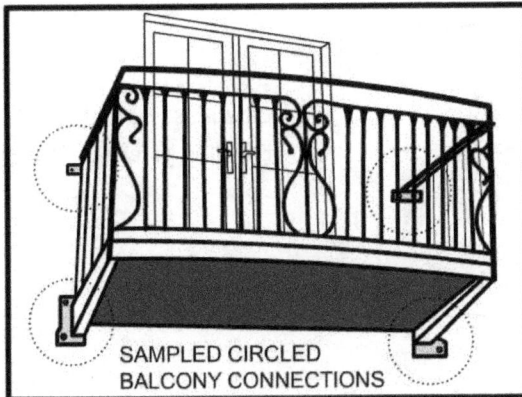

SAMPLED CIRCLED
BALCONY CONNECTIONS

Until this strength testing is attended to, no one should be permitted to use the _____ since structural fatigue or other supportive failure is possible.

50. Request that a viewing be made of the top of the chimney for **spark arrester** provision.

Spark arresters can be helpful especially when the roof is combustible - like a wooden shake or wooden shingle roof.

51. Recognize that the _____ **room(s)** (is) (are) exist **over** the **unheated garage**.

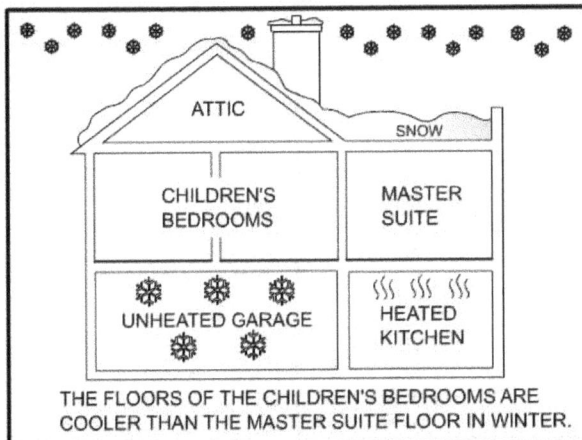

ATTIC

SNOW

CHILDREN'S
BEDROOMS

MASTER
SUITE

UNHEATED GARAGE

HEATED
KITCHEN

THE FLOORS OF THE CHILDREN'S BEDROOMS ARE
COOLER THAN THE MASTER SUITE FLOOR IN WINTER.

The floors in the rooms over the garage are oftentimes cooler than other floors which exist on the same level of the home. This is particularly noticeable in cold weather.

52. Recognize that there is **no direct access** to the
- □ basement
- □ garage

from the interior of the home.

> One must go outside the building to enter the _____.

53. Recognize that there is **little headroom clearance**
- □ at the foot of the steps that lead to the basement
- □ along the steps to the basement
- □ in the basement
- □ in the attic.

Watch your head when
- □ ascending this location.
- □ descending this location.
- □ traversing this location.

> YOU SHOULD ALERT YOUR GUESTS OF THIS.

54. Recognize that the **steps** which lead to the
- □ basement are built (**steep**) (**narrow**).
- □ attic are built (steep) (narrow).

Exercise care while ascending or descending them.

> YOU SHOULD ALERT YOUR GUESTS OF THIS.

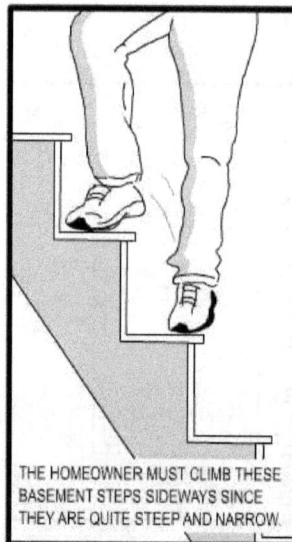

THE HOMEOWNER MUST CLIMB THESE BASEMENT STEPS SIDEWAYS SINCE THEY ARE QUITE STEEP AND NARROW.

55. Request verification of the fact that the house **is tied into** the **sewer lines**.
The _____ assured us that the house was indeed hooked up to sewers; but
> ☐ the drain line exited the back of the house.
> ☐ _____.

56. Recognize that we noted the **presence of a sump pump** in the basement. This might reflect that the home's underfloor location suffers from a chronic water penetration problem; but the pump could also have been provided to control occasional basement flooding.
> ☐ Even though it was working, one takes a risk of basement flooding should the electricity go out during stormy weather.
> ☐ The sump pump should be demonstrated to your satisfaction before closing to see that it works well

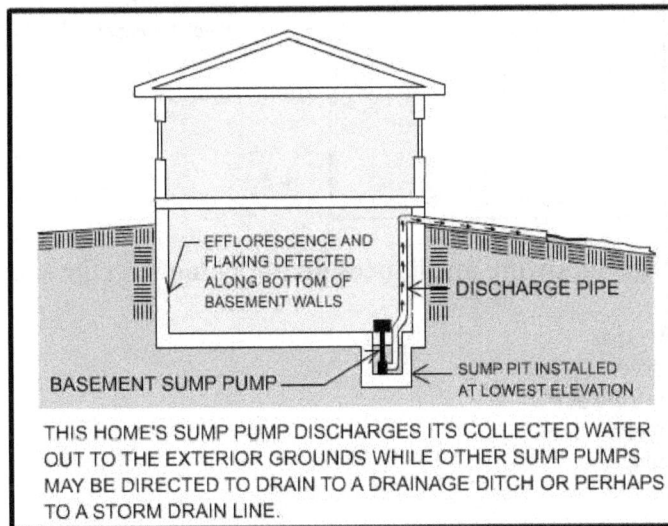

EFFLORESCENCE AND FLAKING DETECTED ALONG BOTTOM OF BASEMENT WALLS

DISCHARGE PIPE

BASEMENT SUMP PUMP

SUMP PIT INSTALLED AT LOWEST ELEVATION

THIS HOME'S SUMP PUMP DISCHARGES ITS COLLECTED WATER OUT TO THE EXTERIOR GROUNDS WHILE OTHER SUMP PUMPS MAY BE DIRECTED TO DRAIN TO A DRAINAGE DITCH OR PERHAPS TO A STORM DRAIN LINE.

57. Recognize that the **kitchen** has been **situated**
> ☐ at a higher elevation than the garage and the home's entry poses an added chore for shoppers to bring bags of grocery items up to the kitchen.
> ☐ at a lower elevation than the garage and the home's entry poses an added chore for shoppers to bring bags of grocery items down to the kitchen.

58. Recognize that
    - □ one of
    - □ some of
    - □ all of the

    appliances which stay(s) with the house (is) (are)
    - □ **old** appliance(s).
    - □ (a) comparatively old appliance(s).

REPLACEMENT PARTS ARE UNAVAILABLE FOR BOTH THE DISHWASHER AND THE REFRIGERATOR.

Frequently, appliance repairmen cannot get parts for old appliances and, consequently, they cannot be repaired because of this.

59. Understand that the following **appliances do not come** with the sale of the house:
    - □ the washer
    - □ the dryer
    - □ the refrigerator
    - □ the freezer
    - □ the range
    - □ the microwave oven
    - □ the room air conditioner
    - □ the barbeque
    - □ _____.

    The (owner) (real estate agent) informed us of this during our inspection. As such, these appliances were not (wholly) checked during our inspection.

60. We recommend that you **determine** exactly which **appliances, equipment and furnishings** are **part of** the seller's **property** and included along with the property sale. For example, do the
    - □ fireplace firescreen(s)
    - □ fireplace andirons
    - □ the exterior potted plants
    - □ _____

    remain with the house?

61. Recognize that the main level of the **building** has been **built on a concrete slab** and that it is normal to find some fine cracking in the slab.

> However, a structural engineer can advise you as to whether the slab distress is structurally significant or not. Note, too, that some plumbing piping may run below the floor slab's surface. Should leakage occur from this plumbing, repair might involve breaking up some areas of the floor slab.

62. Be sure that all **food center attachment(s)** (is) (are) surrendered to you at the time of closing since the replacement of such attachments are pricey.

63. Realize that the _____ **bedroom(s)** lack(s) window(s), but instead have been provided **with sliding glass door**(s). When fresh air is desired, the sliding glass door(s) must be opened.

> What's considered to be unfavorable about this by many from a standpoint of security is the use of sliding screen doors during evening and night hours.

64. Make sure to **keep** the **house burglar-safe**. Remember, an intruder could easily enter the house through the
    ☐ underfloor crawl space hatch opening.
    ☐ pet door opening.
    ☐ _____.

65. Realize that there is **no security alarm system** associated with this home.

66. Realize that there is **no intercom system** associated with this home.

67. Determine **if the fireplace is** designed and capable to be **used only as a gas-burning fireplace** or also, as a wood burning fireplace. We observed the presence of a gas main here, but suspectfully the fireplace is capable of being utilized for both.

68. Understand that the **water heater is an electric unit** which has a lower recovery rate than oil or gas-fired water tanks. As such, once the water in the tank has been used up, one will have to wait a considerable lengthy time for more hot water.

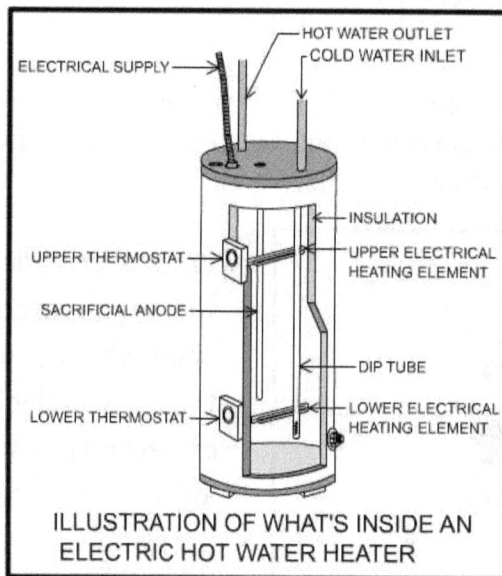

ELECTRICAL SUPPLY —

HOT WATER OUTLET
COLD WATER INLET

— INSULATION

UPPER THERMOSTAT —

— UPPER ELECTRICAL
HEATING ELEMENT

SACRIFICIAL ANODE —

— DIP TUBE

LOWER THERMOSTAT —

— LOWER ELECTRICAL
HEATING ELEMENT

ILLUSTRATION OF WHAT'S INSIDE AN
ELECTRIC HOT WATER HEATER

And that's the reason why when a replacement tank becomes necessary, it is so important to consider the proper tank size to suit your family's hot water needs.

69. Understand that the _____ has **no hookup** at the present time.

70. Understand that the _____ is **disconnected** at the present and, thus, inoperative.

71. Realize that the _____ is an **ineffective** one for the _____.

72. Understand that the _____ we were told is presently **no longer used**.

73. Recognize that the seller reported that the
    - □ dishwasher
    - □ freezer.
    - □ microwave oven
    - □ _____

    is **inoperative and** makes **no representations** regarding it. Consider getting
    a separate estimate of repair from a reputable appliance repairperson.

    > Should the estimate be more than you want to spend, consider
    > asking the seller to remove the _____ before closing so
    > as to avoid future hauling expenses on your part.

74. Request the **bill(s) of sale** for the following newer items:
    - □ _____
    - □ _____
    - □ _____
    - □ _____
    - □ _____
    - □ _____

    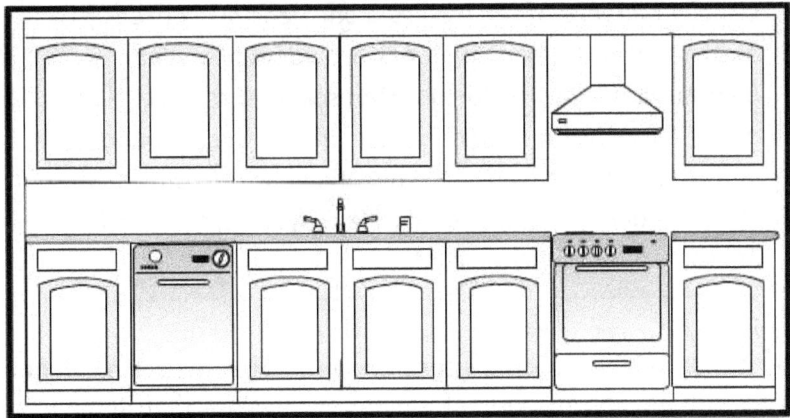

    > Perhaps the bills of sale would assist you should problems arise with those items.
    > Look at the purchase dates to see that the possible guarantees are still in effect
    > and check whether they can be transferred to you. Note that in the above illustration,
    > the seller replaced an old dishwasher and a stove just a few months back and knows that
    > the newer appliances are guaranteed for up to one year for both himself and
    > the purchaser of his home.

75. Learn whether the **security sign** placed in the
    - ☐ front yard
    - ☐ front window
    - ☐ _____

    indicates the presence of a working security alarm system or is just being used as a deterrent to discourage would-be intruders from illegally entering the house.

76. Realize that there is an **incinerator** in the _____ yard.

    > Incinerators are no longer permitted to be used in many communities.

77. Do not use the **heater** in the _____ since it is **unvented** and is no longer permitted.

78. *For buyers of new homes:*

    Request guarantees against defective **workmanship and defects** in materials on roofing, plumbing, electrical work, heating, ventilating and air conditioning work.

    > Usually builders offer buyers a one year guarantee on these items. Many builders provide a one year guarantee against building water seepage as well. You might note that a number of manufacturers of building materials provide longer than a one year guarantee on their products and so, for awhile, buyers are accordingly protected by these guarantees.

79. *For buyers of new homes:*

    Get the **names of** the material **suppliers and subcontracting firms** that were involved with the construction of the house. Ask for their telephone numbers, email addresses and their physical addresses as well.

    > Perhaps this information could prove to be helpful to you in the event that problems arise by dealing with the sub-contractors directly. In this way, you don't need to go through the builder.

80. *For buyers of new homes:*

    Ask the **builder to supply** you with the **manufacturers' guarantees for** the **appliances**, the appliance instruction manuals and any instructional videos which are associated with the appliances.

> In case the builder doesn't have them, demand that they be gotten from the suppliers or from the manufacturers directly.

81. *For buyers of new homes:*

    Request that the builder accordingly furnish you with **samples of** roofing cover **material**, tiling, some wood and masonry, wallpaper, paint, stain and carpeting.

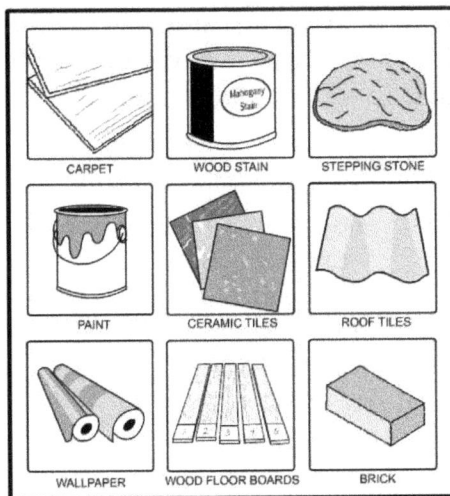

> These samples just might come in handy to you in the future.

82. *For buyers of new homes:*

Recognize that on account of an **agreed allowance** with the builder, the **purchaser provides** the following for this home:

☐ the installation of all finish flooring

☐ _____

☐ _____

We learned of this by the _____ during our inspection.

83. *For buyers of new homes:*

Recognize that we were told that the **builder does not provide** the following:

☐ a furnace humidifier;
☐ a mailbox;
☐ storms and window screens;
☐ perimeter fencing;
☐ a back patio;
☐ an underground lawn sprinkler system;
☐ a lawn, shrubbery and other landscaping;
☐ a washer and dryer;
☐ and _____.

> Some builders may consider these items to be 'optional' items. So know exactly what items are included along with the sale of your new home.

84. *For buyers of new homes:*

Request that the **builder** additionally **provide guarantees** (if any) in connection with the following:

☐ paint and cabinet touch-ups;

☐ _____.

85. *Limitations on your inspection:*

Ask the seller for permission to **move back area rugs and view** the **floors under the carpets**. Doing this will allow you to see the type of floors being covered over and to discover possible existing floor problems.

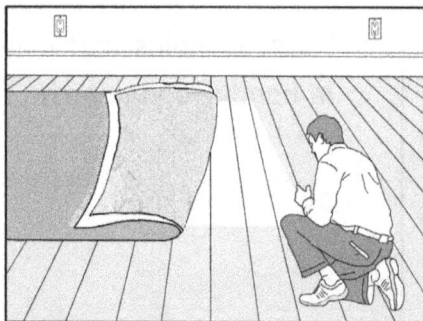

> In this example, the purchaser noticed the yellowing effect of the bleached wood finished floor beneath the area rug's base mat that he just lifted.

86. *Limitations on your inspection:*

Ask that the **security alarm system be** completely **demonstrated** to your satisfaction before closing (for the owner did not fully demonstrate the entire system to us). If need be, request that the seller or the security alarm company itself demonstrate the system to you.

> During the demonstration, determine which apertures and entrances are 'trapped' secure, which locations are 'shunted,' and learn if the fire safety detectors are part of the system.

87. *Limitations on your inspection:*

Since the electricity was off during our inspection, we could not determine general electrical problems and demonstrate

☐ the outlet and fixture performances;
☐ the air conditioning system(s);
☐ the automatic overhead garage door opener;
☐ the doorbell(s);
☐ the electric _____ heating system;
☐ the electric hot water heater;
☐ the _____ exhaust fan(s) of the _____;
☐ the furnace(s)/fan(s);
☐ the heat lamp(s);
☐ the intercom;
☐ the dishwasher (and other remaining appliances);
☐ the electric range oven;
☐ the range hood;
☐ the trash compactor;
☐ _____;

Moreover, request a demonstration of...; etc..

Lastly, request an examination of the following:

☐ the remainder of the garage (after the material removal);
☐ some venting/flue work out to the exterior including for the _____;
☐ the attic space(s) which (was) (were) inaccessible during our inspection. We usually look for evidence of past fires, evidence of roof leaks, any condensation damage, the structural integrity of the rest of the framing members, and any evidences of rodent and termite infestation;
☐ the remainder of the attic space(s). We usually look for evidence of past fires, evidence of roof leaks, any condensation damage, the structural integrity of the rest of the framing members, and any evidences of rodent and termite infestation;
☐ _____.

Unless all these items can be checked and demonstrated to your expectations before closing, we feel you take a big risk in this regard. This is why it is so important to have everything demonstrated and be satisfied that all is in working order.

88. *Limitations on your inspection:*

Since the gas was off during our inspection, we could not demonstrate
  ☐ the furnace(s) and heating (including the thermostat(s) for heating);
  ☐ the furnace's hot water heating capability;
  ☐ the gas-fired hot water heater;
  ☐ the _____ fireplace gas main(s)/loglighter(s);
  ☐ the gas cooktop/range and oven;
  ☐ the gas dryer;
  ☐ the barbeque;
  ☐ the heating capability of the (pool) / (spa heater);
  ☐ the heater in the _____;
  ☐ _____;
  ☐ and determine the hot water temperature(s) nor whether gas odors exist.

Moreover, request a demonstration of...; etc..

Lastly, request an examination of the following:

  ☐ the remainder of the garage (after the material removal);
  ☐ some venting/flue work out to the exterior including for the _____;
  ☐ the attic space(s) which (was) (were) inaccessible during our inspection. We usually look for evidence of past fires, evidence of roof leaks, any condensation damage, the structural integrity of the rest of the framing members, and any evidences of rodent and termite infestation;
  ☐ the remainder of the attic space(s). We usually look for evidence of past fires, evidence of roof leaks, any condensation damage, the structural integrity of the rest of the framing members, and any evidences of rodent and termite infestation;

  ☐ *see item 92 for continuation* _____;

  ☐ _____;

  ☐ _____;

  ☐ _____;

  ☐ _____;

  ☐ _____;

  ☐ _____;

  ☐ _____.

Unless all these items can be checked and demonstrated to your expectations before closing, we feel you take a big risk in this regard. This is why it is so important to have everything demonstrated and be satisfied that all is in working order.

89. *Limitations on your inspection:*

Since the gas and electricity were off during our inspection, we
   □ could not determine whether gas odors exist;
   □ determine the hot water temperature(s);
   □ demonstrate the furnace(s) and heating (including [the] [their] thermostat[s]);
   □ the gas-fired hot water heater;

   □ *see item 88 for continuation*;
   □ also, we could not demonstrate the outlet and fixture performances;

   □ *see item 87 for continuation*;
   □ nor determine (other) general electrical problems, etc...

Moreover, request a demonstration of...; etc..

Lastly, request an examination of the following:

   □ the remainder of the garage (after the material removal);
   □ some venting/flue work out to the exterior including for the _____;
   □ the attic space that was not accessible during our inspection. We usually look
      for evidence of past fires, evidence of roof leaks, any condensation
      damage, the structural integrity of the rest of the framing members, and
      any evidences of rodent and termite infestation;
   □ the remainder of the attic space. We usually look for evidence of past fires,
      evidence of roof leaks, any condensation damage, the structural integrity of
      the rest of the framing members, and any evidences of rodent and termite
      infestation;
   □ *see item 92 for continuation* _____;
   □ _____;
   □ _____;
   □ _____;
   □ _____;
   □ _____;
   □ _____;
   □ _____.

Unless all these items can be checked and demonstrated to your expectations
before closing, we feel you take a big risk in this regard. This is why it is so
important to have everything demonstrated and be satisfied that all is in
working order.

90. *Limitations on your inspection:*

> **Since there was no water to the house** during the inspection, we could not observe the water pressure, nor could we demonstrate the following:
> - ☐ the operation of the plumbing fixtures;
> - ☐ the hot water heating capability;
> - ☐ the dishwasher;
> - ☐ the washing machine;
> - ☐ the laundry drain;
> - ☐ the swimming pool equipment;
> - ☐ the underground lawn sprinkler system;
> - ☐ the well;
> - ☐ and the _____ .

Moreover, request a demonstration of...; etc..

Lastly, request an examination of the following:...

91. *Limitations **in time** on your inspection:*

> - ☐ Understand that **we were limited in our inspection**.
> - ☐ Recognize that we were granted little time in our inspection.
> - ☐ Recognize that we were granted little time in our inspection.
>
>   The (seller) (real estate agent) had to leave and requested that we 'wrap up' our inspection.

Request a demonstration of... *see item 92*; etc..

Moreover, request an examination of the following:
- ☐ the remainder of the garage (after the material removal);
- ☐ some venting/flue work out to the exterior including for the _____ ;
- ☐ the attic space that was not accessible during our inspection. We usually look for evidence of past fires, evidence of roof leaks, any condensation damage, the structural integrity of the rest of the framing members, and any evidences of rodent and termite infestation;
- ☐ the remainder of the attic space. We usually look for evidence of past fires, evidence of roof leaks, any condensation damage, the structural integrity of the rest of the framing members, and any evidences of rodent and termite infestation;
- ☐ *see item 92* _____ ;
- ☐ _____ .

Unless all these items can be checked and demonstrated to your expectations before closing, we feel you take a big risk in this regard. This is why it is so important to have everything demonstrated and be satisfied that all is in working order.

92. *Limitations on your inspection:*

Request a demonstration of:

- some windows (and door[s]) which were not sampled by us;
- the _____ furnace(s) and (its) (their) heating capability(ies), including the operation of (the) (their) thermostat[s])
  - since the gas pilot(s) (was) (were) off during our inspection;
  - since (it) (they) (was) (were) off for the summer;
  - _____ ;
- the balance of the (furnace's) (furnaces') heating capability(ies), including the balance of the operation of (its) (their) thermostat(s);
- the heating and cooling capabilities of the climate control unit(s), including the operation of their thermostat(s);
- the balance of the climate control (unit's) (units') heating and cooling capabilities, including the balance of the operation of (the) (their) thermostat(s);
- the balance of the operation of the radiant ceiling healing (in the _____) to reach (its) (their) ultimate temperature (for [it] [they] felt only slightly warm to the touch moments after the thermostat(s) [has] [have] been activated);
- the dishwasher;
- the other cycles of the dishwasher;
- the self-cleaning operation(s) of the oven(s) (since it takes longer for a self-cleaning 'pyrolytic' oven to clean itself than is the duration of a normal inspection);
- other central vacuum cleaning outlets;
- the _____ fireplace gas main;
  - because its line have been found capped;
  - because _____ ;
- the (fire safety detector[s]) (smoke detector[s]) of the _____ ;
- other intercom outlets;
- the overhead garage door(s) by the use of (its) (their) transmitter(s) (which were not available);
- the exterior area (drain's) (drains') water acceptance ability;
- the _____ gate to the _____ (because it was locked);
- the heating capability(ies) of the (swimming pool) (spa) heater (and their Ortega valve)
  - for (its) (their) gas pilot (was) (were) off (for the winter) (during our inspection);
  - for _____ ;
- the pool heater's water warming capability;
- the (balance of the) operation of the exterior underground lawn sprinkler system (and its [Rainbird] [_____] panel);
- all the timer(s);
- the performance of some electrical receptacles;
- and the lights of the _____ which didn't go on;
- etc..

Moreover, request an examination of the following:

- the remainder of the garage (after the material removal);
- some venting/flue work out to the exterior including for the _____;
- the attic space(s) which (was) (were) inaccessible during our inspection. We usually look for evidence of past fires, evidence of roof leaks, any condensation damage, the structural integrity of the rest of the framing members, and any evidences of rodent and termite infestation;
- the remainder of the attic space(s). We usually look for evidence of past fires, evidence of roof leaks, any condensation damage, the structural integrity of the rest of the framing members, and any evidences of rodent and termite infestation;
- the access for the water and waste connections of the _____ tub(s) (if [this access] [one] [they], in fact exist[s]);
- viewing the water and waste connections within the plumbing access(es) provided for the ____ bathtub(s) (since [the] [their] cover(s) were ____ shut);
- the underfloor crawl space;
- the balance of the crawl space
    - (although [part of] [the majority of] the crawl space had been viewed, some plumbing lines and drain lines, [ductwork] as well as some structural members prevented our complete access to view all areas);
    - (the access opening[s] [was] [were] [too] [quite] small for entrance);
- some rooms that were quickly walked through;
- locating the central air conditioning condensate line location(s);
- locating (the) (some) climate air return register(s);
- some roof and chimney areas;
- other (lengths) (areas) of the _____ exterior _____ wall(s) where (it was) (they were) largely covered by vegetative [over]growth [and other lengths (such as on the neighboring side(s))] ;
- the _____ (since one would have to go onto the neighboring property to examine it fully);
- some (hillside) property which had not been (walked) (climbed);
- locating any waste drainage cleanouts;
- the independent sewage disposal system including
    - verifying the reported septic tank size capacity(ies), whether a drainage field does actually exist as reported (instead of seepage pit[s]) and viewing within its cleanout or inspection opening. What would be helpful in this investigation would be to obtain the (possible) layout plans for this matter, the possible permit(s) and other (possible) prepared documentation, including the bill of sale for this work;
    - requesting verification of the reported fact that this system consists of _____ septic tank(s) which are connected to _____ (leach field[s]) (seepage pit[s]) in the _____ yard, viewing within (its) (their) cleanout or inspection opening(s), and determining the tank capacity size(s). What would be helpful in this investigation would be to obtain the (possible) layout plans for this matter, the possible permit(s) and other (possible) prepared documentation, including the bill of sale for this work;
    - determining what the system actually consists of: for example, is there more than one septic tank and is the septic tank connected to a leach field or to a seepage pit? The owner could not answer this question. Also, determine the tank capacity size(s) and (its) (their) location. If possible, view within (its) (their) cleanout or inspection opening(s). [Lastly], verify whether or not the house and (garage) (_____) utilize the same septic system.] What would be helpful in this investigation would be to obtain the (possible) layout plans for this matter, the possible permit(s) and other (possible) prepared documentation, including the bill of sale for this work;
    - _____ ;
- etc..

Unless all these items can be checked and demonstrated to your expectations before closing, we feel you take a big risk in this regard. This is why it is so important to have everything demonstrated and be satisfied that all is in working order.

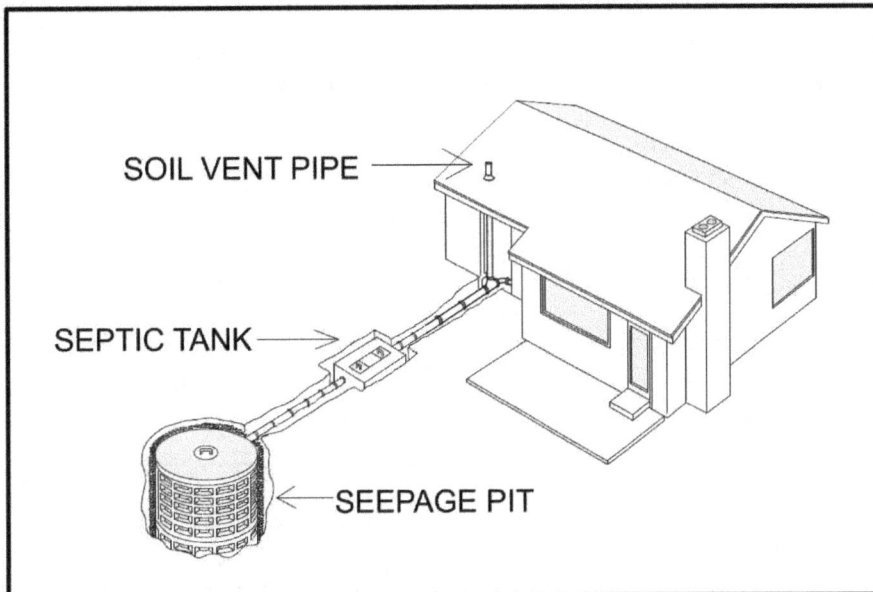

SOIL VENT PIPE

SEPTIC TANK

SEEPAGE PIT

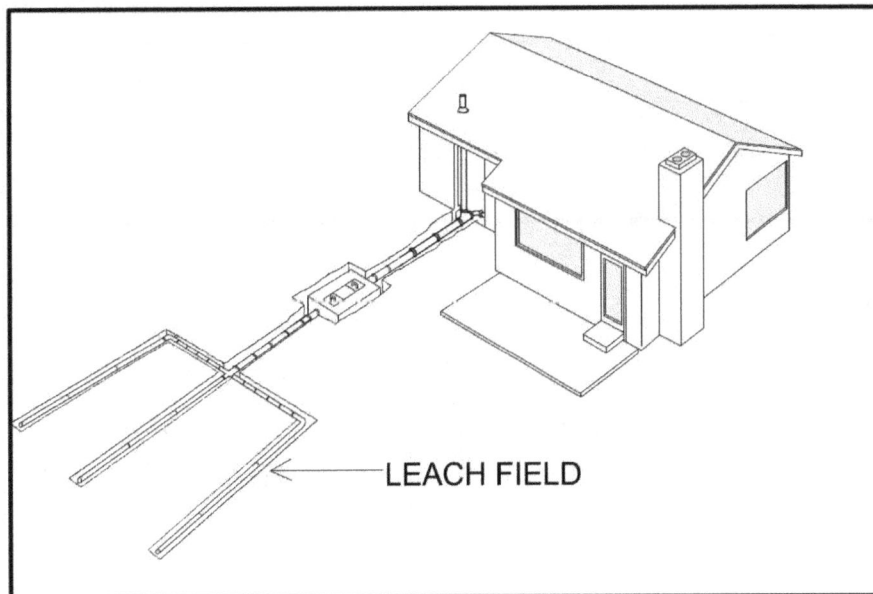

LEACH FIELD

Septic tank's minimum horizontal distance from building structure and from property line is 5 feet. The tank should also not be closer than five feet from either a seepage pit or from a leach disposal field.

93. *Limitations on your inspection:*

Because it snowed heavily, details of the roof, the sidewalk, the driveway and other exterior improvements could not be directly examined. When the snow melts, the following would have to be **carefully look**ed **at:**

☐ the roof;
☐ the grounds;
☐ the sidewalk;

☐ _____ :

☐ _____ :

☐ _____ :

☐ _____ :

☐ _____ :

☐ _____ :

☐ _____ :

☐ _____ :

☐ _____ :

☐ and other exterior improvements.

94. **Locate** the **utility meters**.

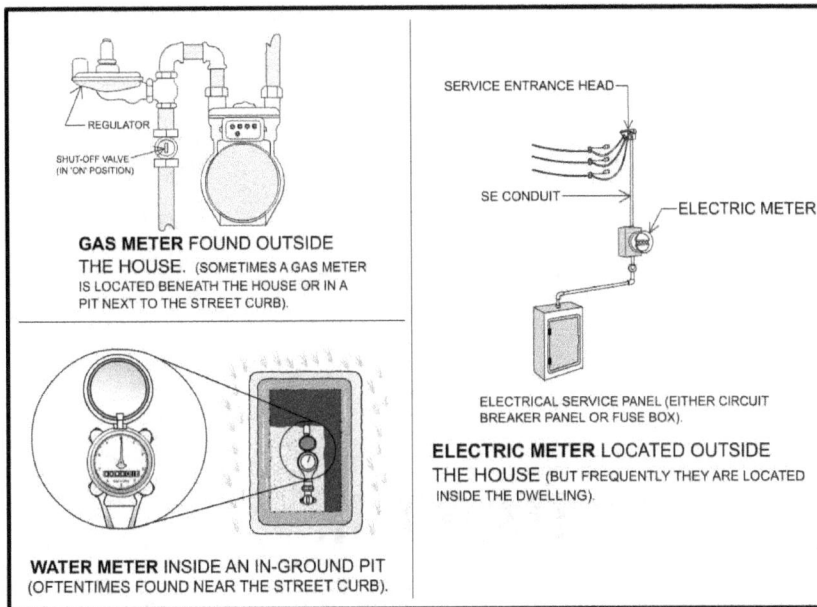

SERVICE ENTRANCE HEAD

REGULATOR

SHUT-OFF VALVE
(IN 'ON' POSITION)

SE CONDUIT

ELECTRIC METER

GAS METER FOUND OUTSIDE
THE HOUSE. (SOMETIMES A GAS METER
IS LOCATED BENEATH THE HOUSE OR IN A
PIT NEXT TO THE STREET CURB).

ELECTRICAL SERVICE PANEL (EITHER CIRCUIT
BREAKER PANEL OR FUSE BOX).

ELECTRIC METER LOCATED OUTSIDE
THE HOUSE (BUT FREQUENTLY THEY ARE LOCATED
INSIDE THE DWELLING).

WATER METER INSIDE AN IN-GROUND PIT
(OFTENTIMES FOUND NEAR THE STREET CURB).

> Learn how to identify your utility meters and
> then locate them.

95. Have the **well water checked**.

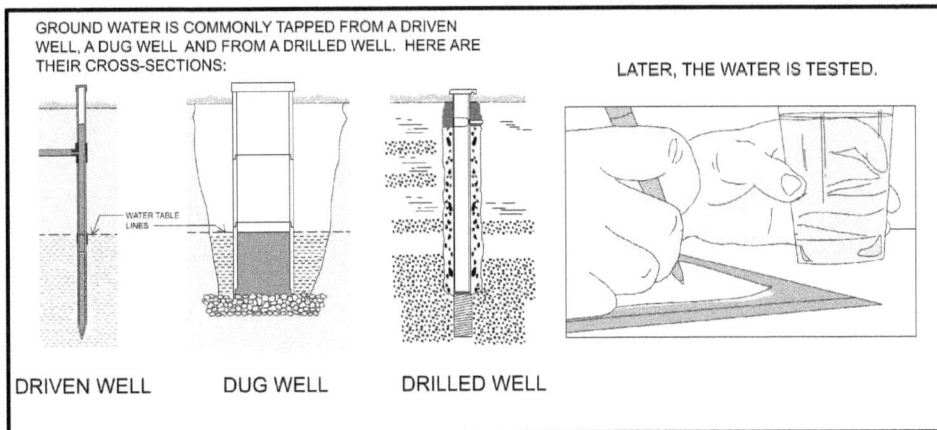

GROUND WATER IS COMMONLY TAPPED FROM A DRIVEN
WELL, A DUG WELL AND FROM A DRILLED WELL. HERE ARE
THEIR CROSS-SECTIONS:

LATER, THE WATER IS TESTED.

WATER TABLE
LINES

DRIVEN WELL   DUG WELL   DRILLED WELL

> Contact a qualified local water testing laboratory to
> determine whether the well water is potable. Ask that
> they check out the water's mineral and bacteria content.

PART II.

Highlights of Home Inspection

Check off and/or fill in the pertaining items which apply:

Air Conditioning

- □ **old** central **air conditioning compressor** unit(s)
    - □ approaching trouble-free life expectancy
    - □ at trouble-free life expectancy
    - □ beyond trouble-free life expectancy
- □ **old** central **air conditioning condensing** unit(s)
    - □ approaching trouble-free life expectancy
    - □ at trouble-free life expectancy
    - □ beyond trouble-free life expectancy
- □ **condensing unit**(s) **miss**(es) seismic **straps**
- □ **secure** condensing **unit**(s)
- □ **bottom of condensing unit** is **short of 3 inches** above gradework
- □ big house has **small** air conditioning **system**

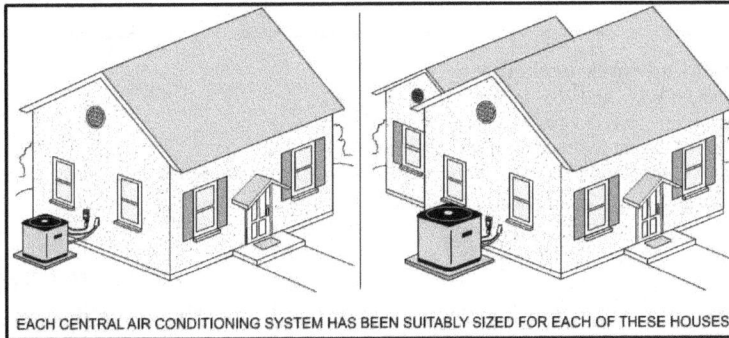

EACH CENTRAL AIR CONDITIONING SYSTEM HAS BEEN SUITABLY SIZED FOR EACH OF THESE HOUSES.

On some very hot summer days, the inside temperature does not remain low to the thermostatic setting. Meanwhile, the air conditioning system virtually runs continuously. It's then desirable to have more air conditioning tonnage.

Appliances

- □ realize **no garbage disposal** unit
- □ **no dishwasher hookup**
- □ **no gas dryer hookup**
- □ **no electric dryer hookup**
- □ **no dishwasher and gas dryer**
- □ **no dishwasher and electric dryer**
- □ _____ **bathroom exhaust fan** needs **reconnecting**
- □ _____ **bathroom exhaust fan** is **noisy**
- □ _____ is **inoperative**. Request a repair estimate.

Banisters and Railings

- □ **no railing** at _____ **steps**

When there are four or more risers along a stairway, handrails are needed. Handrails are also needed at step, stoop or porch landings which are greater than 30 inches above floor or grade.

- □ **no railing** on _____ **stoop**
- □ **resecure shaky** _____ **railing**

Bathroom

- ☐ **bathroom** could stand **modernization**
- ☐ **chipped** _____ **sink**
- ☐ cultured marble **sink counter was burned**
- ☐ **cracked** _____ **sink**

Carpentry

- ☐ **close off** partially **opened** _____ **wall**
- ☐ **door(s) stuck closed** at _____
- ☐ **window(s) stuck closed** at _____
- ☐ **no attic hatch cover**

Caulking

- ☐ **caulking/sealing work needed** at
  - ☐ around window and door frames
  - ☐ between the interfaces of the house's siding/fascia
  - ☐ between the house structure and the chimney
  - ☐ where needed, including sealing off exterior areas of the house open to the elements

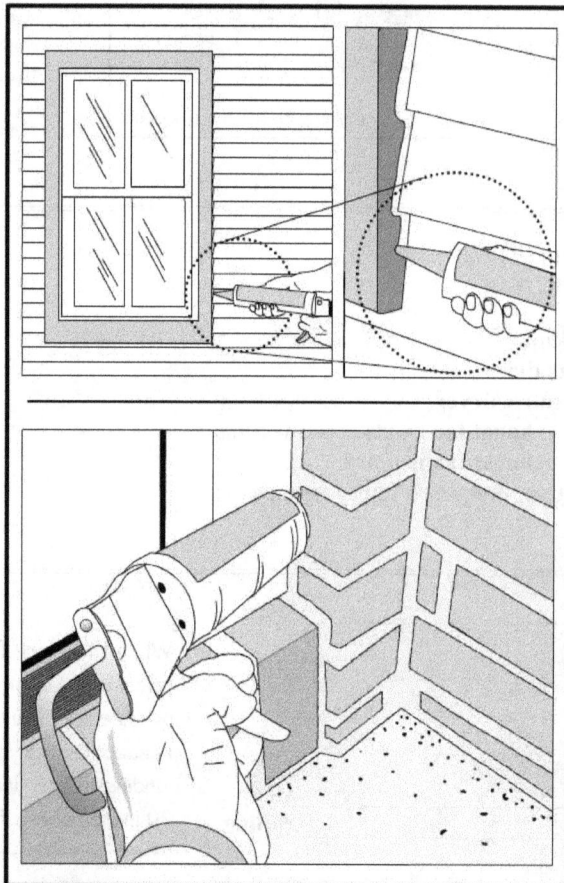

In order to arrest the development of air leakage, the homeowner is caulking between his home's window casing and the exterior wall.

This work is also being conducted around an exterior doorway.

Chimney and Fireplace

□ **check chimney**
- □ masonry **chimney** stack **leans** or is **bending**
- □ masonry **chimney** stack **walls** are built too **thin**
- □ **walls of** the **chimney** feel **hot**
- □ newer **chimney** on exterior wall is **not equipped with** an **air intake** opening
- □ **chimney lacks** an **ashpit** cleanout

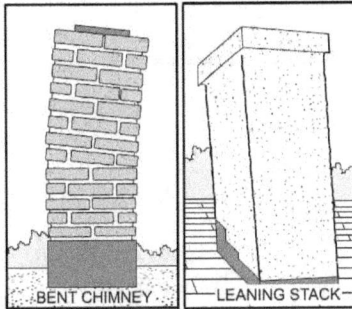

BENT CHIMNEY   LEANING STACK

If the bending chimney serves an oil-fired heating plant, the bending action could be caused by expansion of some masonry joints from fuel oil having a high sulfer content. Leaning stacks should be checked out by a chimney contractor before use. Hopefully chimney re-building costs don't turn out to be needed.

□ **chimney needs proper height**

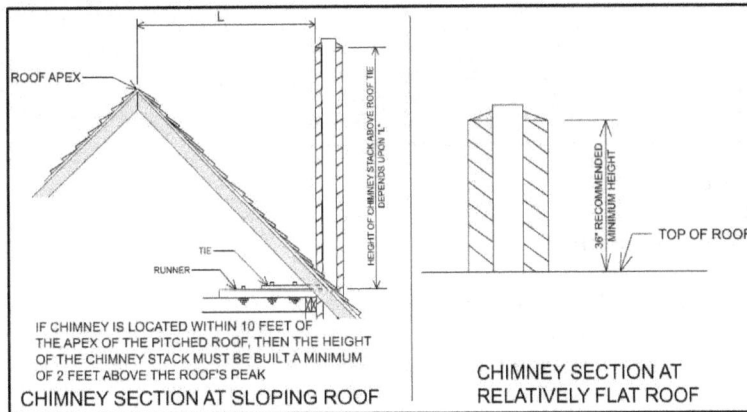

ROOF APEX

HEIGHT OF CHIMNEY STACK ABOVE ROOF TIE DEPENDS UPON 'L'

TIE

RUNNER

IF CHIMNEY IS LOCATED WITHIN 10 FEET OF THE APEX OF THE PITCHED ROOF, THEN THE HEIGHT OF THE CHIMNEY STACK MUST BE BUILT A MINIMUM OF 2 FEET ABOVE THE ROOF'S PEAK

CHIMNEY SECTION AT SLOPING ROOF

36" RECOMMENDED MINIMUM HEIGHT

TOP OF ROOF

CHIMNEY SECTION AT RELATIVELY FLAT ROOF

This helps to prevent fireplace smoking problems.

□ **add spark arrester**

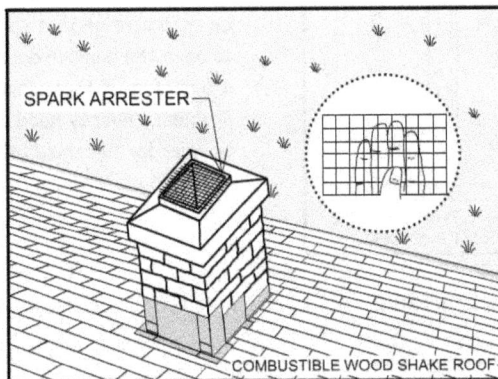

SPARK ARRESTER

COMBUSTIBLE WOOD SHAKE ROOF

A spark arrester is a screen cover usually made up of 12 guage wire mesh having openings not wider than 1/2 inch. They are especially important where there are combustable wood shake or shingle roofs.

☐ **relocate log lighter valve outside chamber**

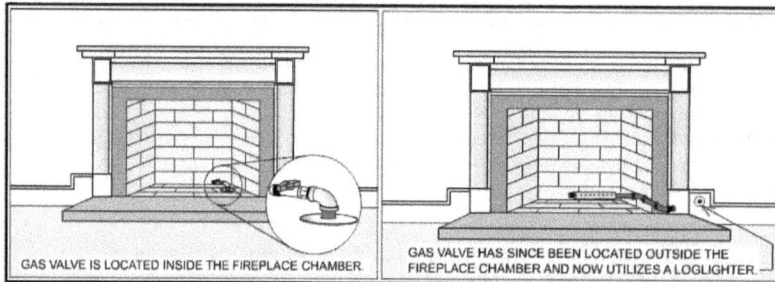

GAS VALVE IS LOCATED INSIDE THE FIREPLACE CHAMBER.

GAS VALVE HAS SINCE BEEN LOCATED OUTSIDE THE FIREPLACE CHAMBER AND NOW UTILIZES A LOGLIGHTER.

In many older homes, log lighter gas valves which have been provided to help ignite a fire have often been positioned inside the fireplace chamber. Once the fire starts, it would not be safe nor easy to shut off the gas with a flame being in the way.

☐ masonry **repair** is **needed to** _____ fireplace **chamber**
☐ **small outer** fireplace **hearth**

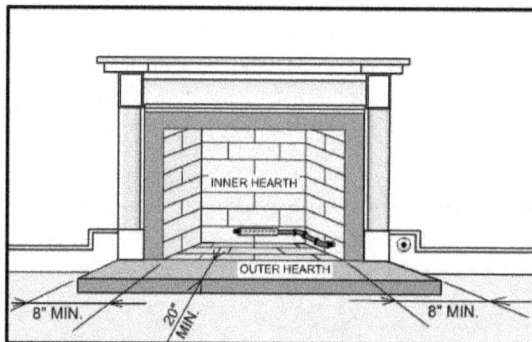

INNER HEARTH

OUTER HEARTH

8" MIN.   20" MIN.   8" MIN.

Because sparks can fly out of the fireplace, it's good to know that a safe fireplace has been built with a properly sized outer hearth.

☐ **outer hearth** is **cracked**
☐ **no damper door**
☐ **damper** door **needs adjustment**
☐ **clean** _____ **fireplace**
☐ **clean** _____ **fireplace** and **adjust damper**
☐ **equip fireplace with firescreening**
☐ **smoke stains** seen **over** the **fireplace opening**

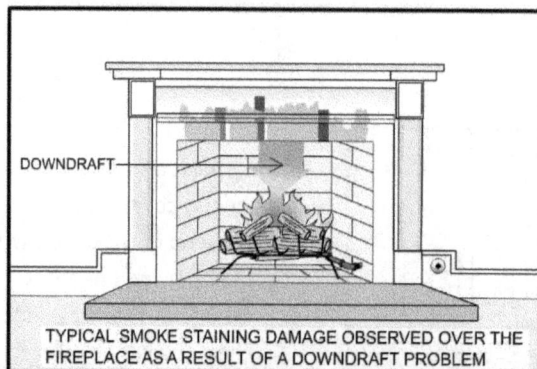

DOWNDRAFT

TYPICAL SMOKE STAINING DAMAGE OBSERVED OVER THE FIREPLACE AS A RESULT OF A DOWNDRAFT PROBLEM

Sometimes smoke staining may merely be an indication that someone neglected to open the damper door when igniting a fire. But, if there is a downdraft problem, chimney hood work may then be in order to remedy the condition.

☐ **wood finish** too **close above** the **fireplace opening**

Doorbells

- ☐ **no doorbells** or **door knockers**
- ☐ **doorbell inoperative**
- ☐ **doorbell** has been **located inside** the storm **door**

Doors

- ☐ **missing door** at _____
- ☐ **door scratches** floor upon extension at _____
- ☐ **jammed door** at _____
- ☐ **door can't fully close** at _____
- ☐ **door failed to remain** in a **closed** position at _____
- ☐ **door didn't close properly** at _____
- ☐ **sliding door** was **off track** at _____
- ☐ **door between house and garage** (is not a fire-rated door) (lacks a fire barrier)

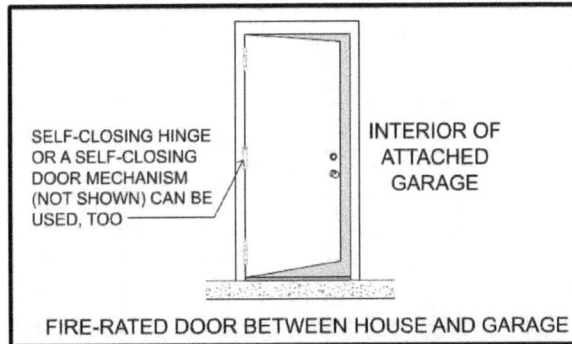

SELF-CLOSING HINGE OR A SELF-CLOSING DOOR MECHANISM (NOT SHOWN) CAN BE USED, TOO

INTERIOR OF ATTACHED GARAGE

FIRE-RATED DOOR BETWEEN HOUSE AND GARAGE

- ☐ the **following door problems** need attention:
  - ☐ _____
  - ☐ _____

DOOR MISSING SELF-CLOSES SELF-OPENS LEAVES GAP WITH DOORWAY DOOR WAS PLANED JAMMED SHUT

DOOR STICKS DOESN'T LOCK SCRAPES FLOOR UPON EXTENSION FAILS TO FULLY CLOSE OR CLOSE PROPERLY FAILS TO FULLY OPEN SLIDING DOOR OFF ITS TRACK

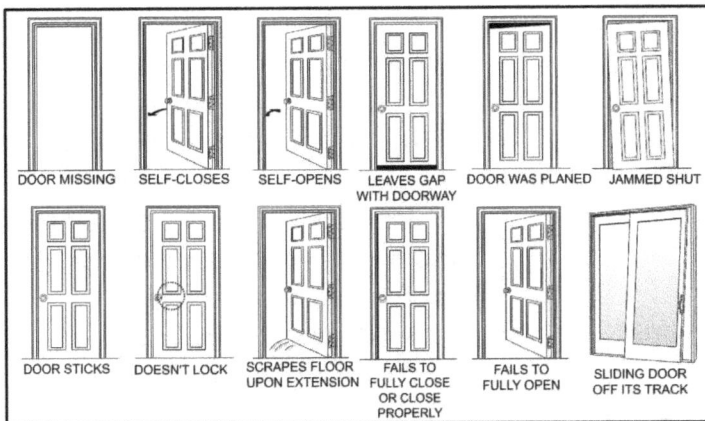

Some of the example problems in the illustration to the left could be due to structural problems.

Drainage

☐ possible **poor grading** at _____

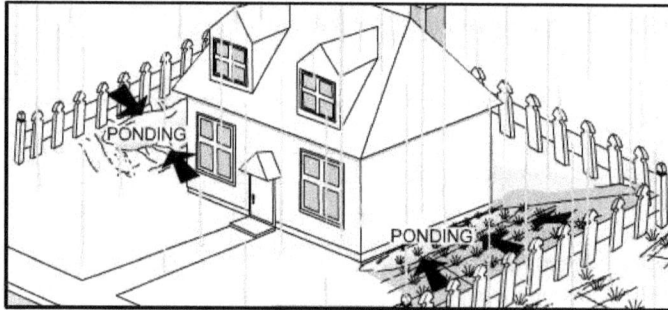

Because of improper gradework, water will tend to accumulate along some yard areas.

What would be helpful in remedying poor drainage conditions would be to accordingly regrade land areas and/or add drainage devices like area drains and swales.

☐ **add drain at driveway**

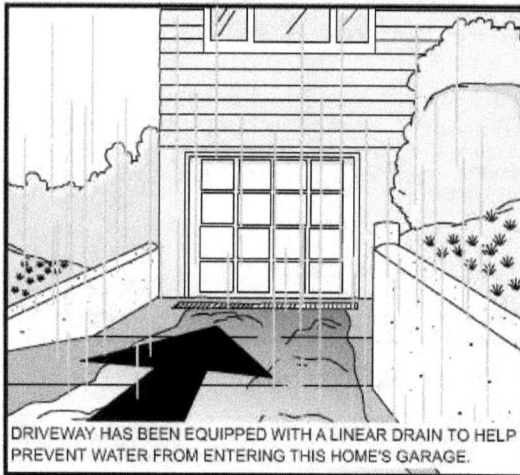

DRIVEWAY HAS BEEN EQUIPPED WITH A LINEAR DRAIN TO HELP PREVENT WATER FROM ENTERING THIS HOME'S GARAGE.

An area drain or a linear drain at the foot of a garage might be a good recommendation to help control flooding in that area.

☐ possibly **add weepholes at** _____ **retaining wall**

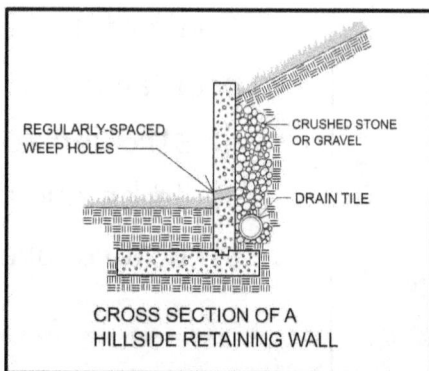

REGULARLY-SPACED WEEP HOLES

CRUSHED STONE OR GRAVEL

DRAIN TILE

CROSS SECTION OF A HILLSIDE RETAINING WALL

Learn what type of drainage system has been provided behind the retaining wall because significant hydrostatic pressure can be exerted on such walls without proper drainage. Look for evidence of cracks in the wall, wall leaning, bowing-out effects and wall bulging, too.

Electrical

□ **bury uncovered** electrical **wiring** at _____

> Uncovered electrical wiring poses a safety hazard.

□ _____ **utility pole leans**

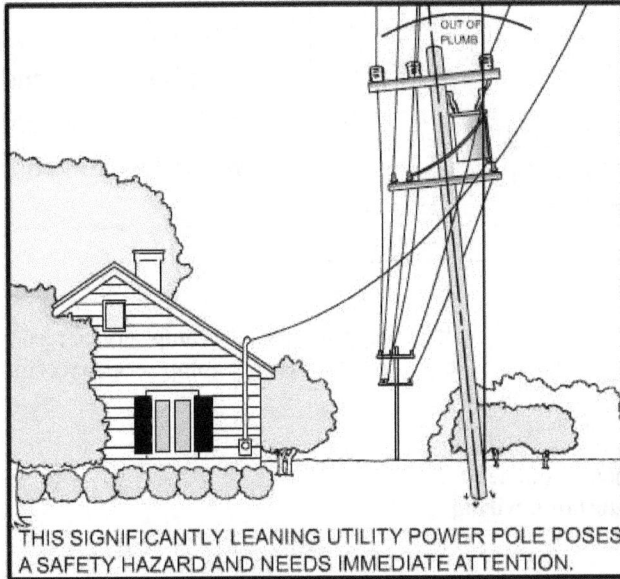

OUT OF PLUMB

THIS SIGNIFICANTLY LEANING UTILITY POWER POLE POSES A SAFETY HAZARD AND NEEDS IMMEDIATE ATTENTION.

□ **frayed** overhead **service lines**

> Advise the seller to contact the local electric company to immediately check out the frayed overhead electrical lines and to make corrective work measures as necessary.

□ **low clearance of** overhead electrical **service lines**

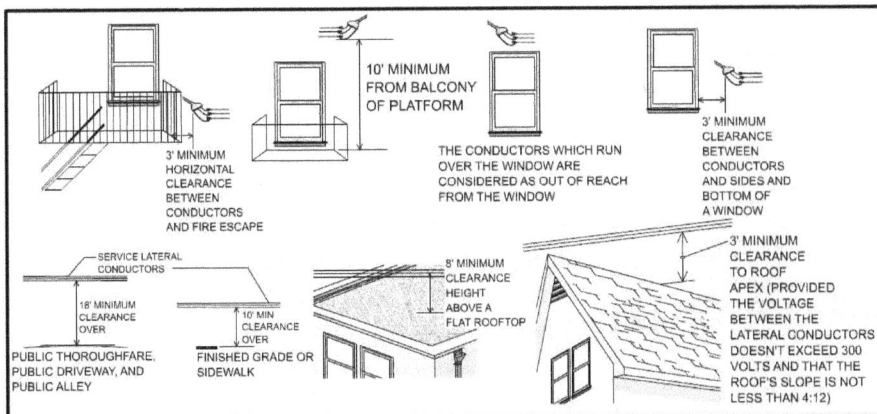

10' MINIMUM FROM BALCONY OF PLATFORM

3' MINIMUM HORIZONTAL CLEARANCE BETWEEN CONDUCTORS AND FIRE ESCAPE

THE CONDUCTORS WHICH RUN OVER THE WINDOW ARE CONSIDERED AS OUT OF REACH FROM THE WINDOW

3' MINIMUM CLEARANCE BETWEEN CONDUCTORS AND SIDES AND BOTTOM OF A WINDOW

SERVICE LATERAL CONDUCTORS

18' MINIMUM CLEARANCE OVER

PUBLIC THOROUGHFARE, PUBLIC DRIVEWAY, AND PUBLIC ALLEY

10' MIN CLEARANCE OVER FINISHED GRADE OR SIDEWALK

8' MINIMUM CLEARANCE HEIGHT ABOVE A FLAT ROOFTOP

3' MINIMUM CLEARANCE TO ROOF APEX (PROVIDED THE VOLTAGE BETWEEN THE LATERAL CONDUCTORS DOESN'T EXCEED 300 VOLTS AND THAT THE ROOF'S SLOPE IS NOT LESS THAN 4:12)

> We also recommend that the local electric company be contacted to check out the clearances of the incoming overhead electrical service lines and to make corrective work measures as necessary. However, it may turn out to be required to additionally engage the services of an electrician.

□ if **house electrical ground connections** do not exist

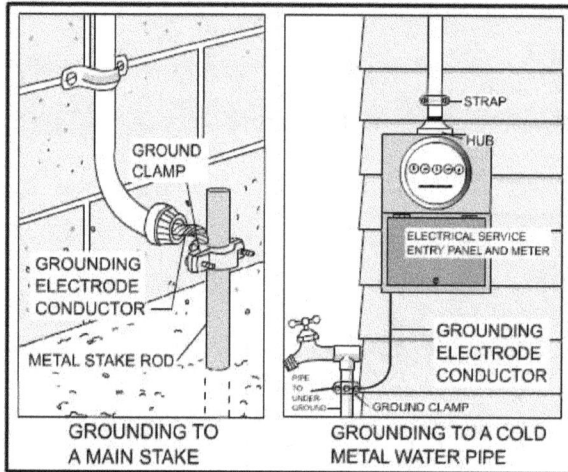

GROUND CLAMP

GROUNDING ELECTRODE CONDUCTOR

METAL STAKE ROD

GROUNDING TO A MAIN STAKE

—STRAP

—HUB

ELECTRICAL SERVICE ENTRY PANEL AND METER

GROUNDING ELECTRODE CONDUCTOR

PIPE TO UNDER GROUND

GROUND CLAMP

GROUNDING TO A COLD METAL WATER PIPE

An electrician should be called in at once to make such connections if none exist. Note that there could be a grounding problem when one feels a "tingling" sensation while touching an appliance.

□ **small electrical service**: _____ wire _____ volt ___ amp service. ___ amp service recommended
□ **electric service marginal** ____ wire ___ volt ___ amp service. ___ amp service recommended
□ **electrical service** is **sufficient** but if you add:
    □ significant or central air conditioning
    □ major electrical appliances (like a self-cleaning range)
       _____ amp service is then recommended
□ home utilizes (some) (all) **aluminum wiring**

Aluminum wiring is considered to be unsafe wiring because the current that travels through it causes oxidation which results in loose connections between the wiring and the receptacle terminal screws. Those loose connections can overheat and turn into a fire.

□ **know your size and type of wiring**: (12 gage) (14 gage) (Copper) (Copper-clad) (_____)
□ **secure** electrical **conduit** at _____

UNSUPPORTED ELECTRICAL CONDUIT LIES ON THE WET CRAWL SPACE FLOOR.

Your local electrical code probably specifies that non-metallic sheathed (romex) or flexible metal cable needs to be secured at least every 4 feet - 6 inches.

☐ **electrician** should be engaged **to check** and make corrective work measures to the following:

    ☐ _____

    ☐ _____

    ☐ _____

☐ close off **open J-boxes** at _____

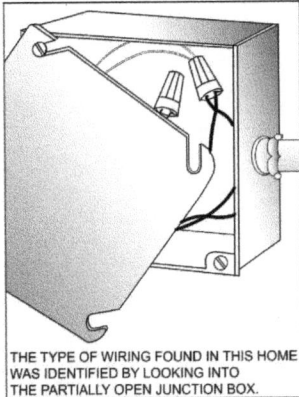

THE TYPE OF WIRING FOUND IN THIS HOME WAS IDENTIFIED BY LOOKING INTO THE PARTIALLY OPEN JUNCTION BOX.

☐ **extension cord(s) (outlet[s])** used

> They should be removed for they are a potential fire hazard. Extension cords / extension outlets are used on account on the limited number of convenience outlets in some rooms.

☐ **ground fault interrupter(s)** recommended

    ☐ at _____ sink(s)

    ☐ at _____ outdoor outlet(s)

    ☐ inside the garage

    ☐ as part of a swimming pool or spa light circuit breaker

    ☐ to control an inside tub spa motor

UNFORTUNATELY, THIS IS NOT A GROUND FAULT INTERRUPTOR OUTLET...

...SUCH AS THIS

RESET

TEST

☐ **no backyard outlet** for general convenience

☐ **no** _____ **bathroom outlet**

☐ **could not cause** _____ **outlet to work**

☐ **tighten** internal screws of **old outlets** for some of these screws tend to loosen up with time

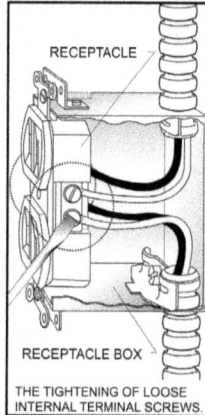

RECEPTACLE

RECEPTACLE BOX

THE TIGHTENING OF LOOSE
INTERNAL TERMINAL SCREWS.

☐ _____ outlet(s) have **reversed polarity**

☐ _____ outlet(s) have **open ground connection**

☐ **dangerously located receptacle** at:
    ☐ behind a kitchen cooktop
    ☐ within arms reach of a bathtub
    ☐ low hanging light fixture directly over a bathtub
    ☐ _____

☐ _____ **exterior outlet(s)** and **switch(es) lack protection** from the elements

☐ **flickering light** in _____

☐ **light** was (**hanging** by its wiring) (**loose**)

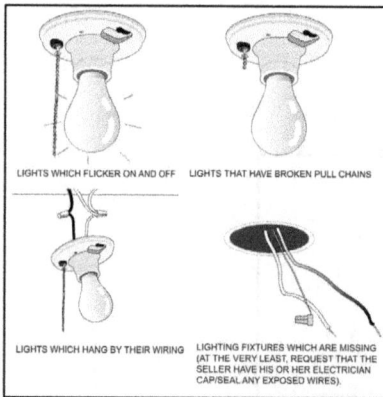

LIGHTS WHICH FLICKER ON AND OFF   LIGHTS THAT HAVE BROKEN PULL CHAINS

LIGHTS WHICH HANG BY THEIR WIRING   LIGHTING FIXTURES WHICH ARE MISSING
(AT THE VERY LEAST, REQUEST THAT THE
SELLER HAVE HIS OR HER ELECTRICIAN
CAP/SEAL ANY EXPOSED WIRES).

☐ **light inside small closet** poses a **fire hazard**

☐ further **specific items of electrical repair** include:
    ☐ _____
    ☐ _____
    ☐ _____
    ☐ _____

Exterior Improvements

☐ **uprooted sidewalk**

> Repave the affected area since, for example, someone can trip on the raised edge(s) and, also, a child whose skateboard overturns can fall.

☐ **patching concrete cracks** noted in:
- ☐ front sidewalk
- ☐ driveway
- ☐ pathway to the front porch
- ☐ _____
- ☐ _____

☐ corrective **masonry repair** is needed to:
- ☐ _____
- ☐ _____
- ☐ _____

☐ **replace** sections of **stone and mortar** _____ when this **improvement** reaches this state of deterioration for:
- ☐ it possessed numerous cracked joints
- ☐ it was settled
- ☐ it was uprooted

☐ **provide access route** to _____ yard

> With some hillside properties, proper access routes to side yards or to backyards have not been provided. Or it could be that the existing routes to these locations are hazardous ones. Easy access is important, especially when there is a need for quick egress in the event of emergencies. Expensive exterior improvement work might include the provision of steps, railings and walkways.

☐ **recommend retaining wall** at _____

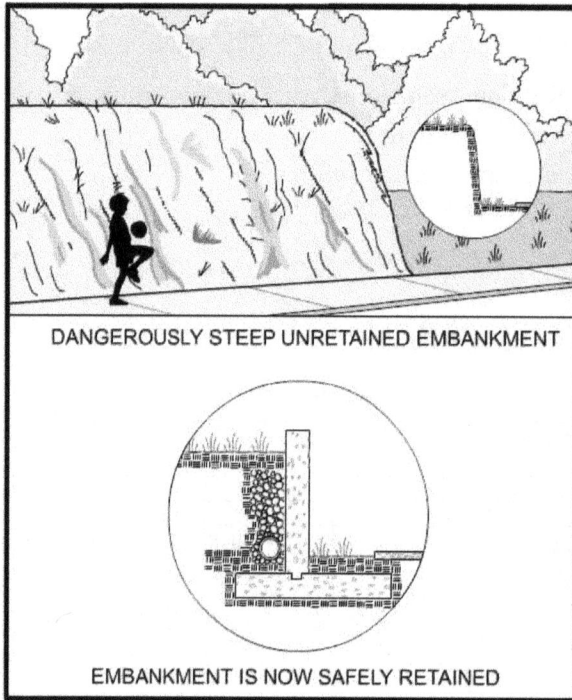

DANGEROUSLY STEEP UNRETAINED EMBANKMENT

EMBANKMENT IS NOW SAFELY RETAINED

The construction of a retaining wall along a length of steeply sloped earth embankment might be (or soon become) necessary even though the soil grade has been unretained like that for years.

☐ **increase** height and length of **retaining wall**

Or, perhaps even provide debris fencing because of some soil conditions.

☐ _____ **outdoor wall leans**

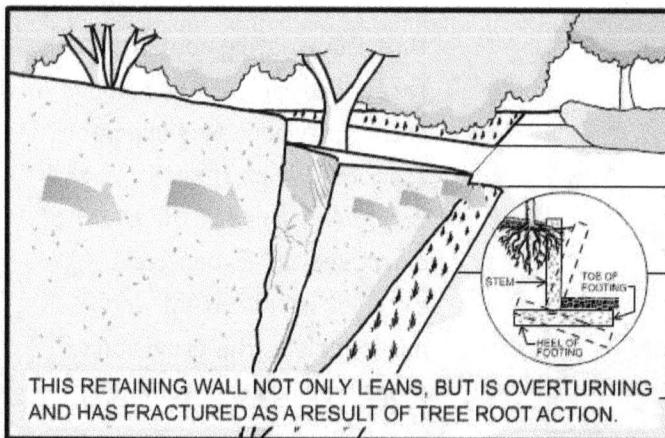

THIS RETAINING WALL NOT ONLY LEANS, BUT IS OVERTURNING AND HAS FRACTURED AS A RESULT OF TREE ROOT ACTION.

Retaining walls which lean might have to be rebuilt. The cause of leaning could be caused by such factors as earth movement, hydrostatic pressure, tree root action or by poorly designed, undersized walls. Note that additional modes of retaining wall failure include lateral and shift displacement failure, wall bowing or bulging, and serious cracking.

□ **discount** _____ that is in poor condition

□ **(repave) (resurface) (seal) blacktop driveway** that was (cracked) (quite worn)

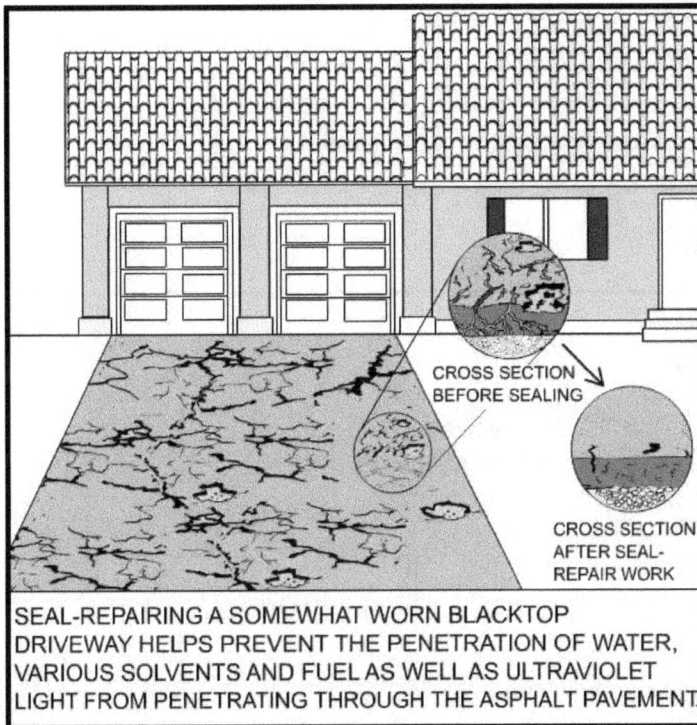

SEAL-REPAIRING A SOMEWHAT WORN BLACKTOP DRIVEWAY HELPS PREVENT THE PENETRATION OF WATER, VARIOUS SOLVENTS AND FUEL AS WELL AS ULTRAVIOLET LIGHT FROM PENETRATING THROUGH THE ASPHALT PAVEMENT.

□ **seal blacktop driveway** that shows signs of wear

□ **repave** (areas of) distressed **concrete driveway** that was (severely cracked) (in poor condition)

□ **oil stains** mark driveway

□ differential **settlement of** swimming **pool**

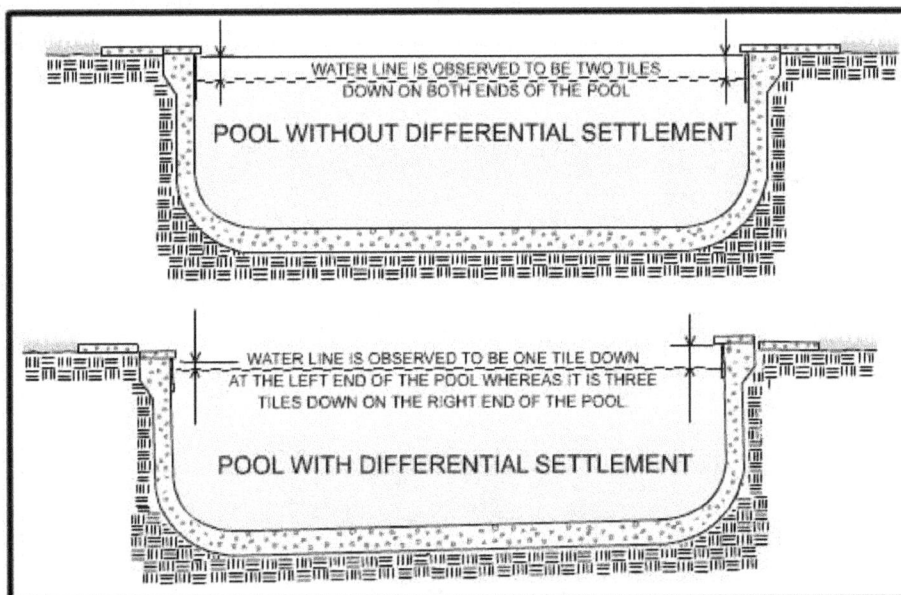

□ **rusted diving board bolts**

> Because diving board bolt connections rust and
> weaken, they shouldn't be neglected to be examined
> for their structural condition for safety reasons.

□ **low height patio cover**

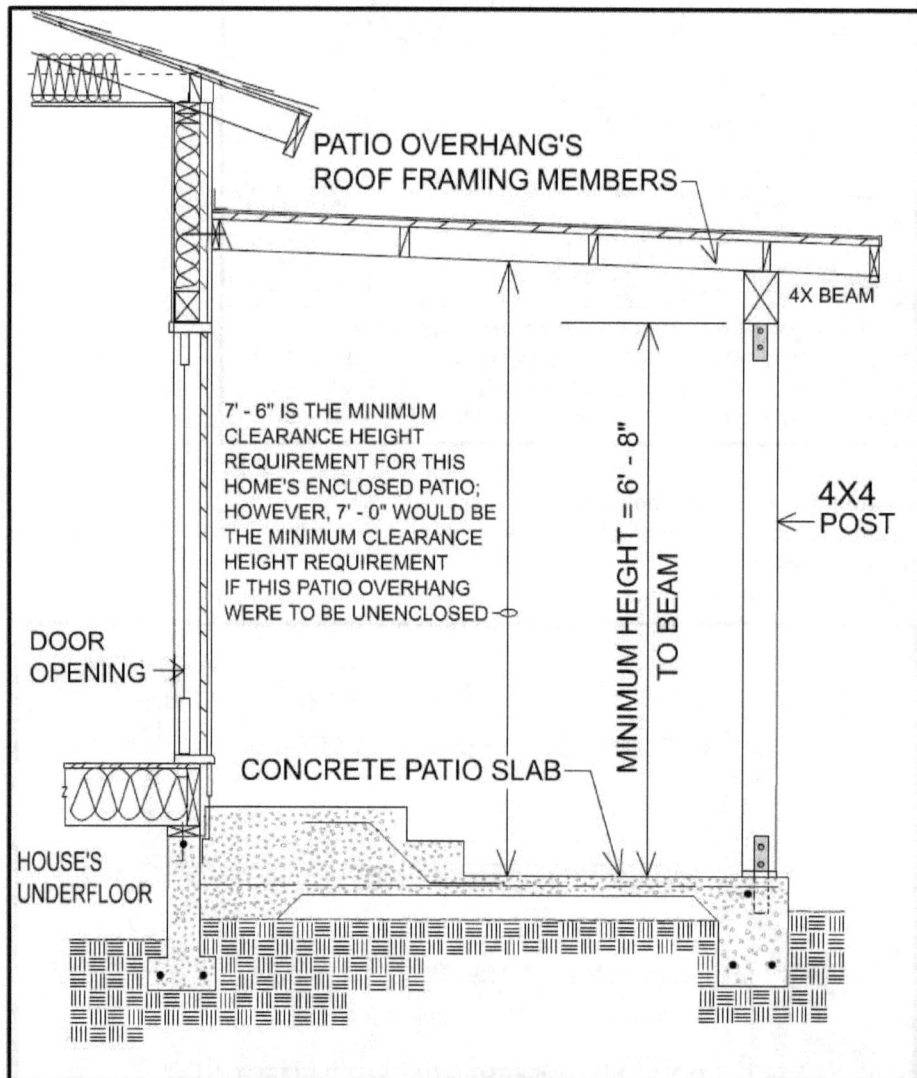

PATIO OVERHANG'S
ROOF FRAMING MEMBERS

4X BEAM

7' - 6" IS THE MINIMUM
CLEARANCE HEIGHT
REQUIREMENT FOR THIS
HOME'S ENCLOSED PATIO;
HOWEVER, 7' - 0" WOULD BE
THE MINIMUM CLEARANCE
HEIGHT REQUIREMENT
IF THIS PATIO OVERHANG
WERE TO BE UNENCLOSED

MINIMUM HEIGHT = 6' - 8"
TO BEAM

4X4
POST

DOOR
OPENING

CONCRETE PATIO SLAB

HOUSE'S
UNDERFLOOR

Exterior Siding

☐ recommend **corrective wooden siding** / weatherproofing work which includes:
- ☐ closing up / sealing off sections open to weather and insect exposure;
- ☐ replacing damaged siding members;
- ☐ securing looser wood siding members
- ☐ and caulking/sealing around window and door frames, at the interfaces of the siding and fascia, etc. (where needed) so as to protect against the elements.

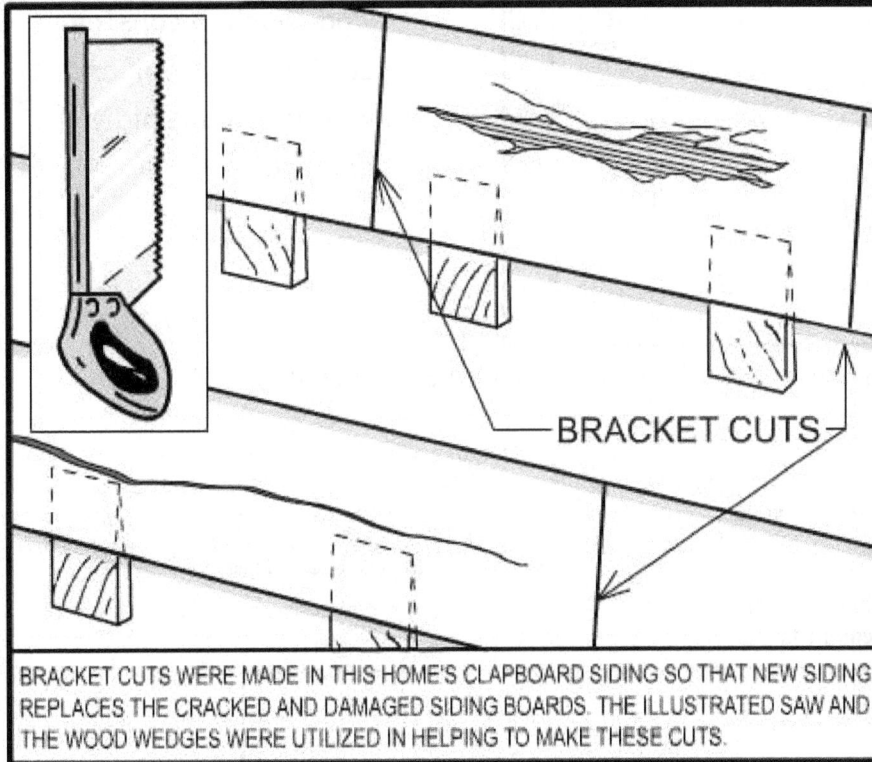

BRACKET CUTS WERE MADE IN THIS HOME'S CLAPBOARD SIDING SO THAT NEW SIDING REPLACES THE CRACKED AND DAMAGED SIDING BOARDS. THE ILLUSTRATED SAW AND THE WOOD WEDGES WERE UTILIZED IN HELPING TO MAKE THESE CUTS.

☐ **crawl space access cover** was _____

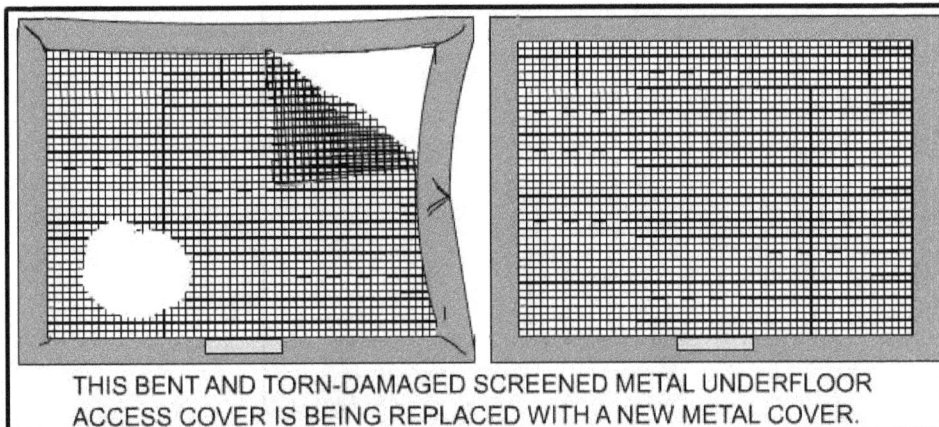

THIS BENT AND TORN-DAMAGED SCREENED METAL UNDERFLOOR ACCESS COVER IS BEING REPLACED WITH A NEW METAL COVER.

☐ **replace** affected **damprotted post** base

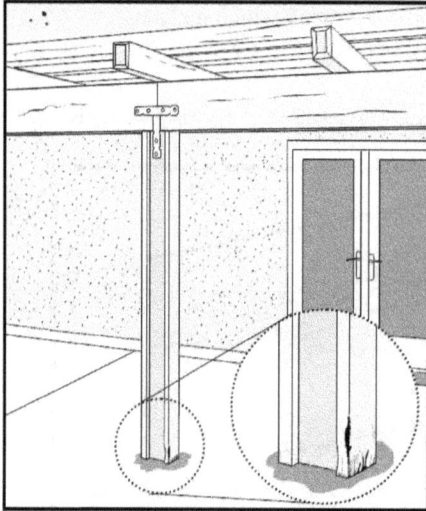

> Unprotected exterior woodwork in constant contact with soil and water could rapidly damprot.

☐ **replace** the following **exterior woodwork** which was damprotted:

      ☐ _____

      ☐ _____

      ☐ _____

☐ some **cracks in** the exterior **stucco walls**

☐ **monitor stucco cracks**

> Patching helps stop cracks from becoming larger ones and prevents the possibility of insect entry or water entry through them. The more severe cracks may require periodic inspections after the patchwork to see whether they reappear.

☐ **reparge** fallen/missing exterior **plaster cement fascia**

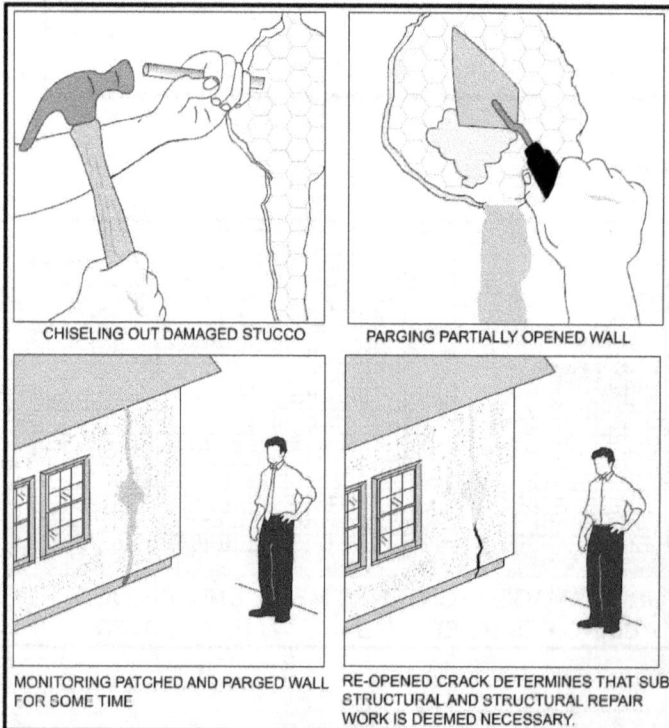

CHISELING OUT DAMAGED STUCCO

PARGING PARTIALLY OPENED WALL

MONITORING PATCHED AND PARGED WALL FOR SOME TIME

RE-OPENED CRACK DETERMINES THAT SUB-STRUCTURAL AND STRUCTURAL REPAIR WORK IS DEEMED NECESSARY.

□ **re-point** the _____

When masonry loses some of its mortar, it is time to "re-point." Masons 're-point' when they fill in the small cracks and holes which occur between masonry blocks and their mortar with new mortar. They additionally replace missing masonry. In the illustration above, the stone and mortar wall is being re-pointed.

□ **install fence** where none exists at
    □ alongside the foot edge of the hillside slope for a fall down this embankment could be dangerous
    □ _____

WIRE ROPE FENCE OFFERS PROTECTION FROM
ONE FALLING OFF THIS STEEP HILLSIDE SLOPE EDGE.

□ **fence off** the swimming **pool**

THIS HOME'S 8 FEET DEEP SWIMMING POOL HAS BEEN ENCLOSED BY A MINIMUM
4.5 FEET FENCE ABOVE THE GROUND. ITS 4.5 FEET GATE SELF-LATCHES CLOSED.

Building codes usually require that bodies of water which
are more than 18 inches deep be fenced off and gated.

☐ **discount** _____ **fence** in state of disrepair

THIS PICKET FENCE IS IN A STATE OF DISREPAIR FOR IT HAS LOOSE, FALLEN PICKETS, PARTIALLY LEANS AND IS AFFECTED BY TERMITES.

☐ the _____ **fence** is in **worn** condition and needs attention:
    ☐ several lengths of which _____
    ☐ we saw its damaged sections as well
    ☐ _____

> Learn who will be faced with the responsibility of repairs.

☐ **repair** sections of **leaning fence** in the _____ yard

Garage

☐ due to **garage's poor condition** and/or the fashion of its construction, the following corrective work measures will be needed:
    ☐ structural retrofitting work, including _____
    ☐ _____
    ☐ _____

☐ repair **dented/knocked-in section of rear garage wall** noted by car impact damage

☐ **add concrete carstops** to (garage) (carport)

☐ **garage floor incorrectly pitched**

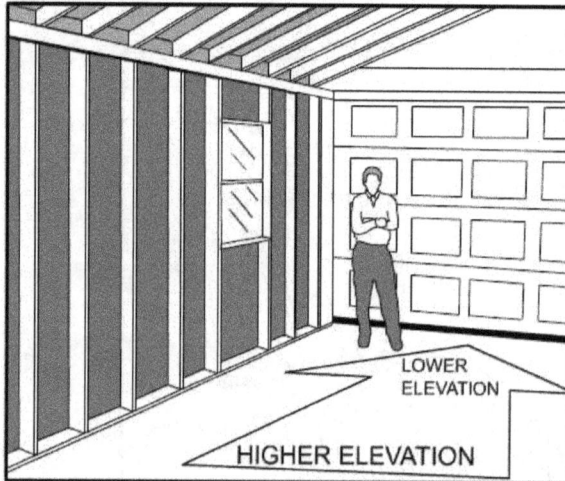

LOWER ELEVATION

HIGHER ELEVATION

> Garage floors are required to be of non-combustible materials (such as of concrete or asphalt pavement) and are normally pitched toward garage entries. (A downward floor slope run of 1/8" per foot is recommended). That way, during a rainstorm, water that drips from a wet car that has just entered the garage can then exit it readily rather than form puddles therein.

☐ **no overhead garage door**

☐ **side-by-side garage doors** noted

☐ **no** automatic **garage door opener**

> Where applicable, it is recommended that an emergency key release is provided at the time of installation for the purpose of operating the overhead garage door manually in the event of a neighborhood electrical power failure.

☐ overhead **garage door springs in way of pathway**

> The dangerous condition illustrated here clearly signals some unpermitted construction.

☐ **broken** overhead **garage door spring**

> The installation of new safety springs for both sides of the lift door so as to equalize tension is recommended.

Glazing

□ **replace cracked panes** detected at _____

THIS CRACKED WINDOW PANE IS BEING REPLACED.

□ **cracked glazing** detected at the (_____ bathroom tub) (_____ bathroom stall shower)
□ **reputty around** _____ **panes** of window glass due to their:
      □ cracked glazing compound
      □ loosened glazing compound
      □ fallen glazing compound

That way, the window joints are kept both airtight and watertight.

□ **check whether there is safety tempered glass** at the following:
- □ the _____ sliding glass door(s)
- □ all other exterior glass door(s)
- □ the transom window(s)
- □ the sidelights
- □ the _____ stall shower door(s) and enclosure(s)
- □ the _____ bathtub sliding doors
- □ the _____

THIS IS A TYPICAL BREAKAGE PATTERN OF SAFETY TEMPERED GLASS.

THIS IS WHAT A SAFETY TEMPERED CLASS 'BUG' LOOKS LIKE.

□ **low-to-floor windows** of the _____ **need safety tempered glazing**

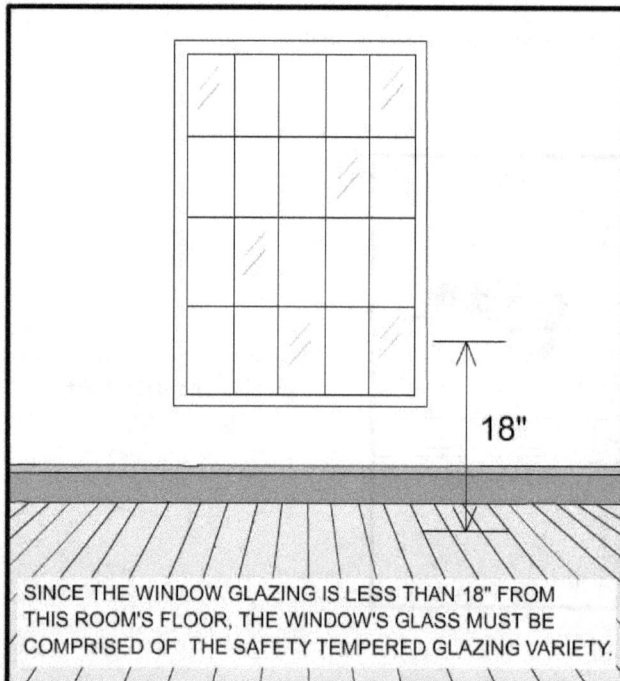

18"

SINCE THE WINDOW GLAZING IS LESS THAN 18" FROM THIS ROOM'S FLOOR, THE WINDOW'S GLASS MUST BE COMPRISED OF THE SAFETY TEMPERED GLAZING VARIETY.

Heating

□ realize _____ **room** is **absent of** direct **heating**

Surprisingly, the added master bedroom lacks direct heating provision and, because of this, the homeowner in winter feels cold.

□ **heat failed to emanate** from _____

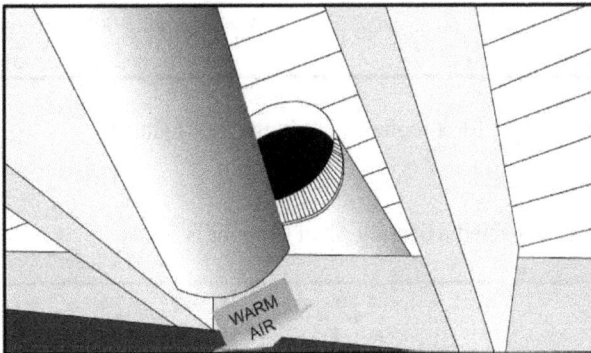

Because this duct had gotten separated in the underfloor crawl space, the bedroom the duct serves is no longer being heated.

□ **furnace ventilation** is **restricted**

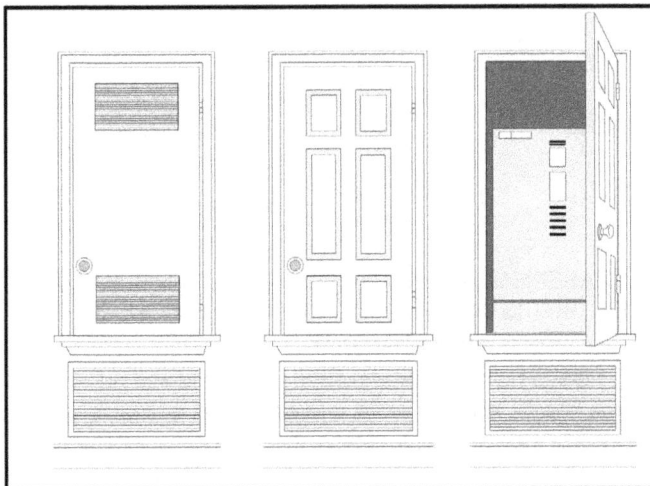

The homeowner replaced the partially louvered door with a paneled door to make this furnace closet more attractive. Unfortunately, upper and lower vents within the closet are absent and, thus, the new door restricts ventilation to this gas-fired heating plant.

☐ **furnace** has _____ problem while in operation - seller should have his contractor check this out and repair as deemed necessary

☐ **firebox cracked (and crumbling)** - recommend replacing it

☐ **old gravity furnace** - budget for a modern forced air furnace replacement in the years ahead

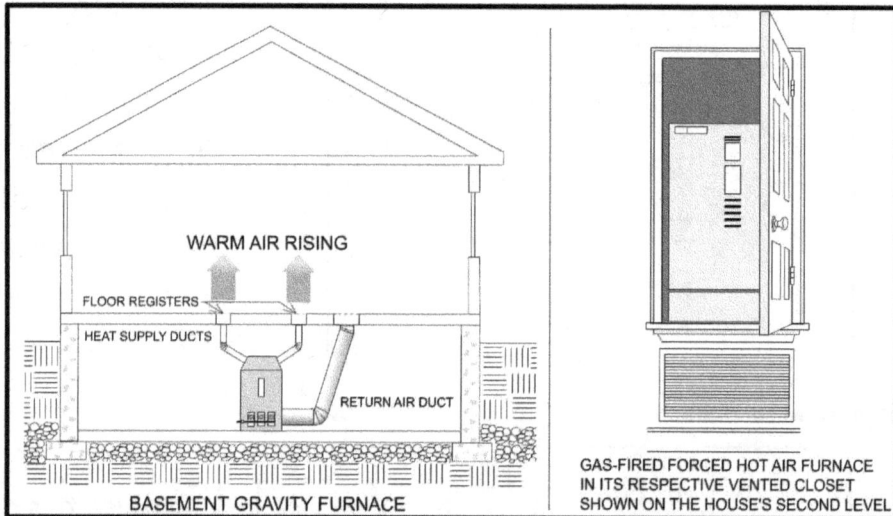

WARM AIR RISING

FLOOR REGISTERS

HEAT SUPPLY DUCTS

RETURN AIR DUCT

BASEMENT GRAVITY FURNACE

GAS-FIRED FORCED HOT AIR FURNACE
IN ITS RESPECTIVE VENTED CLOSET
SHOWN ON THE HOUSE'S SECOND LEVEL

☐ **old furnace** - because of its age, budget for a replacement in the years ahead
   ☐ nearing its rated life
   ☐ at its rated life
   ☐ past its rated life

☐ **skimpy furnace** - we would have expected a heating plant of more B.T.U.s

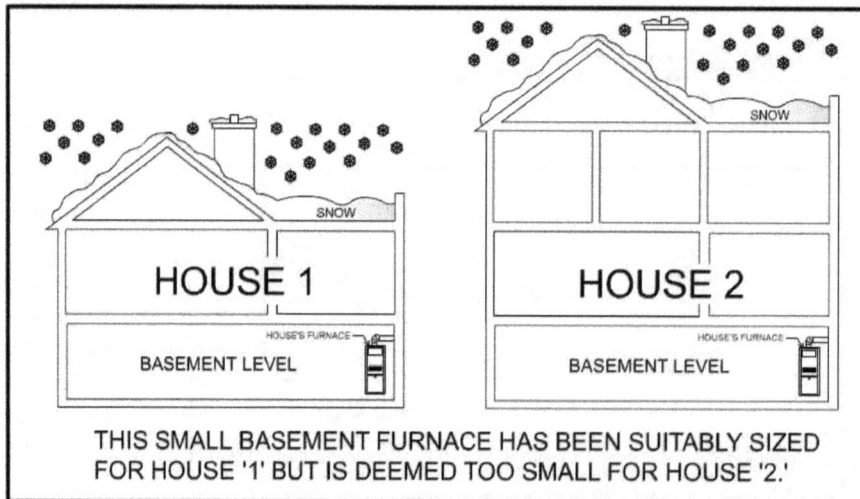

HOUSE 1

BASEMENT LEVEL

HOUSE'S FURNACE

SNOW

HOUSE 2

BASEMENT LEVEL

HOUSE'S FURNACE

SNOW

THIS SMALL BASEMENT FURNACE HAS BEEN SUITABLY SIZED
FOR HOUSE '1' BUT IS DEEMED TOO SMALL FOR HOUSE '2.'

On real cold winter days, the temperature inside the house might not keep up with the setting of the thermostat. Perhaps adding a separate small furnace system would help resolve this condition.

☐ **separated** heating plant **exhaust flue** - notify the owner to have this condition corrected at once

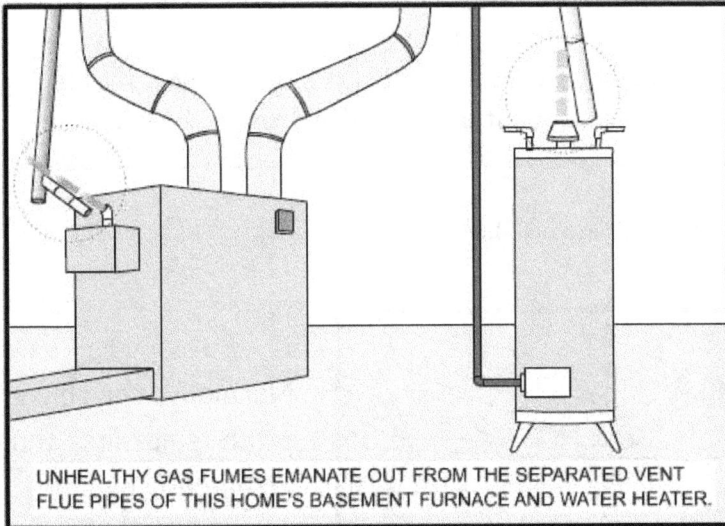

UNHEALTHY GAS FUMES EMANATE OUT FROM THE SEPARATED VENT
FLUE PIPES OF THIS HOME'S BASEMENT FURNACE AND WATER HEATER.

☐ **soot streaks** noted off _____

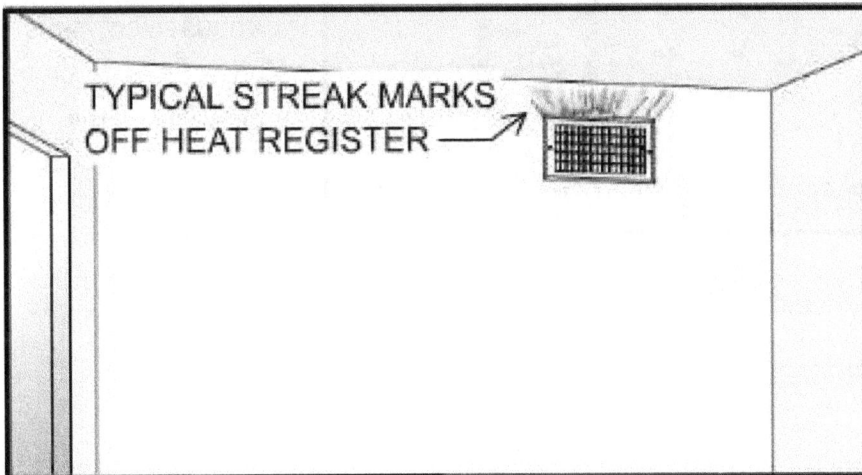

TYPICAL STREAK MARKS
OFF HEAT REGISTER ——→

Soot streaks could reflect evidence of a cracked heat exchanger inside the furnace which would allow fumes of carbon dioxide and carbon monoxide to flow out of the heating element and circulate throughout the house.

□ **asbestos duct** thermal **wrapping possible**

> Have a laboratory make a positive identification of it since with old friable asbestos ducting wrapping replacement ducting might prove to be necessary.

□ **long flat run of** fuel-fired furnace's **exhaust duct**

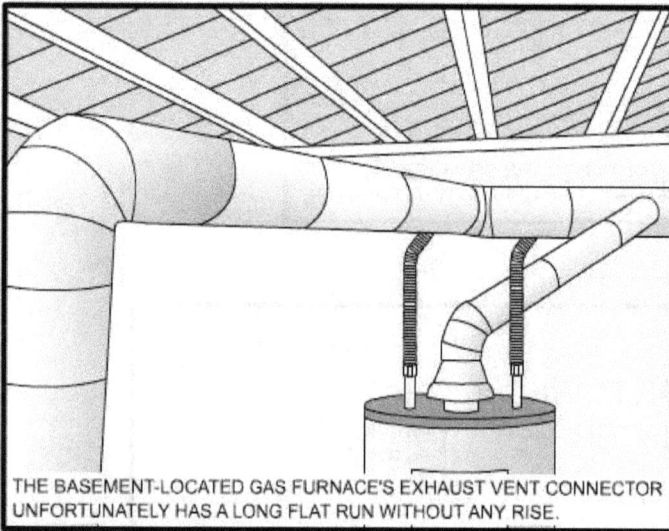

THE BASEMENT-LOCATED GAS FURNACE'S EXHAUST VENT CONNECTOR UNFORTUNATELY HAS A LONG FLAT RUN WITHOUT ANY RISE.

> Normally, the rise or pitch is not less than 1/4 inch for each foot of run. Note that direct vertical exhaust venting is considered to be more favorable.

□ **dented ducting** at _____

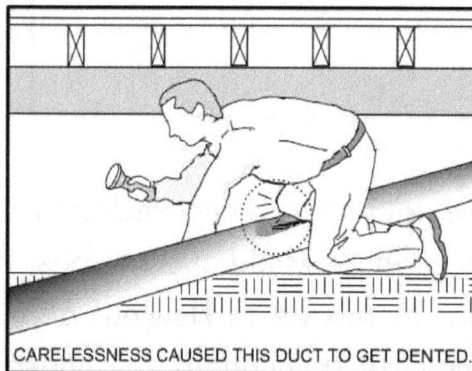

CARELESSNESS CAUSED THIS DUCT TO GET DENTED.

> Ducts develop holes and get separated, also. Look out for damaged ducts.

□ **no humidifier** on the furnace

> Warm air heated homes become dry without good humidification.

Hot Water Heating

□ **water heater works inefficiently**

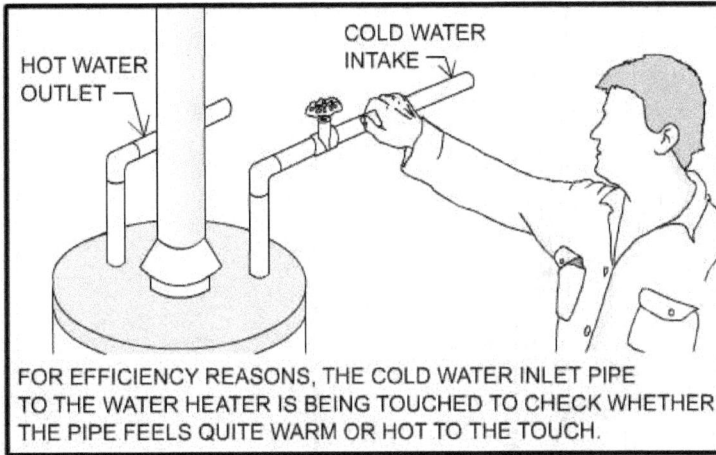

HOT WATER OUTLET

COLD WATER INTAKE

FOR EFFICIENCY REASONS, THE COLD WATER INLET PIPE TO THE WATER HEATER IS BEING TOUCHED TO CHECK WHETHER THE PIPE FEELS QUITE WARM OR HOT TO THE TOUCH.

Sometimes the hot and cold water lines at a hot water heater are reversed, causing the tank to operate energy-wise in an uneconomical manner.

□ **old hot water heater**
  □ nearing its rated life
  □ at its rated life
  □ past its rated life

Budget for a new tank in the years ahead.

□ **small hot water heater**: existing capacity _____ proposed capacity _____

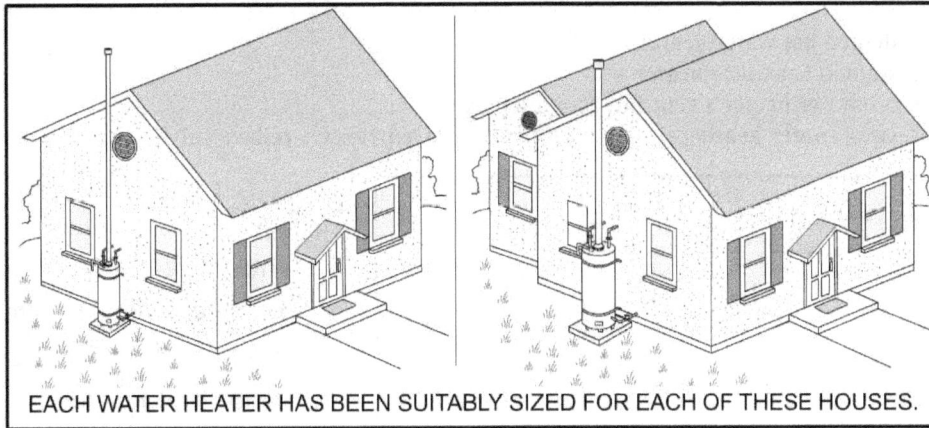

EACH WATER HEATER HAS BEEN SUITABLY SIZED FOR EACH OF THESE HOUSES.

□ **small and old hot water heater**: existing capacity _____ proposed capacity _____

If the water tank is of minimal size for normal family needs and is rapidly aging, a larger replacement tank is recommended.

□ **popping sounds** from **hot water heater**

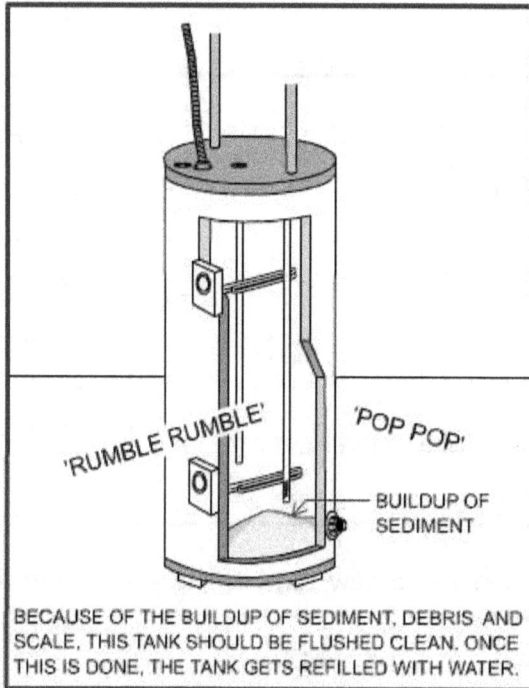

'RUMBLE RUMBLE'

'POP POP'

BUILDUP OF SEDIMENT

BECAUSE OF THE BUILDUP OF SEDIMENT, DEBRIS AND SCALE, THIS TANK SHOULD BE FLUSHED CLEAN. ONCE THIS IS DONE, THE TANK GETS REFILLED WITH WATER.

□ **dented hot water heater**
□ **stained hot water heater**
□ hot **water heater's vent flue** found **separated**
□ **equip water heating system with temperature/pressure relieve valve**

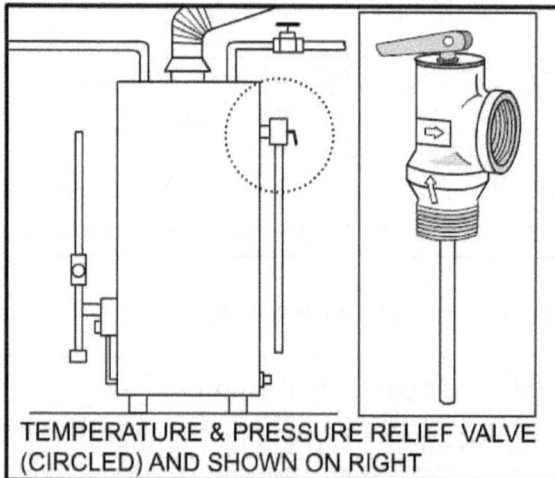

TEMPERATURE & PRESSURE RELIEF VALVE (CIRCLED) AND SHOWN ON RIGHT

This valve acts as a safeguard which will allow steam to escape safely, for instance, should the heater's thermostat malfunction / when excess pressure can virtually destroy the tank.

□ **pressure relief valve leaks**

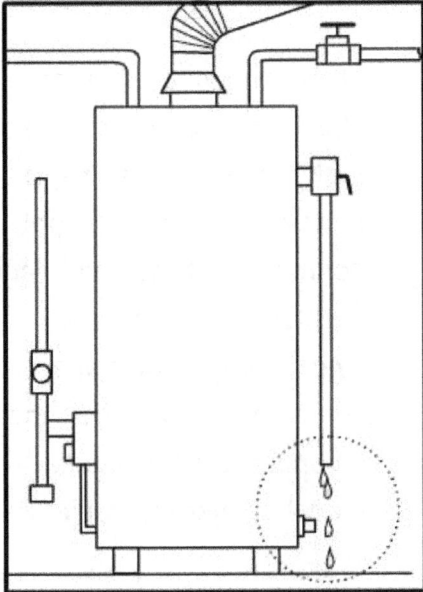

This could mean that the water temperature is too high for this valve's setting or, that too much pressure is being built up in the hot water line. The valve may need replacement.

□ **water heater's cleanout drain drips**

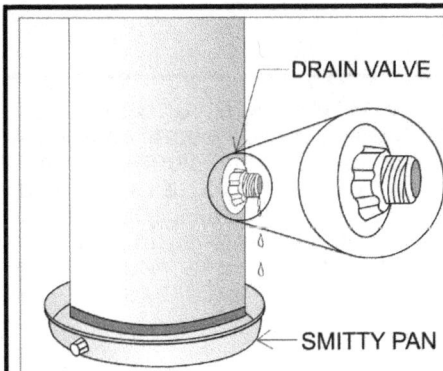

DRAIN VALVE

SMITTY PAN

THE HOMEOWNER TIGHTENS HIS WATER HEATER DRAIN VALVE TO ARREST ITS DRIPPING WATER.

HE THEN CLEANS THE SEDIMENT IN THE TANK BY DRAINING THE HEATER.

☐ **water heater is not anchored**

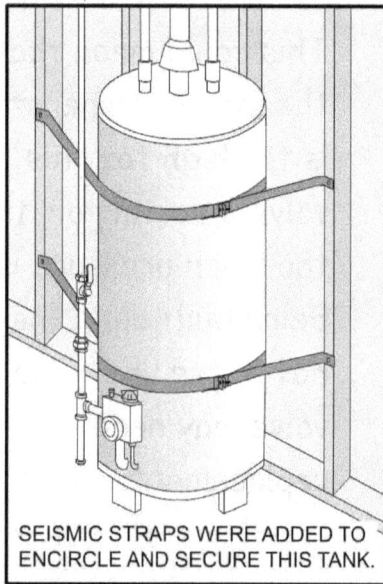

SEISMIC STRAPS WERE ADDED TO
ENCIRCLE AND SECURE THIS TANK.

In earthquake country, there is a danger of gas leakage from semi-rigid aluminum tube gas supply connectors that can break with seismic movement. That's why homeowners are replacing them with those of an approved corrugated metal connector variety.

Insulation

☐ **uninsulated attic**

HEAT LOSS THROUGH...

ROOF/ATTIC - 25-30%

WINDOWS & DOORS- 15-25%

EXTERIOR WALLS - 25-35%

FLOOR - 10-15%

HEAT FLOWS FROM WARMER SPACES TO COOLER SPACES. IT DOES SO BY MEANS OF CONVECTION, CONDUCTION, AND RADIATION. FOR EXAMPLE, DURING COLD WINTER MONTHS, HEAT TRAVELS OUT FROM THE HEATED LIVING SPACES TO THE EXTERIOR, TO UNHEATED ATTICS, GARAGES AS WELL AS TO UNDERFLOOR LOCATIONS - PROVIDED THERE IS A VARIATION IN TEMPERATURE. THUS, TO REDUCE THE AMOUNT OF HEATING AND COOLING IN THE HOME, INSULATION IN CEILINGS, WALLS AND FLOORS OFFERS RESISTANCE TO THE FLOW OF HEAT.

HERE ARE SOME COMMONLY USED INSULATION MATERIALS IN HOUSES:

BATT AND BLANKET FIBERGLASS INSULATION IS MINERAL FIBER OF ROCK, GLASS OR SLAG

LOOSE FILL INSULATION
CAN BE MINERAL FIBER OF ROCK, GLASS OR SLAG; OR ALSO CAN BE CELLUOSE*, EXFOLIATED VERMICULITE, OR EXPANDED PERLITE

LOOSE FILL INSULATION
BOARD USED TO LEVEL FILL INSULATION

FOAM INSULATION (CAN BE BLOWN INTO SMALL AREAS TO CONTROL AIR LEAKS)

RIGID BOARD INSULATION CAN BE EXPANDED POLYSTYRENE

REFLECTIVE INSULATION

*NOTE THAT CELLULOSE WHICH IS NOT TREATED IS HIGHLY FLAMMABLE, WHILE SYRENE AND URETHANE FOAMS MIGHT PRESENT FLAME-SPREAD AND SMOKE PROBLEMS IF THEY ARE NOT USED PROPERLY.

□ **minimal insulation** found **in attic**

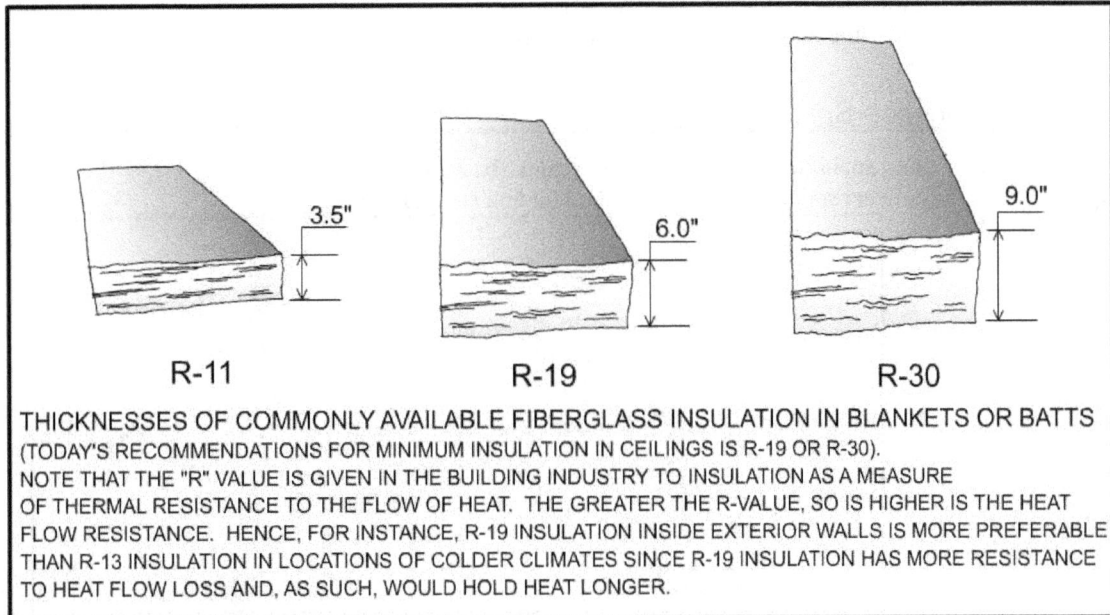

3.5"

6.0"

9.0"

R-11   R-19   R-30

THICKNESSES OF COMMONLY AVAILABLE FIBERGLASS INSULATION IN BLANKETS OR BATTS
(TODAY'S RECOMMENDATIONS FOR MINIMUM INSULATION IN CEILINGS IS R-19 OR R-30).
NOTE THAT THE "R" VALUE IS GIVEN IN THE BUILDING INDUSTRY TO INSULATION AS A MEASURE
OF THERMAL RESISTANCE TO THE FLOW OF HEAT. THE GREATER THE R-VALUE, SO IS HIGHER IS THE HEAT
FLOW RESISTANCE. HENCE, FOR INSTANCE, R-19 INSULATION INSIDE EXTERIOR WALLS IS MORE PREFERABLE
THAN R-13 INSULATION IN LOCATIONS OF COLDER CLIMATES SINCE R-19 INSULATION HAS MORE RESISTANCE
TO HEAT FLOW LOSS AND, AS SUCH, WOULD HOLD HEAT LONGER.

□ **re-lay attic insulation**

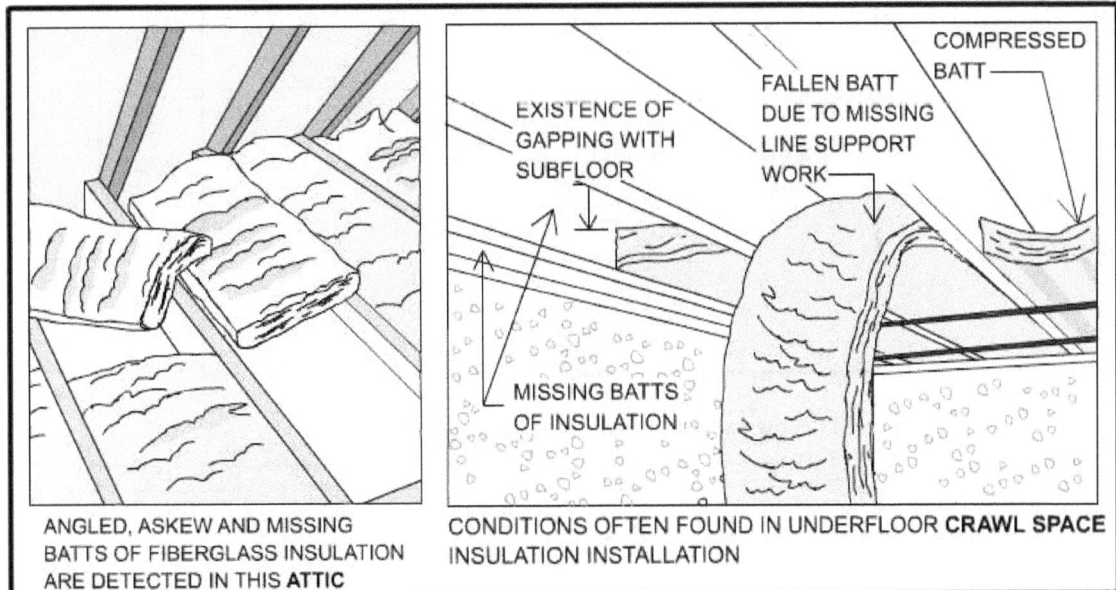

EXISTENCE OF
GAPPING WITH
SUBFLOOR

FALLEN BATT
DUE TO MISSING
LINE SUPPORT
WORK

COMPRESSED
BATT

MISSING BATTS
OF INSULATION

ANGLED, ASKEW AND MISSING
BATTS OF FIBERGLASS INSULATION
ARE DETECTED IN THIS **ATTIC**

CONDITIONS OFTEN FOUND IN UNDERFLOOR **CRAWL SPACE**
INSULATION INSTALLATION

Kitchen

- ☐ **kitchen** could stand **modernization**
- ☐ **kitchen and bathroom** need **modernization**

Irrigation Sprinklers

- ☐ **no sprinkler system in** (front) (side) (back) **yard(s)**
- ☐ **divert** sprinkler **spray from** the building **structure** at _____

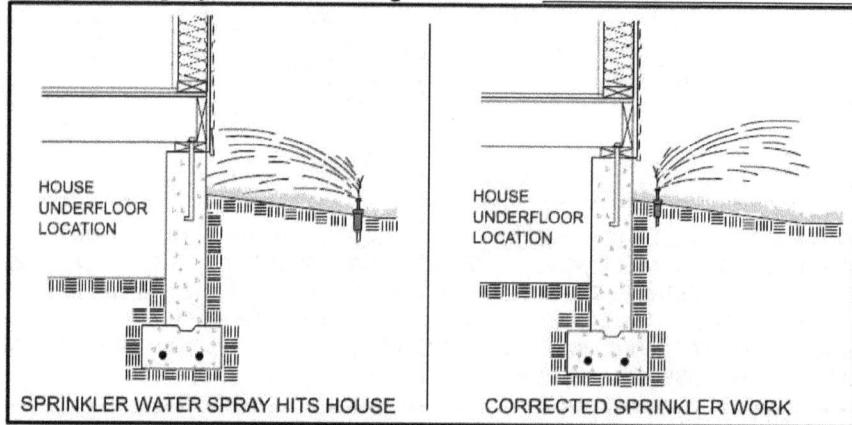

HOUSE UNDERFLOOR LOCATION

HOUSE UNDERFLOOR LOCATION

SPRINKLER WATER SPRAY HITS HOUSE | CORRECTED SPRINKLER WORK

- ☐ **sprinkler line leaks** at _____
- ☐ old **sprinkler system lacks anti-syphon valves**

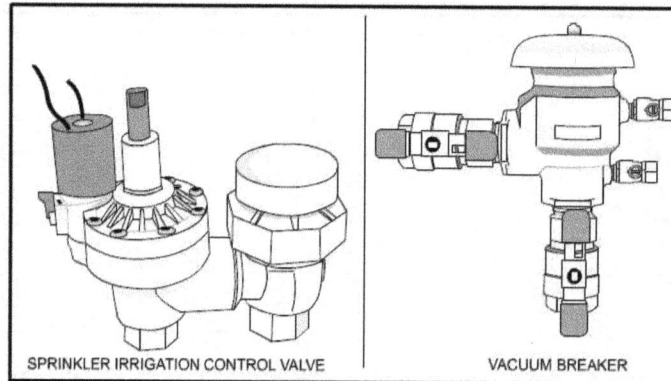

SPRINKLER IRRIGATION CONTROL VALVE | VACUUM BREAKER

- ☐ **several problems with irrigation system** include:
    - ☐ _____
    - ☐ _____
    - ☐ _____

Leaders and Rain Gutters

□ (no) (some areas lack) **leaders and gutters**

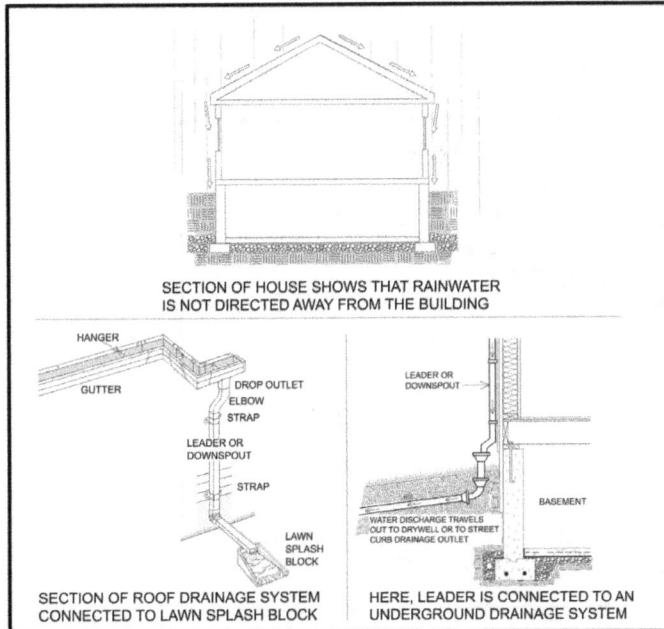

SECTION OF HOUSE SHOWS THAT RAINWATER
IS NOT DIRECTED AWAY FROM THE BUILDING

HANGER

GUTTER

DROP OUTLET
ELBOW
STRAP

LEADER OR
DOWNSPOUT

STRAP

LAWN
SPLASH
BLOCK

SECTION OF ROOF DRAINAGE SYSTEM
CONNECTED TO LAWN SPLASH BLOCK

LEADER OR
DOWNSPOUT

BASEMENT

WATER DISCHARGE TRAVELS
OUT TO DRYWELL OR TO STREET
CURB DRAINAGE OUTLET

HERE, LEADER IS CONNECTED TO AN
UNDERGROUND DRAINAGE SYSTEM

A roof drainage system serves to manage the direction of water from a roof. The system helps prevent damage to the foundation and exterior walls caused by water action.

□ **add extension leader(s)** to _____

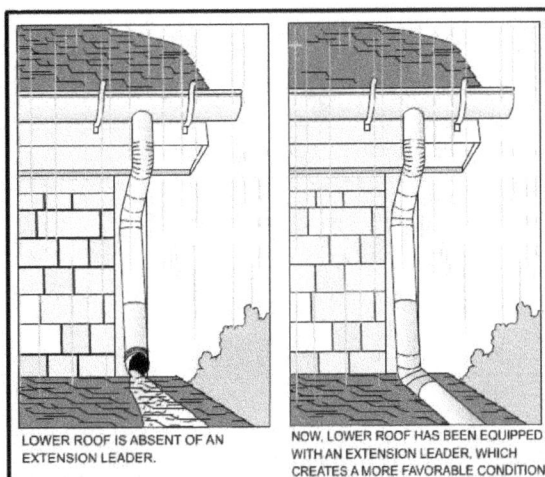

LOWER ROOF IS ABSENT OF AN
EXTENSION LEADER.

NOW, LOWER ROOF HAS BEEN EQUIPPED
WITH AN EXTENSION LEADER, WHICH
CREATES A MORE FAVORABLE CONDITION.

In the absence of extension leaders, water from downspouts is permitted to drain directly onto lower roof areas below them.

☐ **leaders and gutters aging**

☐ some **items of** corrective **roof drainage system work** include:

    ☐ _____

    ☐ _____

    ☐ _____

☐ **poor pitch of** rain **gutters**

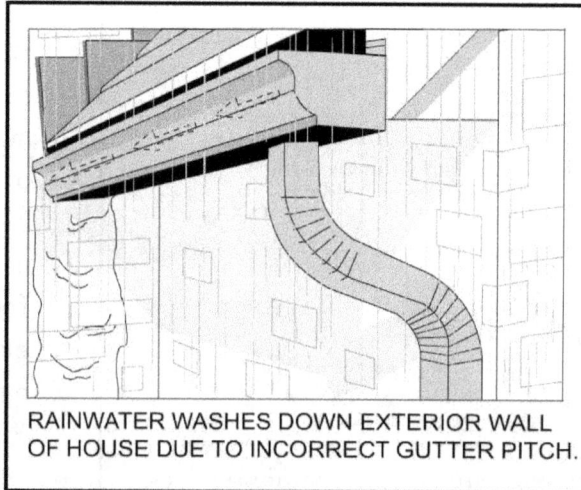

RAINWATER WASHES DOWN EXTERIOR WALL
OF HOUSE DUE TO INCORRECT GUTTER PITCH.

☐ **clear leaders and gutters**

Under certain circumstances when roof drainage systems
become clogged, water could back up beneath the eaves of
some houses and penetrate down into exterior walls.

Legal (Items of Conformance)

☐ **low ceiling height** in _____

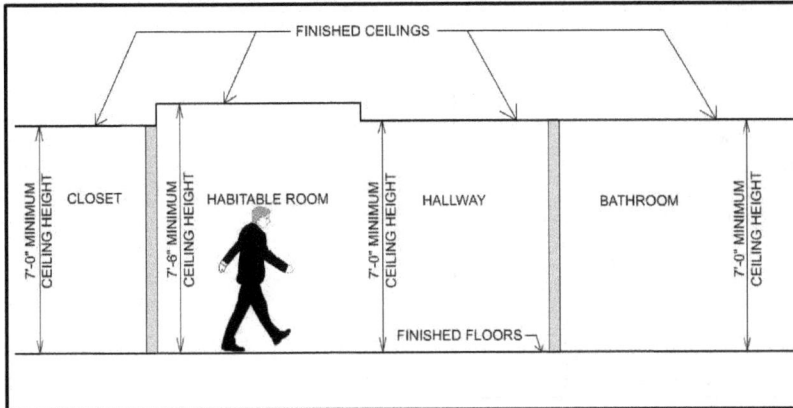

> A local building code might specify the heights in these illustrated locations as their required minimum clear ceiling heights.

☐ **narrow width of room** in _____

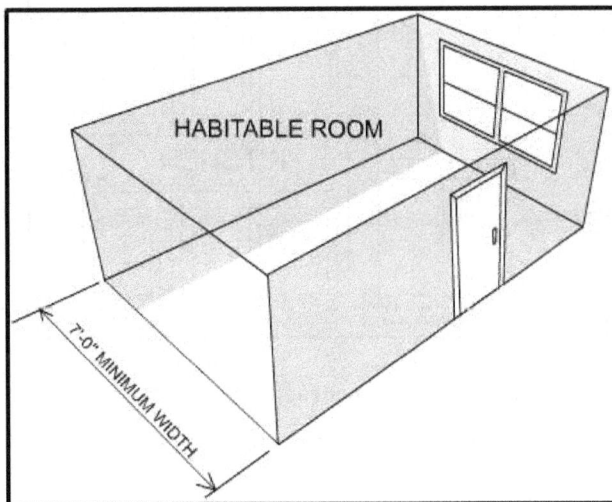

> Except for kitchens, many building codes require that in order for a room to qualify as a 'habitable room,' it should measure at least 7' - 0" along its width.

☐ **small room** area in _____

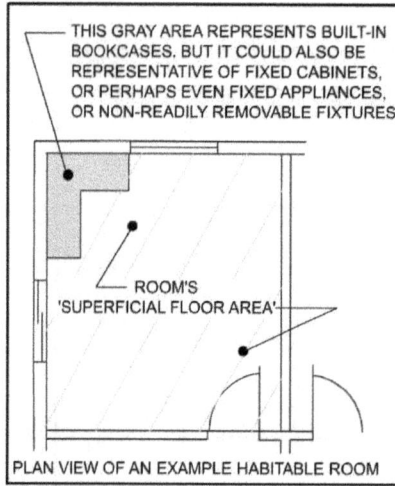

THIS GRAY AREA REPRESENTS BUILT-IN
BOOKCASES. BUT IT COULD ALSO BE
REPRESENTATIVE OF FIXED CABINETS,
OR PERHAPS EVEN FIXED APPLIANCES,
OR NON-READILY REMOVABLE FIXTURES

ROOM'S
'SUPERFICIAL FLOOR AREA'

PLAN VIEW OF AN EXAMPLE HABITABLE ROOM

☐ **bathroom opens to kitchen**

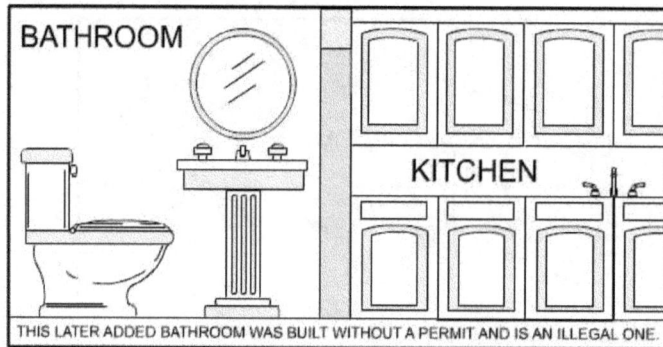

BATHROOM

KITCHEN

THIS LATER ADDED BATHROOM WAS BUILT WITHOUT A PERMIT AND IS AN ILLEGAL ONE.

☐ what looks to be a **bedroom is not a bedroom**

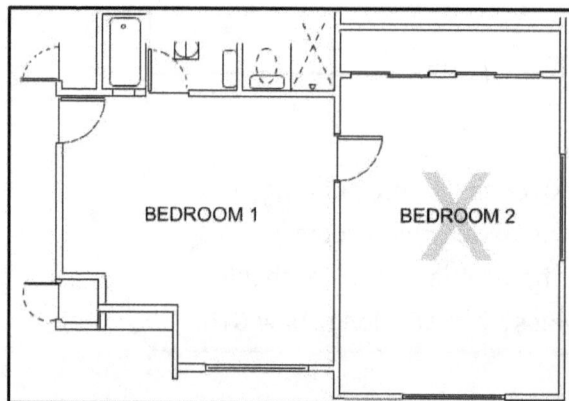

BEDROOM 1

BEDROOM 2

Bedroom '1' might be
called an 'anteroom' or a
dressing room. In theory,
'1' could not be a bedroom
inasmuch as it is used as a
passageway. Note,
however, that many may
use '1' as a bedroom with
'2' being its walk-in
wardrobe closet.

☐ realize **bedroom has no closet**

Bedrooms don't have to have closets.

☐ **improper clearance in** underfloor crawlspace

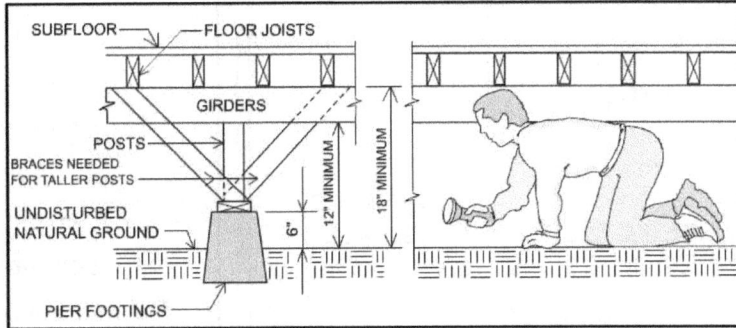

☐ **doorway at** _____ **fails to meet minimum size** dimensions

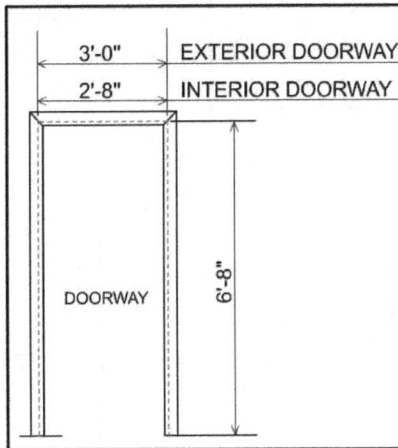

In this drawing and in the illustration above, these are minimum size dimensions as called for by one local example building code.

☐ hinged **shower door opens inwardly**

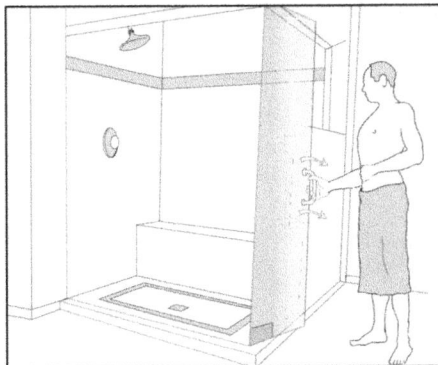

Hinged doors of bathtub and shower enclosures are required to open outwardly.

□ **garage door does not lead to a "bedroom"**

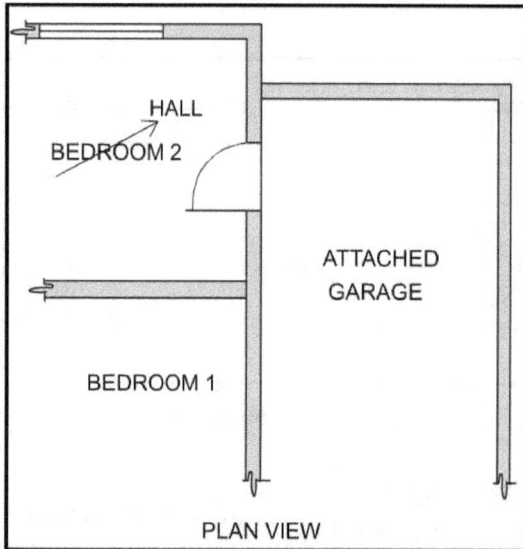

HALL

BEDROOM 2

ATTACHED
GARAGE

BEDROOM 1

PLAN VIEW

Although local building codes prohibit an attached garage's walk-in door from entering a bedroom, it is a commonly found hazardous improvement addition which many homeowners later do.

□ **fire-rated door between house and garage**

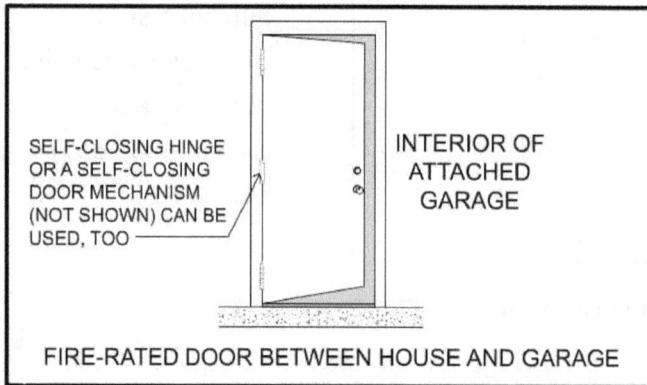

SELF-CLOSING HINGE
OR A SELF-CLOSING
DOOR MECHANISM
(NOT SHOWN) CAN BE
USED, TOO

INTERIOR OF
ATTACHED
GARAGE

FIRE-RATED DOOR BETWEEN HOUSE AND GARAGE

Fire-rated doors are usually 1 3/8 inch thick solid core doors which must self-close.

□ **improper** dimensions of **stairway run and riser**

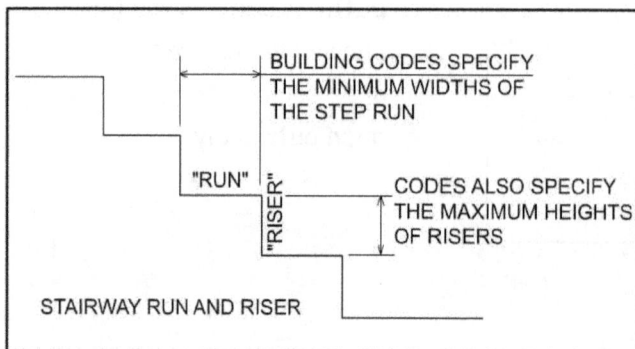

BUILDING CODES SPECIFY
THE MINIMUM WIDTHS OF
THE STEP RUN

"RUN"

"RISER"

CODES ALSO SPECIFY
THE MAXIMUM HEIGHTS
OF RISERS

STAIRWAY RUN AND RISER

☐ **step** risers **vary in height**

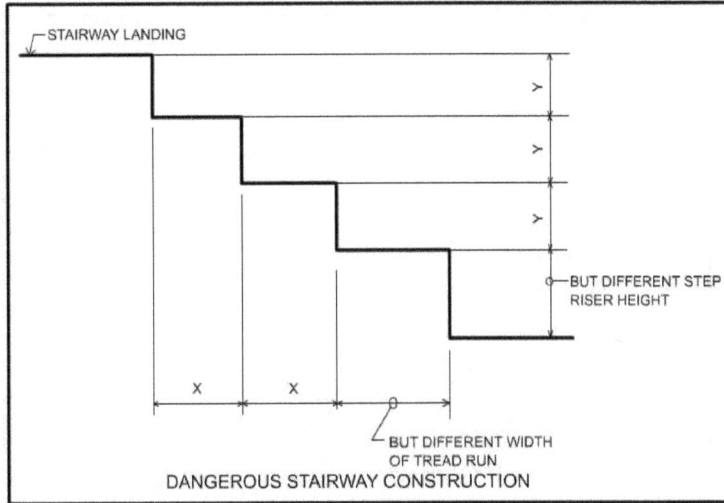

DANGEROUS STAIRWAY CONSTRUCTION

Good construction practice dictates that the variation in step riser heights ought not to exceed 1/4" between steps.

☐ **small clearance** height **along stairway**

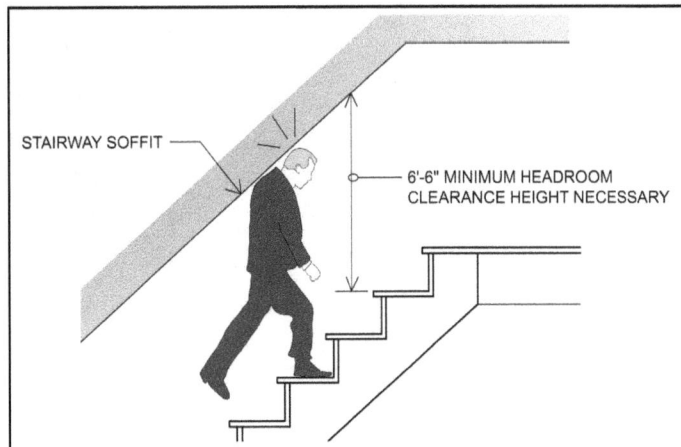

Building codes in general are known to specify this clearance to be at least 6 feet - 6 inches in height.

☐ **baluster** stairway **spacing** is **too wide**

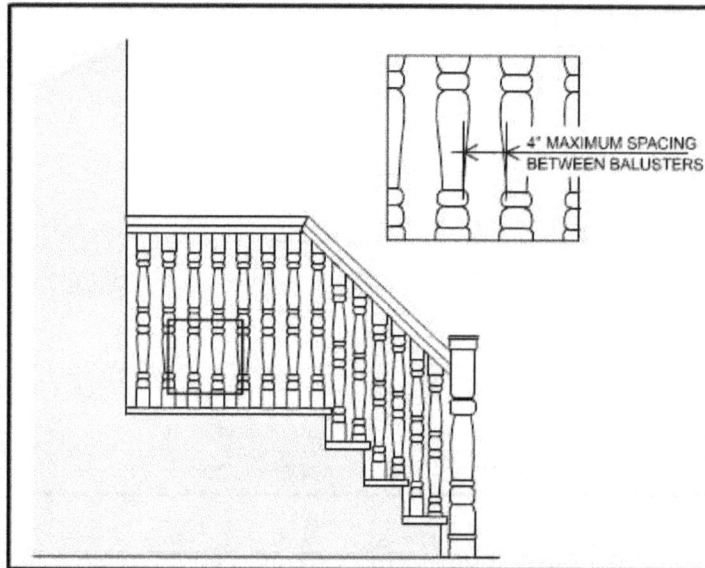

☐ **incorrect** stair **handrail's** wall **projection**

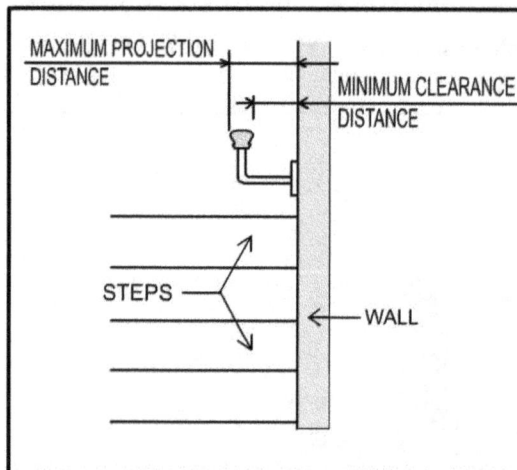

There should be at least 1 1/2" distance between the rail bar and the stair wall. But it is not recommended that handrails project more than 3 1/2" from the stairway wall into the width of the stairs.

□ **window too small** in _____

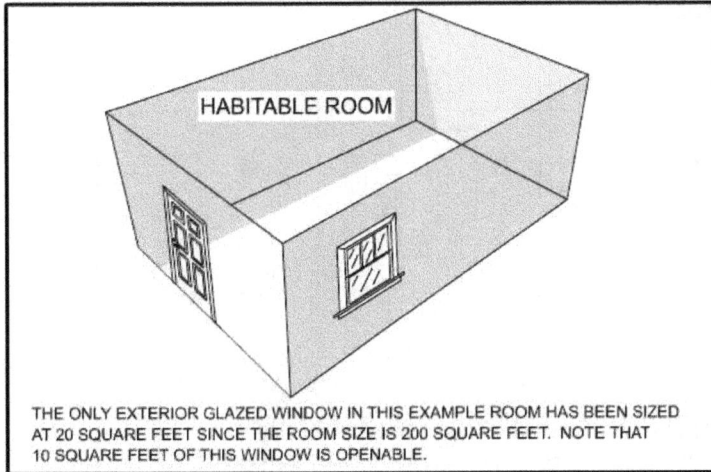

HABITABLE ROOM

THE ONLY EXTERIOR GLAZED WINDOW IN THIS EXAMPLE ROOM HAS BEEN SIZED
AT 20 SQUARE FEET SINCE THE ROOM SIZE IS 200 SQUARE FEET. NOTE THAT
10 SQUARE FEET OF THIS WINDOW IS OPENABLE.

There are building codes that specify the minimum size of windows to be 1/10th of the room's superficial floor area to satisfy light and ventilation requirements for a habitable room of a house. For bathrooms, laundry rooms etc., that requirement is different.

□ **window sill too high** over _____ bedroom floor

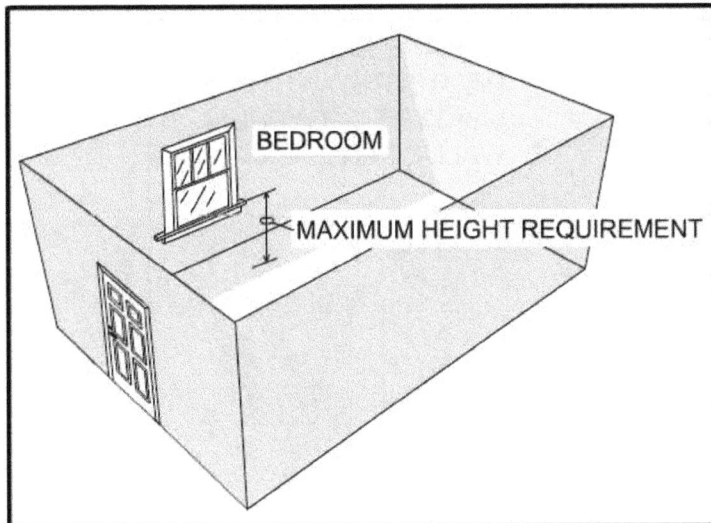

BEDROOM

MAXIMUM HEIGHT REQUIREMENT

For those bedroom windows which are dependent upon ease of access in the event of an emergency, your building code likely specifies 44 inches as the maximum common height allowed.

□ _____ **bedroom window security bars** are **absent of interior release** handle

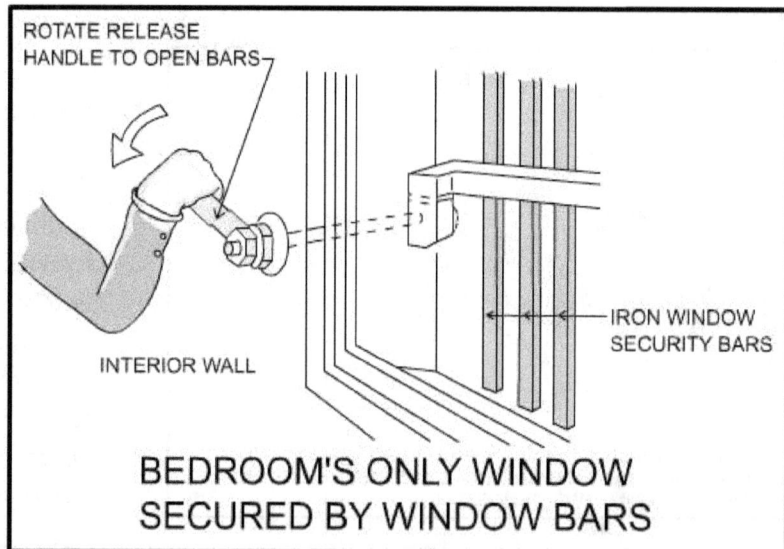

ROTATE RELEASE
HANDLE TO OPEN BARS

INTERIOR WALL

IRON WINDOW
SECURITY BARS

BEDROOM'S ONLY WINDOW
SECURED BY WINDOW BARS

□ **wall between house and** attached **garage** isn't of adequate fire resistive construction

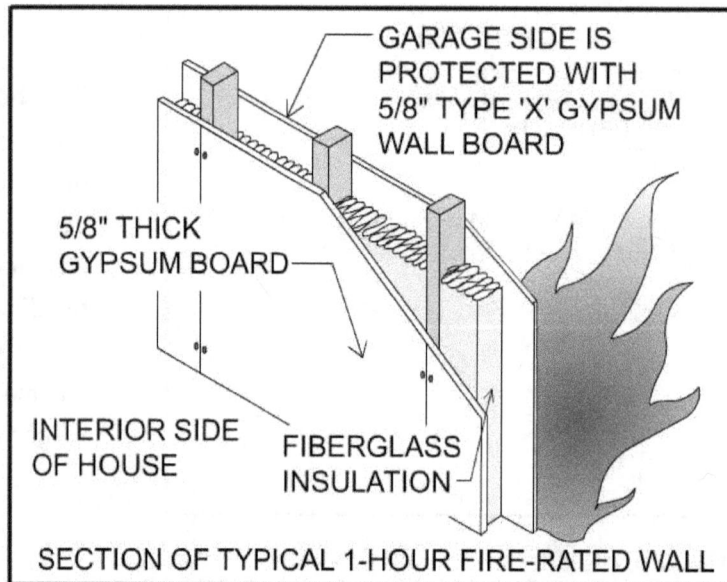

GARAGE SIDE IS
PROTECTED WITH
5/8" TYPE 'X' GYPSUM
WALL BOARD

5/8" THICK
GYPSUM BOARD

INTERIOR SIDE
OF HOUSE

FIBERGLASS
INSULATION

SECTION OF TYPICAL 1-HOUR FIRE-RATED WALL

☐ **no attic access**

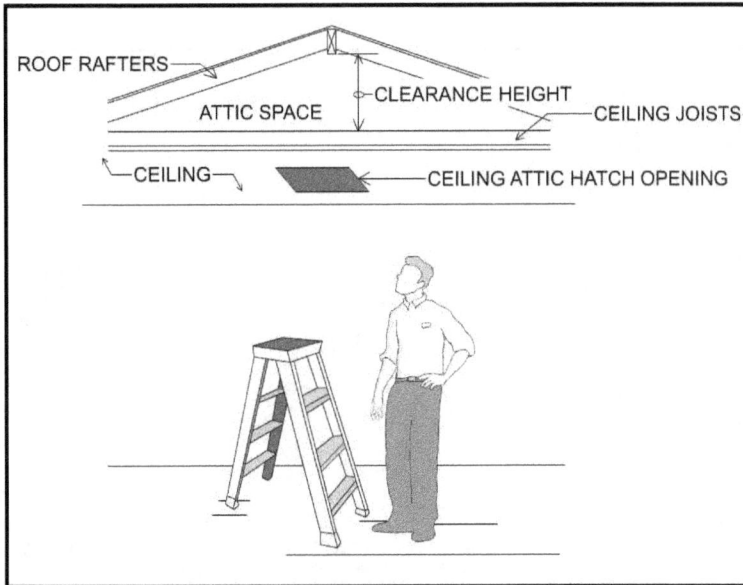

ROOF RAFTERS
CLEARANCE HEIGHT
ATTIC SPACE
CEILING JOISTS
CEILING
CEILING ATTIC HATCH OPENING

In many homes, a scuttle hatch has not been provided nor required because the attic clearance height is less than 30 inches.

☐ exterior wood **siding** starts too **low-to-grade** along _____

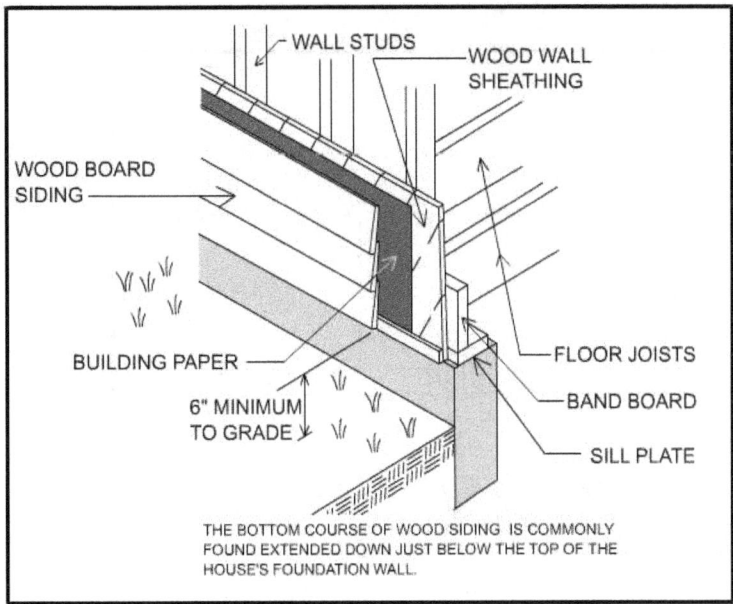

WALL STUDS
WOOD WALL SHEATHING
WOOD BOARD SIDING
BUILDING PAPER
6" MINIMUM TO GRADE
FLOOR JOISTS
BAND BOARD
SILL PLATE

THE BOTTOM COURSE OF WOOD SIDING IS COMMONLY FOUND EXTENDED DOWN JUST BELOW THE TOP OF THE HOUSE'S FOUNDATION WALL.

Watch out for low-to-grade woodwork since there is the possibility that termite damage or wood rotting action could have already taken place.

□ separate electrical **service lines cross** a later added non-permitted **swimming pool**

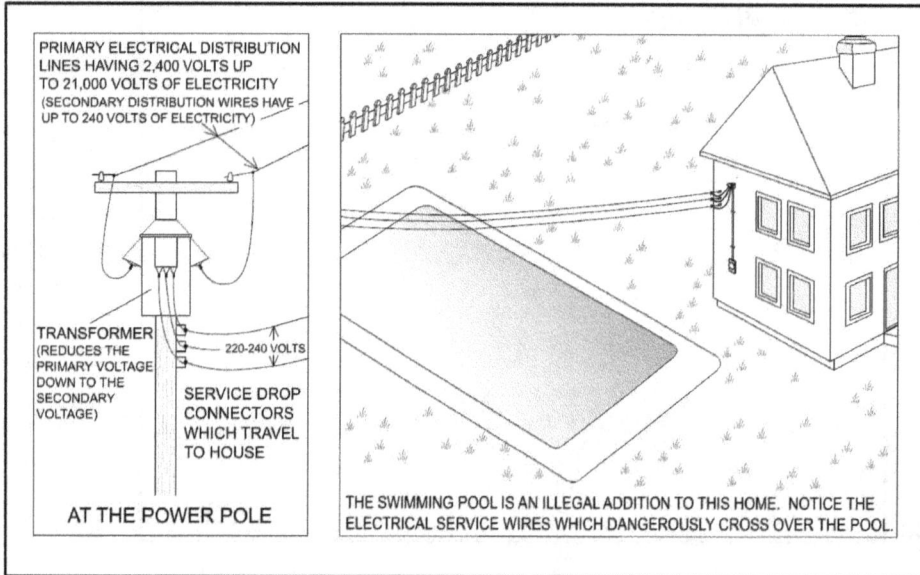

PRIMARY ELECTRICAL DISTRIBUTION
LINES HAVING 2,400 VOLTS UP
TO 21,000 VOLTS OF ELECTRICITY
(SECONDARY DISTRIBUTION WIRES HAVE
UP TO 240 VOLTS OF ELECTRICITY)

TRANSFORMER
(REDUCES THE
PRIMARY VOLTAGE
DOWN TO THE
SECONDARY
VOLTAGE)

220-240 VOLTS

SERVICE DROP
CONNECTORS
WHICH TRAVEL
TO HOUSE

AT THE POWER POLE

THE SWIMMING POOL IS AN ILLEGAL ADDITION TO THIS HOME. NOTICE THE
ELECTRICAL SERVICE WIRES WHICH DANGEROUSLY CROSS OVER THE POOL.

□ **fuel heating plants** are located **under stairs**

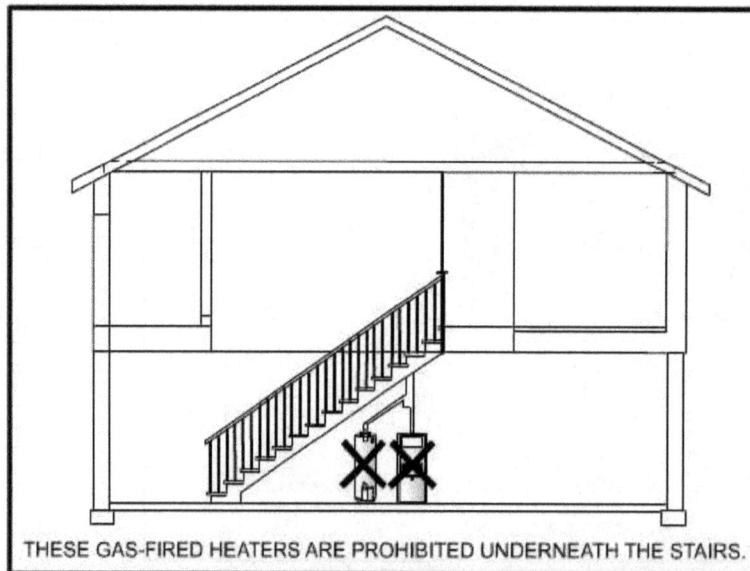

THESE GAS-FIRED HEATERS ARE PROHIBITED UNDERNEATH THE STAIRS.

If a fire or an explosion caused by either of these heaters were to destroy the steps, there would be no easy
access route for one to exit the dwelling from an upper level. Fuel-fired heating plants are also prohibited,
for instance, in a bathroom, in a bedroom and inside a closet that opens into a bedroom or a bathroom.

□ **garage size is too small**

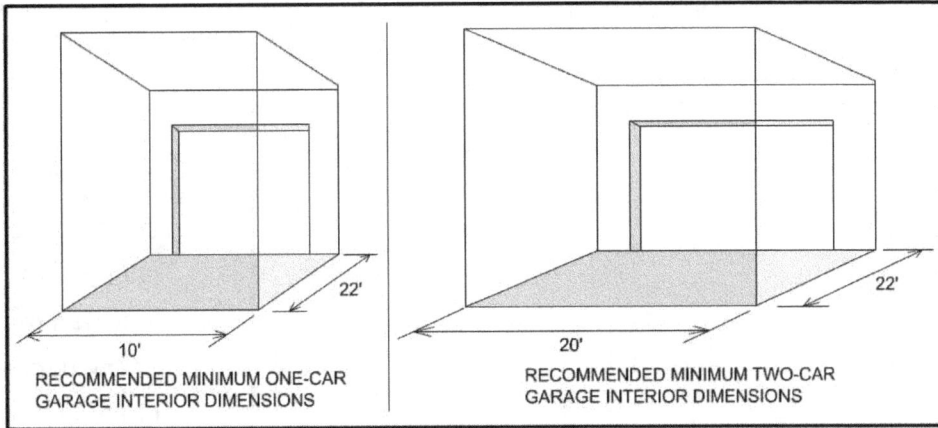

RECOMMENDED MINIMUM ONE-CAR
GARAGE INTERIOR DIMENSIONS

RECOMMENDED MINIMUM TWO-CAR
GARAGE INTERIOR DIMENSIONS

□ **room entry** is **absent of a light switch** or a switch controlling an electrical outlet

□ **wonder whether approvals are in order** for the following:

□ _____
□ _____
□ _____

Lighting

☐ **exterior lighting** is **recommended outside** the _____ yard

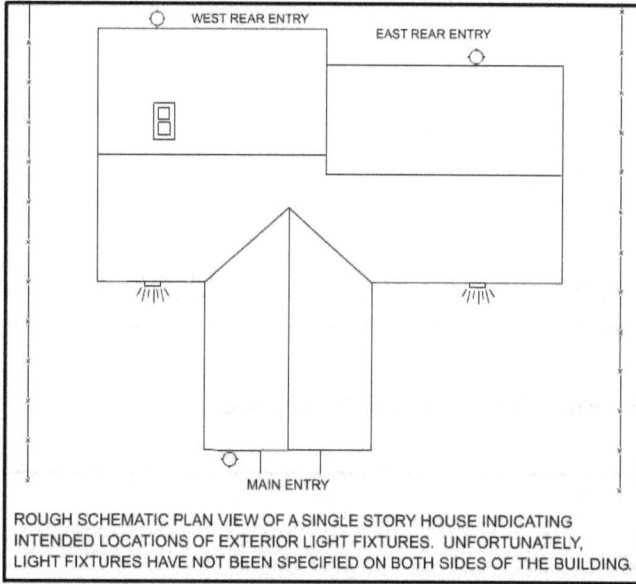

WEST REAR ENTRY

EAST REAR ENTRY

MAIN ENTRY

ROUGH SCHEMATIC PLAN VIEW OF A SINGLE STORY HOUSE INDICATING
INTENDED LOCATIONS OF EXTERIOR LIGHT FIXTURES. UNFORTUNATELY,
LIGHT FIXTURES HAVE NOT BEEN SPECIFIED ON BOTH SIDES OF THE BUILDING.

Today's electrical codes generally require that the location of a house entry receive illumination, although it is not necessary to place a light fixture at each exterior doorway.

☐ **replace missing light fixture** at _____
☐ hanging **light fixture** at _____ **may sway** against _____
☐ hanging **light fixture** at _____ **hangs too low**

Besides someone inadvertently walking into this low hanging light fixture, wind or seismic forces could cause it to sway against a wall resulting in falling, broken glass.

☐ **light** fixture **hangs low over** _____ **bathtub**

> This low hanging light is an electrical hazard. In fact, switches and outlets are not even supposed to be located within arms reach of a bathtub. Lastly, it's not a good idea to have an outlet located directly behind a kitchen cooktop.

☐ **clearance** is **needed around light canister** in attic

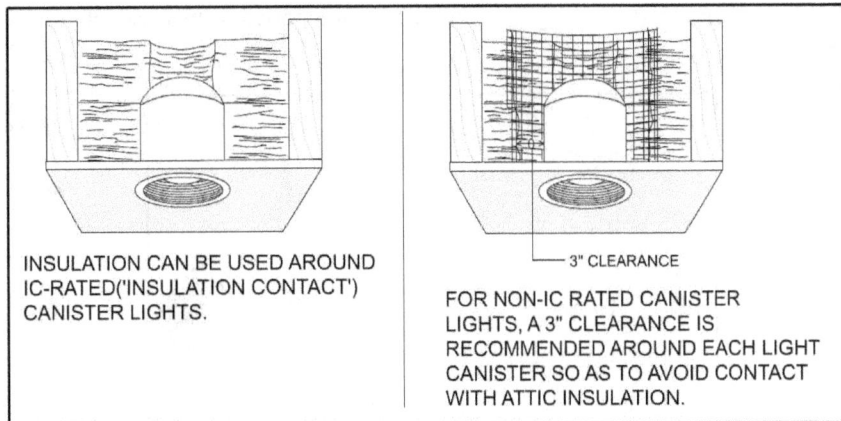

INSULATION CAN BE USED AROUND IC-RATED('INSULATION CONTACT') CANISTER LIGHTS.

—— 3" CLEARANCE

FOR NON-IC RATED CANISTER LIGHTS, A 3" CLEARANCE IS RECOMMENDED AROUND EACH LIGHT CANISTER SO AS TO AVOID CONTACT WITH ATTIC INSULATION.

Locks

☐ **provide lock** at _____

☐ realize (master bedroom) (smaller bedroom) **entry door(s) did not contain locks**

☐ recommend an **emergency key release** for operating the garage door manually in the event of an electrical power failure

☐ **provide** a **lock at** the _____ **bathroom door for privacy**

Painting

- □ **paint** a marking **to make** the existence of the **elevation differential obvious** at _____
- □ **exterior of (house) (building) could stand a paint job** for aesthetic reasons
- □ **exterior trim needs painting**

> Sanding work prepares this clapboard siding for priming and painting.

- □ **touch up trim** where some peeling paint
- □ exterior **metal trim needs painting**
- □ **repair fine cracking** during painting at _____

Patchwork

- □ **patched** _____ **ceiling from** reported former **leak** above

> This ceiling was just patched as a result of a reported former leak that had developed above this area. The ceiling is presently dry and we don't see any reason to dispute the claim. But we recommend that you ask for the bill of sale for the repair in the event of any implied warranties or actual guarantees.

- □ **patched** _____ **ceiling from** lighting **fixture removal**
- □ **patched** _____ **ceiling - ask the owner** and get any guarantees regarding this work
- □ **ask** the **owner about the patchwork / or staining** that was noted at the following example locations:
    - □ _____
    - □ _____

Peeling Paint

☐ **peeling paint** noted on _____ **wall - hoping no rot**

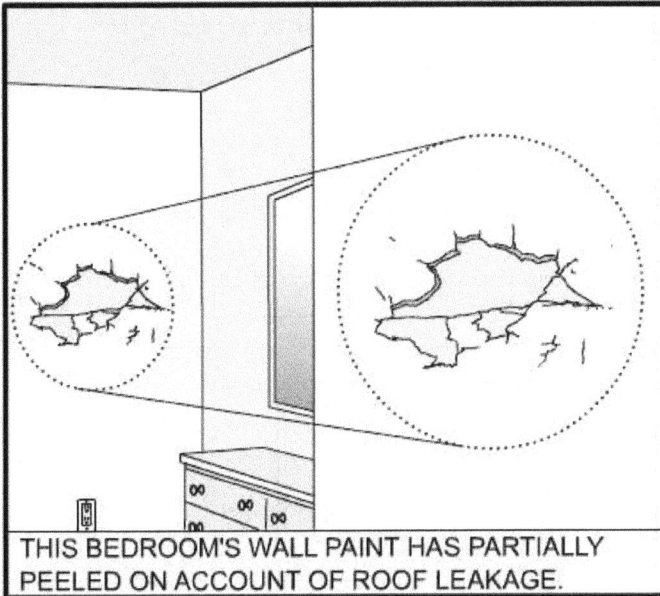

Peeling paint could reflect poor bonding between the base primer paint and the surface paint. But it also could represent (possible past) moisture / water problems inside the wall that can cause mold / or wood rot. By cutting open the wall before the next paint job, this would divulge the wall's interior condition. If a rot / or mold condition(s) do exist, the cost to retrofit can be high and you take a risk in this regard.

THIS BEDROOM'S WALL PAINT HAS PARTIALLY PEELED ON ACCOUNT OF ROOF LEAKAGE.

☐ **peeling paint** noted on _____ **wall - likely from poor bonding**

Pest Control

☐ **presence of** _____, **a monthly service** with a licensed pest control contractor is recommended for at least a year
☐ **presence of numerous bees** noted in the _____, **call** an **exterminator**
☐ **call exterminator to remove** an active _____ **nest** at _____
☐ **presence of the following pests**, we recommend a monthly service with a licensed pest control contractor for at least a year
    ☐ _____
    ☐ _____
    ☐ _____

Plumbing

☐ standing **water inside water meter pit**

> It could reflect a leakage problem from the water main, but the condition could merely have resulted from sprinkler or rain water entry, or a matter of having developed meter or valve leakage. Note that the cost of a new water main can be expensive.

☐ **plumber to check** the following:
    ☐ _____
    ☐ _____
    ☐ _____
☐ **wet** area along the _____ **yard** probably caused **by damaged pipe**
☐ **lower water pressure:**
    ☐ (hot) (cold) water (low) (somewhat low) at _____ sink faucet
    ☐ (hot) (cold) water (low) (somewhat low) at _____ sink faucet
    ☐ (hot) (cold) water (low) (somewhat low) at _____ sink faucet

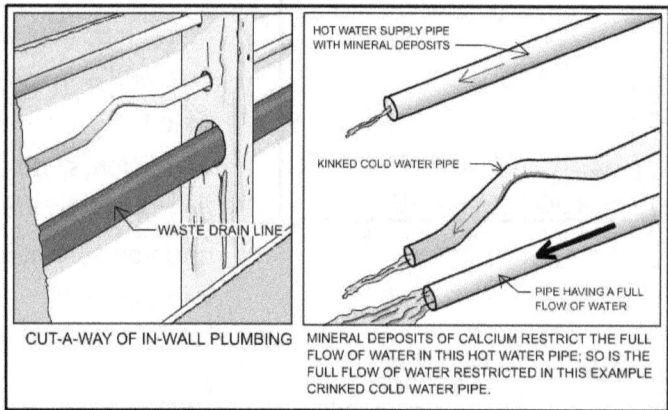

CUT-A-WAY OF IN-WALL PLUMBING

HOT WATER SUPPLY PIPE WITH MINERAL DEPOSITS

KINKED COLD WATER PIPE

PIPE HAVING A FULL FLOW OF WATER

MINERAL DEPOSITS OF CALCIUM RESTRICT THE FULL FLOW OF WATER IN THIS HOT WATER PIPE; SO IS THE FULL FLOW OF WATER RESTRICTED IN THIS EXAMPLE CRINKED COLD WATER PIPE.

☐ **clogged aerator(s)** detected at:
    ☐ _____ sink faucet
    ☐ _____ sink faucet
    ☐ _____ sink faucet

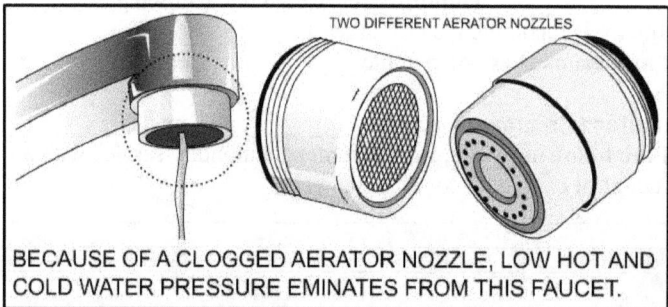

TWO DIFFERENT AERATOR NOZZLES

BECAUSE OF A CLOGGED AERATOR NOZZLE, LOW HOT AND COLD WATER PRESSURE EMINATES FROM THIS FAUCET.

☐ **high water pressure**

WATER RESERVOIR

HOMES WITH HIGH WATER PRESSURE

HOMES HAVING LESSER PRESSURE

HOMES WITH GREATEST WATER PRESSURE

WATER PRESSURE REDUCING VALVE

WATER PRESSURE TEST GAUGE

50 to 60 psi is normal, workable pressure for the interior of a home.

☐ **rusty water** likely reflects rusty galvanized piping:
>   ☐ (hot) (cold) water at ___ sink faucet - but (cleared) (did not clear) after a moment of running water
>   ☐ (hot) (cold) water at ___ sink faucet - but (cleared) (did not clear) after a moment of running water
>   ☐ (hot) (cold) water at ___ sink faucet - but (cleared) (did not clear) after a moment of running water

☐ because of (some) (most) (all) **old galvanized plumbing** (with pressure loss) (with rusting), **budget** for new copper piping

☐ **galvanized plumbing with no pressure loss and rusting** - believe it doesn't pose a serious problem in the immediate future

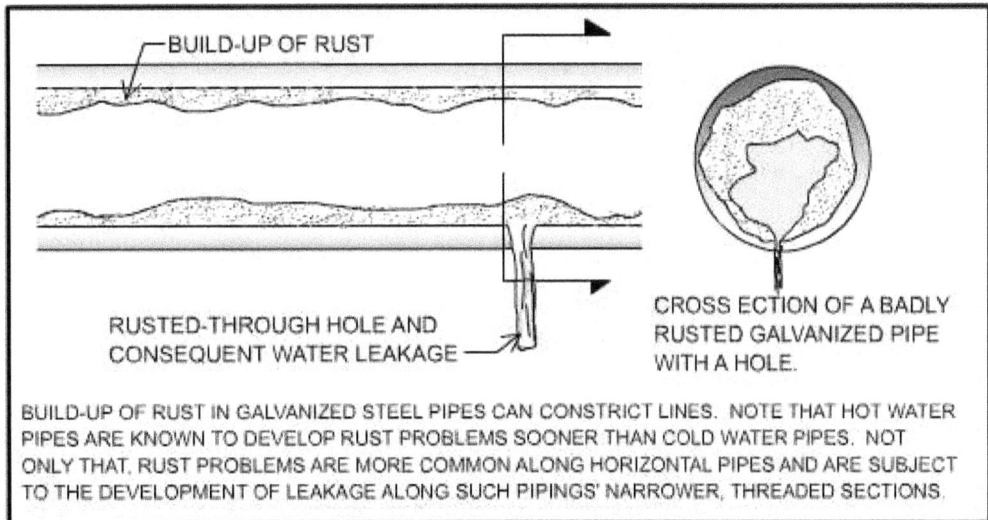

BUILD-UP OF RUST

RUSTED-THROUGH HOLE AND CONSEQUENT WATER LEAKAGE

CROSS ECTION OF A BADLY RUSTED GALVANIZED PIPE WITH A HOLE.

BUILD-UP OF RUST IN GALVANIZED STEEL PIPES CAN CONSTRICT LINES. NOTE THAT HOT WATER PIPES ARE KNOWN TO DEVELOP RUST PROBLEMS SOONER THAN COLD WATER PIPES. NOT ONLY THAT, RUST PROBLEMS ARE MORE COMMON ALONG HORIZONTAL PIPES AND ARE SUBJECT TO THE DEVELOPMENT OF LEAKAGE ALONG SUCH PIPINGS' NARROWER, THREADED SECTIONS.

☐ **ask extent of copper piping** installation
☐ **active leakage** at _____
☐ **corrosion of pipe** at _____

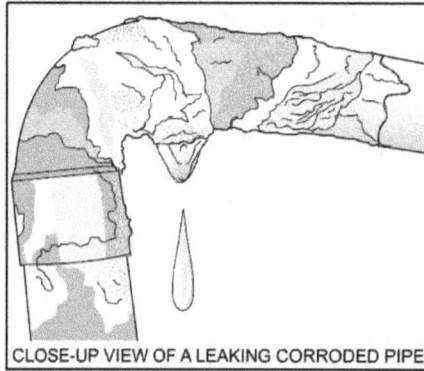

CLOSE-UP VIEW OF A LEAKING CORRODED PIPE

When pipes show corrosion, they could be so deeply pitted and so weak that they require immediate replacement.

☐ **corrosion of pipe atop water heater** from electrolysis

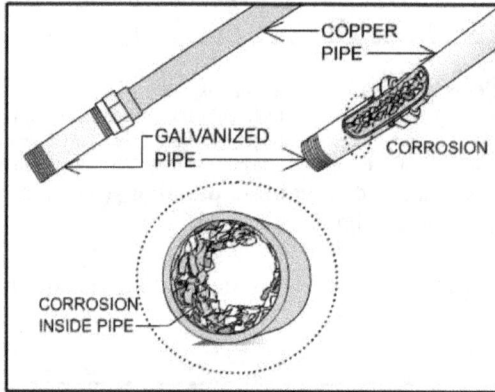

COPPER PIPE

GALVANIZED PIPE

CORROSION

CORROSION INSIDE PIPE

Heavy corrosion of juncture piping typically occurs as a result of electrolytic action. This is a process of unusually rapid destruction of the pipe joint which sets up when two different types of metals are brought together in the presence of water. Indeed, nonconducting adapters should be used for these connections. The corrective plumbing action should be taken before significant leakage occurs. You might detect an example of this above a water heater.

☐ length(s) of **water line(s) rest on soil**
☐ **piping touches wood** member(s)
☐ **banging water hammer noise** at _____ faucet when water turned off
☐ **chattering noise** when _____ faucet is turned on
☐ **gas odor** at (meter) (_____)

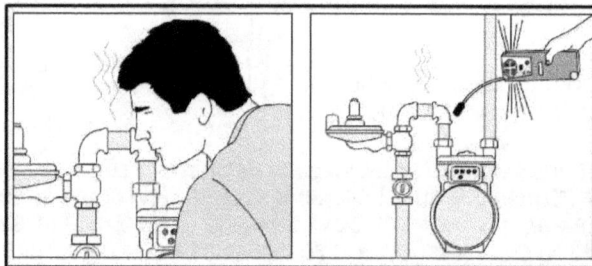

A gas leak was detected at the gas meter location by sense of odor as well as by the use of a gas leak detector. The local gas company should be notified at once so that their personnel could take care of the repair.

☐ **waste backup** at _____

THE OVERFLOWING TOILET AND THE WASTE BACKUP ARE CAUSED BY THIS HOME'S DAMAGED DRAIN LINE.

Search, also, for stained or wetted drain pipes since the cost of possible waste plumbing replacement work can be expensive.

☐ **old sewer lines**

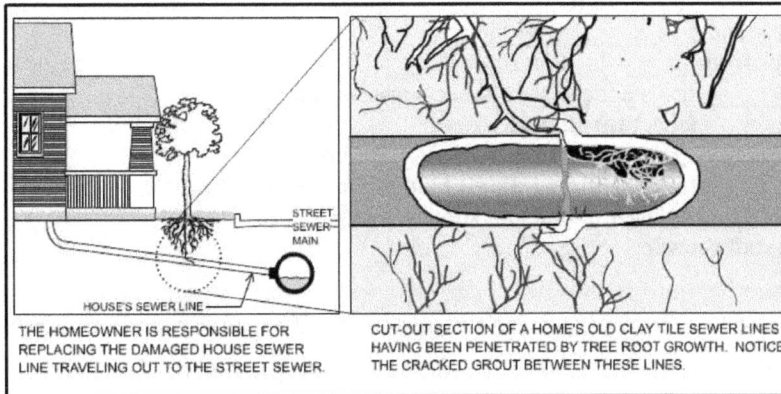

STREET SEWER MAIN

HOUSE'S SEWER LINE

THE HOMEOWNER IS RESPONSIBLE FOR REPLACING THE DAMAGED HOUSE SEWER LINE TRAVELING OUT TO THE STREET SEWER.

CUT-OUT SECTION OF A HOME'S OLD CLAY TILE SEWER LINES HAVING BEEN PENETRATED BY TREE ROOT GROWTH. NOTICE THE CRACKED GROUT BETWEEN THESE LINES.

Sewer lines which are more than 40 years old are considered to be getting old.

☐ **septic system (aging)**(at its rated life)(beyond its rated life expectancy)

THE OCCURRENCE OF SOME FAILURE OF A HOME'S LEACH FIELD.

☐ later **added bedrooms, but** private **waste system wasn't increased**
☐ **examine private sewage disposal system and have periodically cleaned**

□ **no air gap**

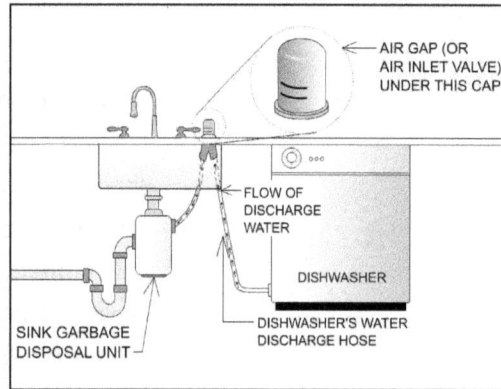

AIR GAP (OR
AIR INLET VALVE)
UNDER THIS CAP

FLOW OF
DISCHARGE
WATER

DISHWASHER

SINK GARBAGE
DISPOSAL UNIT

DISHWASHER'S WATER
DISCHARGE HOSE

> The purpose of this device is to prevent a vacuum in the waste line that could cause siphoning of waste water back into the dishwasher.

□ **water empties through air gap**

□ (_____sink) (_____bathtub) **water was slow to drain**

□ **cracked** _____ **sink**

□ **leak** at _____ **under** _____ sink

□ **taped elbow** under _____ sink

□ **water drips from** _____ **faucet**

□ _____ sink's left and right **faucets are reversed**

□ _____ **faucet turns clockwise**

□ replace **missing pop-up drain plug** at _____ sink

□ _____ sink's **drain plug didn't hold** its basin **water**

□ possible need for **replacement of stall shower pan**

□ **small size stall shower**

> Your local building code likely doesn't allow shower stalls to have an interior dimension having less than 30", nor have a floor area smaller than 900 square inches in size.

□ **wrong finish of stall shower**

□ **back water siphonage at** old _____ tub

□ **no tub plumbing access** for _____ tub

□ **leakage at** _____ **diverter valve**

□ **drain mechanism didn't work** - stopper used at _____

□ **rubber stopper used** at _____ tub

□ _____ **tub's plug didn't hold water**

□ **cramped clearance**(s) offered **at** _____ **toilet**

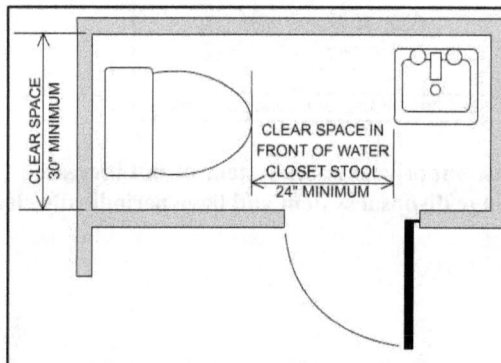

CLEAR SPACE
30" MINIMUM

CLEAR SPACE IN
FRONT OF WATER
CLOSET STOOL
24" MINIMUM

☐ eventually replace _____ **toilet finely cracked** - but no leakage
☐ _____ **toilet tank cover broken**
☐ _____ **toilet leaks at** its **base**

INSTALLATION OF NEW WAX RING

DETECTION OF LEAKAGE
AT THE TOILET BASE

CROSS SECTION OF TOILET DRAIN

☐ _____ **toilet moves**
☐ **water trickles into** _____ **toilet bowl**
☐ **dripping water after** _____ **toilet** was **flushed**
☐ _____ **toilet runs**
☐ _____ **toilet flushed weakly**
☐ **hold lever at** _____ **toilet**
☐ some **plumbing fixture problems noted**:
      ☐ _____
      ☐ _____
      ☐ _____

Pool

☐ differential **settlement of** swimming **pool**

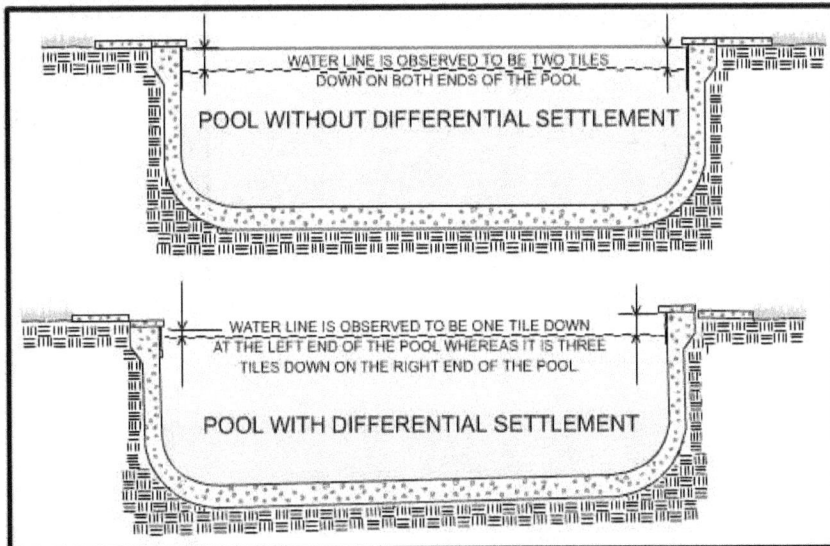

WATER LINE IS OBSERVED TO BE TWO TILES
DOWN ON BOTH ENDS OF THE POOL

POOL WITHOUT DIFFERENTIAL SETTLEMENT

WATER LINE IS OBSERVED TO BE ONE TILE DOWN
AT THE LEFT END OF THE POOL WHEREAS IT IS THREE
TILES DOWN ON THE RIGHT END OF THE POOL

POOL WITH DIFFERENTIAL SETTLEMENT

□ **worn pool** needs attention
□ **pool needs resurfacing**
□ **re-seal coping joint**
□ **unheated** swimming **pool**
□ **pool's water heater aging**
□ **old pool filter**
□ **old pool pump**/motor
□ **pool** was **not fenced off**

This home's 8 feet deep swimming pool has been enclosed by a minimum 4.5 feet fence above the ground. Its 4.5 feet gate self-latches closed.

□ **diving board bolts rusted**

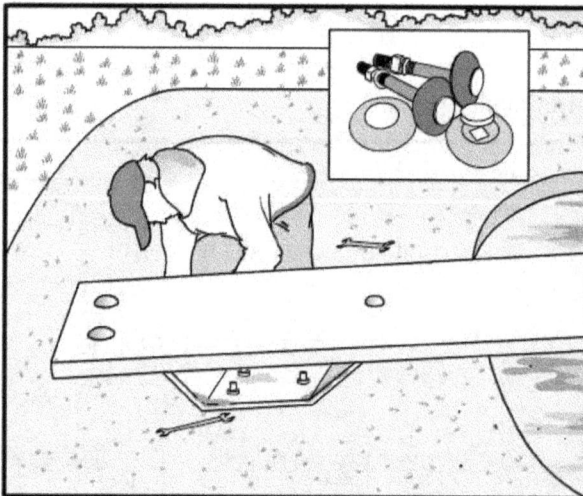

Not only have these diving board bolts rusted, but the diving board's support is beginning to show signs of rust as well.

Regrout

☐ **regrout** _____ sink
☐ **regrout** _____ bathtub
☐ **regrout** _____ stall shower

A PROFESSIONAL TILEMAN WAS CALLED IN TO REGROUT THIS STALL SHOWER'S CERAMIC TILE WALLS ON ACCOUNT OF THE MANY GAPS AND HOLES WHICH EXIST IN THE SHOWER'S GROUTING.

Because water could seep through holes and gaps in old groutings around sinks, tubs and stall showers and cause the wood below and in back of these plumbing fixtures to eventually rot, regrouting work is recommended to be done periodically.

Removal

☐ **clear underfloor** crawl space free of debris

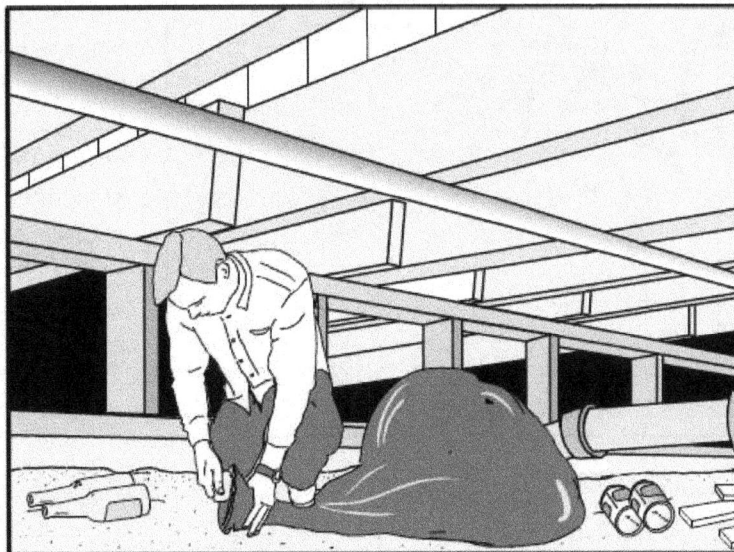

□ **remove** stored **material near (furnace)** (water heater)

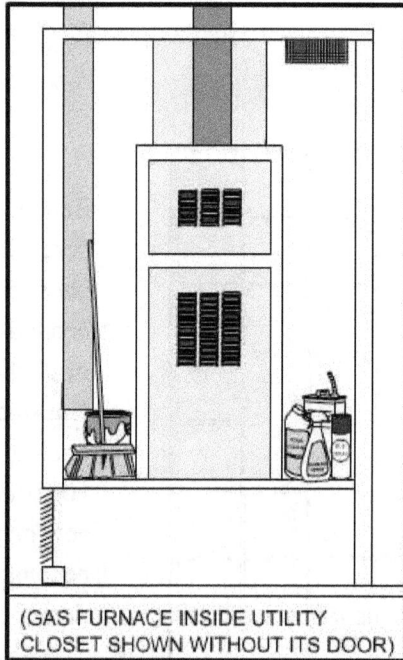

(GAS FURNACE INSIDE UTILITY
CLOSET SHOWN WITHOUT ITS DOOR)

All stored material that is located inside fuel-fired heating plant closets should be removed from these closets for safety reasons.

□ **remove rodent droppings** from (attic) (_____)
□ **clean roof** free of leaves and debris

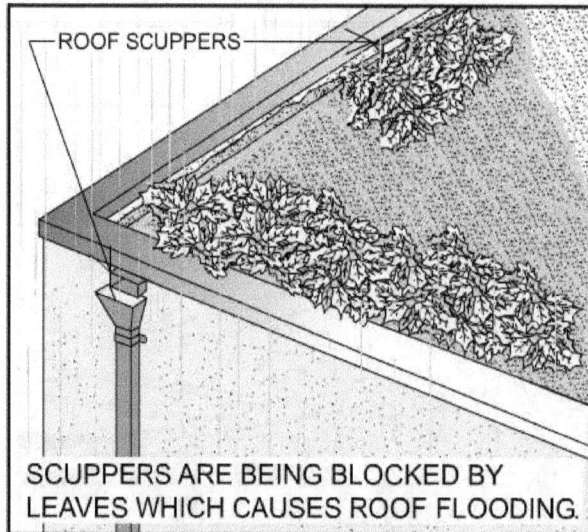

ROOF SCUPPERS

SCUPPERS ARE BEING BLOCKED BY
LEAVES WHICH CAUSES ROOF FLOODING.

A clean and properly pitched roof with adequate drainage helps to prevent water backup and consequent roof leakage. It can also help reduce the chance of structural failure occurrences often caused by the weight of standing water which collects upon relatively flat roofs.

□ **remove** _____ **resting on roof**

Roof

☐ **replace** _____ **roof** (at) (beyond) **rated life:**
- ☐ evidence of leakage on _____
- ☐ some roofing repairs already made of late
- ☐ _____ causes us to believe that replacement time is now

WIND-LIFTED SHINGLES

ATTIC

LARGE WET STAIN ON CEILING

LEAKS HERE BUT DRIPS THERE

POINT OF LEAKAGE IS LOCATED IN ATTIC.

☐ **replace soon** _____ **roof** (at) (beyond) rated life:
- ☐ evidence of leakage on _____
- ☐ brace for periodic patching
- ☐ immediate roofing repair should be instituted

☐ **replace soon** _____ **roof rapidly aging:**
- ☐ no significance evidence of leakage could be found
- ☐ brace for periodic patching
- ☐ immediate roofing repair should be instituted

☐ **repair** _____ **roof** which appears to be **in generally** _____ **condition:**
- ☐ no significance evidence of leakage could be found
- ☐ some _____ (was) (were) noted
- ☐ some _____ (was) (were) noted

Screens

☐ **re-screen** _____ **underfloor vent screens** that were (torn) (damaged) (missing)

THESE TORN-DAMAGED SCREENED UNDERFLOOR WALL VENT OPENINGS ARE SCHEDULED TO BE RE-SCREENED.

These ventilation wall openings need re-screening work to bar the entry of small animals. Typically, 1/4" square corrosion - resistant metal mesh is used for this purpose.

- ☐ **no screen door** at _____ entrance to the house
- ☐ **missing** _____ **sliding screen door**
- ☐ **no window screens** provided on house
- ☐ **window screens missing** at _____
- ☐ **ripped screen** found at _____
- ☐ **vent openings** at _____ **need re-screening** work

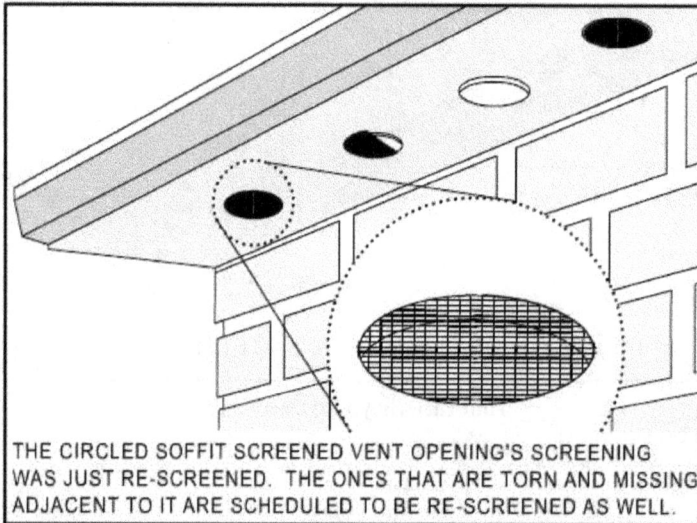

THE CIRCLED SOFFIT SCREENED VENT OPENING'S SCREENING WAS JUST RE-SCREENED. THE ONES THAT ARE TORN AND MISSING ADJACENT TO IT ARE SCHEDULED TO BE RE-SCREENED AS WELL.

Note that if the condition is left unattended, bees and other insects might utilize the attic's space for their nesting area.

- ☐ **add screening to attic vents**

Seek Information

It is recommended that you further inquire about the following:

- ☐ determining whether mineral rights come along with the sale of the property;
- ☐ learning whether there are any underground utilities and plumbing supply and waste lines which cross the home site to any of the neighboring properties;
- ☐ more about the history and use of the site and additional information about the site's subdivision. For instance, was the property part of a fruit grove?
- ☐ determining whether the house has been later equipped with a new water main;
- ☐ additional information about the adequacy of street drainage in the neighborhood, especially in front of the house;
- ☐ the cost of fire insurance for the house and learning whether it would be difficult to obtain. Ask if there has been any known fire to have occurred in the locality of the home. For instance, the known "Malibu Fire" burned the neighbor's house down. You may also wish to learn more about the extent of water spray action from the irrigation sprinklers present;
- ☐ more about the neighboring parcels of land, including what they have been zoned for and who owns them. For instance, the seller spoke of zoning for 2-family homes across the street from this house. Ask if there are any neighboring land parcels which are presently landlocked;

□ more about the environmental locality of this dwelling. This includes, for example, determining with certainty whether the nearby electrical transformer vault, the not-too-distant utility pole and wiring pose any possible harmful health effects to the residents of the house such as during seismic activity or by means of possible radiation;

□ additional information about the nearby water channel. For example, learn who cleans and maintains this channel. Ask, too, if water which runs along it attracts insects or emits odors;

□ determining whether gnats or other flying insects frequent the home's yards where a multitude of such insects are noted to hover about the property;

□ determining whether a vehicle has ever run into the home and, if so, learn exactly what damage did it do;

□ determining whether the street storm drain in front of the house poses a safety hazard to small children for it has a wide unprotected opening. Learn, too, whether foul odors are emitted from this storm drain or whether it attracts insects at times;

□ more about the lot size relative to the minimum size zoned lot permitted in the locality

□ determining whether cable television is now possible in the neighborhood or, perhaps, will be possible in the near future;

□ learning whether the exterior tiles have been recently sealed

□ determining that sewage which exits the house is done by gravity flow and does not require pumping through the waste lines. If this is so, is there a hermetically sealed pump to do this work?

□ determining whether it is required for the house to be connected to city sewers when they are installed along the street in front of the house;

□ determining the exact route of the home's sewer lines in exiting the home site;

□ why the street curb in front of the house has been marked with painted numerals;

□ learning of any possible encroachments;

□ how the perimeter fences, walls and curbing run relative to the property lines. For example, one fence doesn't run straight, but juts to one side at its mid-length;

□ what remedy(ies) (if any) does the seller intend to correct before closing;

□ where the collected water from the outside area drains exit. Could it be to the drainage outlet in the street curb?

□ determining whether the swimming pool has been equipped with overflow drains;

□ determining whether the planter along the outside wall of the house has been waterproofed;

□ learning whether the close-to-grade wood used in the construction of this home utilizes pressure-treated wood with an approved preservative, or is of a durable variety;

□ determining whether anchor bolts have been used along mud sillplates to help secure the house framing (called the superstructure) to its respective foundation in the event of seismic activities. The finished walls prohibit examination of this condition;

□ learning for what kind of pests does the extermination service treat against;

□ learning the age of the house's tile roof, including learning whether it has a new underlayment (since many homeowners of tile roofs merely replace the old underlayment and any damaged tiles);

□ determining whether tub, door and shower glazing as well as low-to-floor window and transom window glazing consist of safety tempered glazing which is appropriate for these glass sections;

□ how well secure is the climate control unit mounted upon the roof;

□ how well the mirrored panels have been fastened to the wall. Are they glue-adhesive fastened?

☐ verifying the existence of vinyl asbestos tile finish flooring in this home. A laboratory can make a positive identification of it;

☐ learning whether the mineral asbestos is present in all acoustical ceiling spray material. Again, a laboratory can make a positive identification of it;

☐ learning whether acoustical ceiling spray, which was reportedly recently removed from the house, was performed by a certified or licensed asbestos abatement contractor (if asbestos was, in fact, found to be present in that acoustical spray material);

☐ additional information about the community's shared well water supply system that the house is connected onto. This was provided by a private company with each homeowner having been granted transferable shares of well usage. The home's private well was disconnected and is not in use;

☐ determining whether the efflorescence which was seen in the fireplace chamber reflects a chimney water penetration problem possibly because of faulty flashing. A chimney contractor/or a roofer will have to check this out;

☐ determining whether the self-cleaning oven requires exterior venting and, if this is so, learn whether it has been so equipped;

☐ determining if there is pre-wiring already installed underground to serve an outside post lamp. If so, ask then if all that would be required is the post lamp itself

☐ what the timer controls;

☐ determining whether or not the firm which architecturally designed the home or the home's remodeling work is a duly licensed architectural firm and, further, had been engaged to oversee the construction;

☐ and whether or not the installation of fire sprinklers are (or have been) required in the building;

☐ determining whether belonging to the local homeowners association is mandatory or not;

☐ (new home) determining whether any possible design changes conform to the issued plans (which should, of course, be approved plans). If not, then request to see possible final amended documentation or addenda for any possible changes. For instance, the builder spoke of a shared connecting bathroom to serve two bedrooms but, instead, it was later decided after the plans were building department -approved that each bedroom was to have its own bathroom and was so accordingly built that way. The building department inspector red-lined in and signed off this change at the job site;

☐ (new home) for what length of time is the structural integrity of the house guaranteed for;

☐ (new home) determining if the builder offers guarantees relative to paint and cabinet touch-ups;

☐ (condominium) learning whether the homeowners of the building are involved in any possible existing litigation matters or other possible action taken with respect to possible building defects and deficiencies;

☐ (condominium) requesting verification of the fact that the common walls which separate the apartment units are of the correct fire-rated wall variety;

☐ (condominium) and determining whether guarantees exist for the building's fire sprinkler system and elevators, or possibly whether there are service contracts to maintain them.

Soils/Geological

☐ **poor grading** on _____ side(s)

NOTE THAT WATER AROUND AND UNDER BUILDINGS CAN UPHEAVE STRUCTURES AND CAUSE INTERIOR CRACKS TO TAKE PLACE. THIS IS KNOWN TO HAPPEN PARTICULARLY IN BUILDINGS OVER EXPANSIVE (CLAY) SOILS.

MAIN FLOOR

BASEMENT LEVEL

LAND SLOPES TOWARDS THE HOUSE AND FLOODS THE YARD THERE. AS SUCH, THE SURFACE WATER IN THIS EXAMPLE PRODUCES ENOUGH HYDROSTATIC PRESSURE TO CAUSE CONSEQUENT BENDING IN OF THE HOUSE'S FOUNDATION AND EXTERIOR WALLS.

SURFACE WATER RUN-OFF EXAMPLE CONDITION

SILLPLATE

DISTRESSED AND BOWED-IN CONCRETE FOUNDATION WALL WITH WATER PENETRATION
SECTION A

MAIN FLOOR

BASEMENT LEVEL

HYDROSTATIC PRESSURE

WATER TABLE

FOOTING DRAIN NO LONGER EFFECTIVE OR CLOGGED (PERHAPS BY SILT)

HYDROSTATIC PRESSURE

BECAUSE OF SIGNIFICANT HYDROSTATIC PRESSURE, WATER COMES UP THROUGH SLAB'S FLOOR CRACK AND THROUGH LENGTHS OF THE JUNCTURE WHERE THE CONCRETE FLOOR MEETS THE FOUNDATION WALL

HYDROSTATIC PRESSURE FROM SUB-SURFACE DRAINAGE CAN BEND AND CRACK FOUNDATION WALLS AND FLOOR SLAB.

SUB-SURFACE DRAINAGE EXAMPLE CONDITION

SILLPLATE

CRACKED AND BOWED-IN CONCRETE BLOCK FOUNDATION WALL WHICH ALLOWS THROUGH-THE-WALL WATER PENETRATION
SECTION A1

Unfavorable grading of the land might mean that the land slopes toward the house whereby the hydraulic pressure on the building can be increased. Also, this can lead to water seepage problems.

☐ **geologist to examine** the premise grounds before commitment including for:
- ☐ hillside sloughing / debris or rock slides
- ☐ slump slippage
- ☐ subsidence
- ☐ lateral creep
- ☐ soil erosion
- ☐ the building's close proximity to the hillside slope
- ☐ _____ geological condition

HOUSE STRUCTURE IS TOO CLOSE TO EDGE OF HILLSIDE SLOPE.

SLOUGHAGE

ENTIRE BACK PORTION OF FLOOR OF HOUSE SLOPES DOWNWARDLY.

☐ **distress** at _____ **probably** resulted **from settlement** - but verify with geologist
☐ **provide ground cover** at bare _____ slope

EROSION CREVICES OBSERVED ALONG BARE SLOPED AREAS OF HILLSIDE BEHIND THIS HOUSE.

Staining

□ old dry **stains on underfloor members** likely by past plumbing leakage-but ask owner

AS A RESULT OF WATER SPRINKLER ACTION HAVING SPRAYED AGAINST THE HOUSE FOR AN EXTENDED PERIOD OF TIME, WATER STAINS, STREAK MARKS AND DISCOLORATION NOW MARK THIS HOME'S BOTTOM EXTERIOR WALL.

□ **old** water **stains on** _____ **ceiling probably** from a **past** plumbing **leak**
□ **old** water **stains on** _____ **ceiling reported** from a **past** plumbing **leak**
□ **water stains mark** _____ **but** appear **old and inactive** at the present time
□ **old** water **staining marks** ____ but **ask the seller** about this and obtain any guarantees
□ **old, dry** water **stains** seen **at** the following **example locations** and hopefully corrected:
  □ old staining exists on _____;
  □ _____;
  □ _____.
□ **old stains in attic - antedate latest roofing** installation work
□ **old, dry** water **staining / blister damage / patchwork** were seen **at** the following **example locations** and hopefully the problems which caused the conditions have been corrected:
  □ old staining exists on _____;
  □ blister damage exists along _____;
  □ patchwork detected at _____.

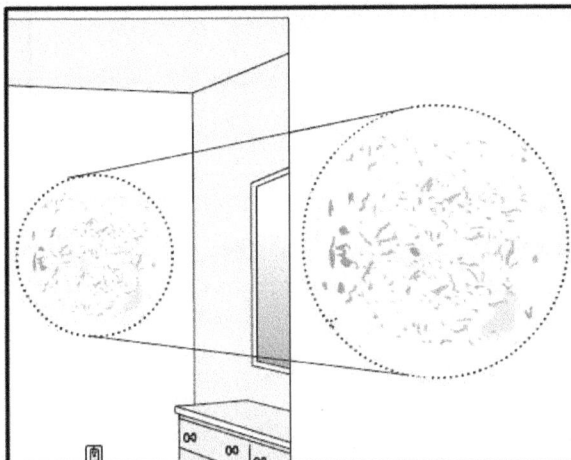

Water or moisture penetration can cause an interior wall to blister. The illustrated blistered bedroom's plaster wall example points up the necessity to ensure that all exterior walls are weathersealed/or patch-repaired, and that all roof and roof/flashing be appropriately maintained.

Stairs

☐ **reinforce** _____ **weak steps**

THE CRACKED STRINGER, STEP RISER, STEP TREAD AND KICK PLATE WERE ALL SISTER-REINFORCED TO STRENGTHEN THIS STAIRWAY.

Structural

☐ **re-point and patch** (vertical) (horizontal) **crack in** ____ **foundation wall** and monitor

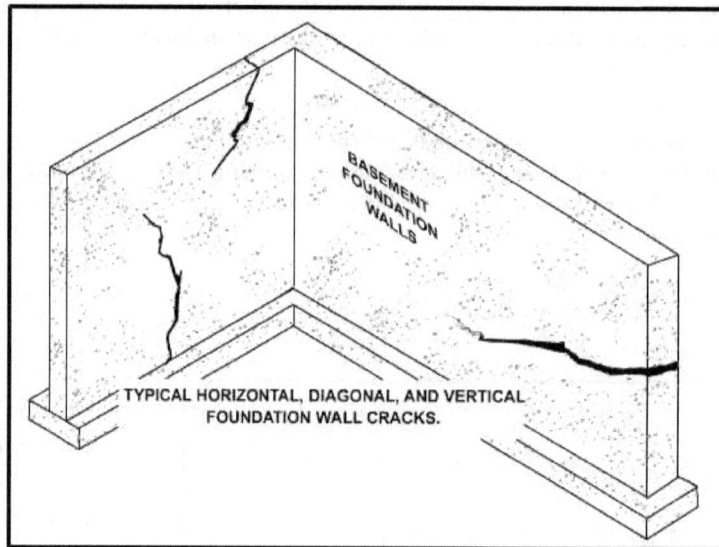

BASEMENT FOUNDATION WALLS

TYPICAL HORIZONTAL, DIAGONAL, AND VERTICAL FOUNDATION WALL CRACKS.

Numerous foundation wall cracks can be pointed and patched in their entirety. Should significant cracking reappear following the patchwork, costly sub-structural "underpinning" work may then be in order.

☐ **following crawl space structural work** is **required:**

    ☐ _____

    ☐ _____

☐ **recommend** house **framing be secured to** its **foundation**

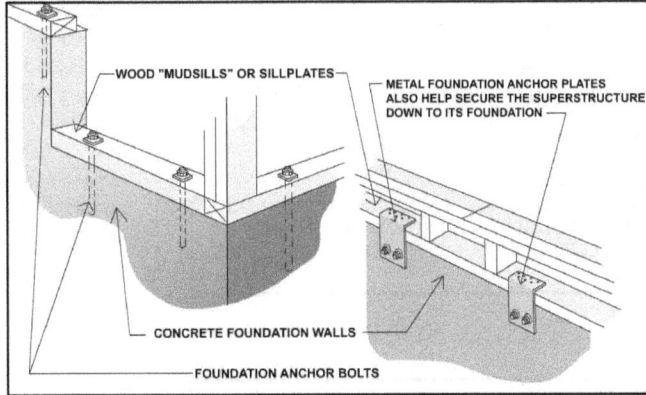

WOOD "MUDSILLS" OR SILLPLATES

METAL FOUNDATION ANCHOR PLATES ALSO HELP SECURE THE SUPERSTRUCTURE DOWN TO ITS FOUNDATION

CONCRETE FOUNDATION WALLS

FOUNDATION ANCHOR BOLTS

Realize that there are many old houses which have not been tie-down secured. The tying is normally done by utilizing anchor bolts. Look for their existence.

☐ **deteriorated foundation wall(s)** at _____

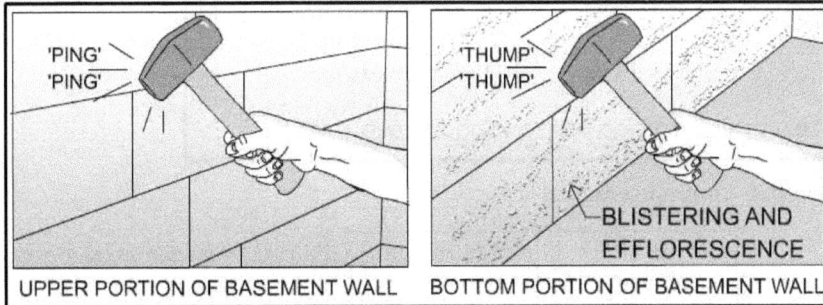

'PING' 'PING'

'THUMP' 'THUMP'

BLISTERING AND EFFLORESCENCE

UPPER PORTION OF BASEMENT WALL   BOTTOM PORTION OF BASEMENT WALL

Chronic underfloor water seepage problems can eventually deteriorate foundation walls.

☐ **structural damage** detected **from termites** at _____

☐ **off-center post loading**

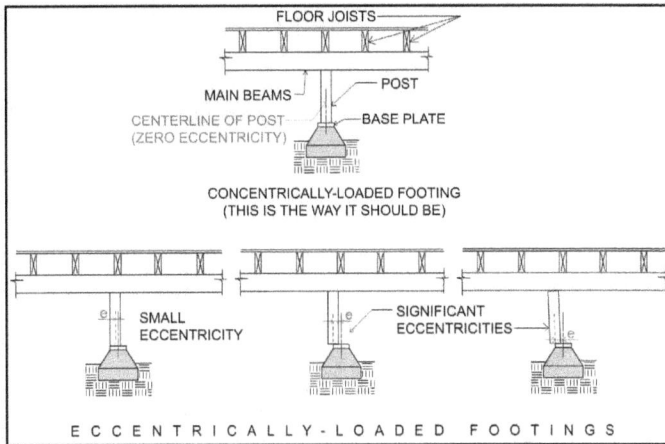

FLOOR JOISTS

MAIN BEAMS   POST

CENTERLINE OF POST (ZERO ECCENTRICITY)   BASE PLATE

CONCENTRICALLY-LOADED FOOTING
(THIS IS THE WAY IT SHOULD BE)

SMALL ECCENTRICITY   SIGNIFICANT ECCENTRICITIES

E C C E N T R I C A L L Y - L O A D E D   F O O T I N G S

☐ **temporary shoring under house** at _____

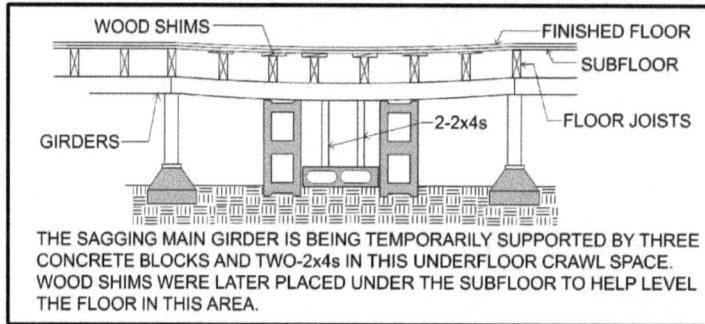

WOOD SHIMS — FINISHED FLOOR
SUBFLOOR
GIRDERS — 2-2x4s — FLOOR JOISTS

THE SAGGING MAIN GIRDER IS BEING TEMPORARILY SUPPORTED BY THREE CONCRETE BLOCKS AND TWO-2x4s IN THIS UNDERFLOOR CRAWL SPACE. WOOD SHIMS WERE LATER PLACED UNDER THE SUBFLOOR TO HELP LEVEL THE FLOOR IN THIS AREA.

Sometimes, the type of 'shoring' work that is used is that which is found in only temporary construction. The removal of the support work could lead to floor deflection.

☐ **main beams** at _____ are **in poor condition**

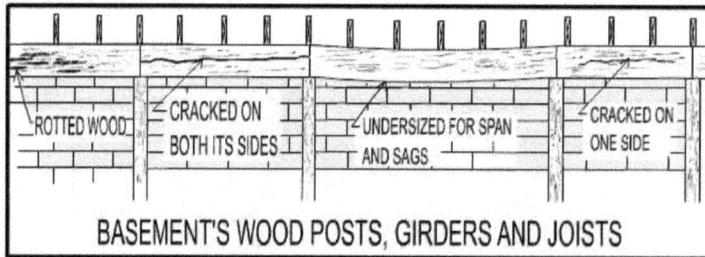

ROTTED WOOD — CRACKED ON BOTH ITS SIDES — UNDERSIZED FOR SPAN AND SAGS — CRACKED ON ONE SIDE

BASEMENT'S WOOD POSTS, GIRDERS AND JOISTS

☐ concrete **slab-on-grade cracked** at _____

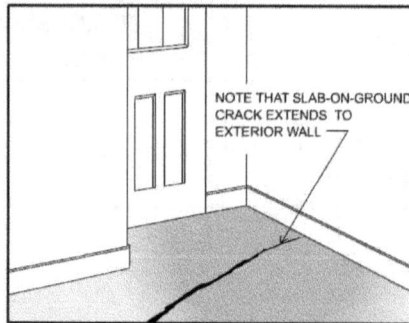

NOTE THAT SLAB-ON-GROUND CRACK EXTENDS TO EXTERIOR WALL

Most distresses are not deemed to be structurally significant for typical house slabs basically serve as earth covers. Slab cracks which develop at exterior walls and at other footing locations are of concern, however.

☐ add (bracing) (reinforcement support work) for **bouncy** _____ **floor**

RATTLE RATTLE

Test jump all raised floors in the building. They could be bouncier than what might be normally expected since the floor joists may have been undersized for their long span. Or perhaps, the condition could be the result of the use of an improper grade and species of wood.

□ **out-of-plumb** _____ **wall(s)**

LINE OF SIGHT | PLUMB LINE

Cite the building from a distance to more easily observe possible leaning, bowed-out or bulging exterior walls.

□ **crack in** _____ **exterior wall** at line of new addition

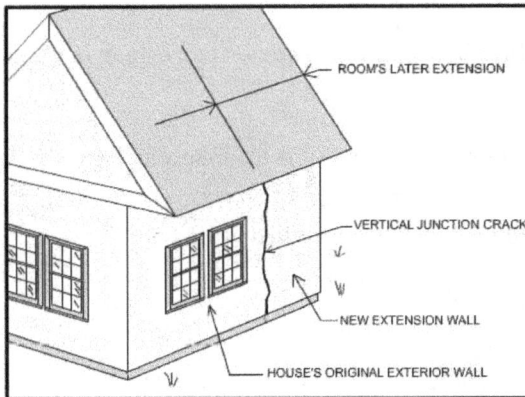

ROOM'S LATER EXTENSION

VERTICAL JUNCTION CRACK

NEW EXTENSION WALL

HOUSE'S ORIGINAL EXTERIOR WALL

Such vertical cracks are usually typical distresses which are the result of differential settlement.

□ **cracks radiating out over** _____ **window(s) and** _____ **door(s)**
□ **crack at** _____ **ceiling and wall juncture** in the _____

CRACK SEPARATIONS NOTED
ALONG WALL RETURN AND CEILING

In some newer homes, interior cracks at wall corners or along wall junctures with ceilings could have developed, for instance, from wood shrinkage as part of the framing's drying process.

□ area of _____ **floor slopes**
□ area of _____ **floor slopes - get access** to see whether there are supportive problems

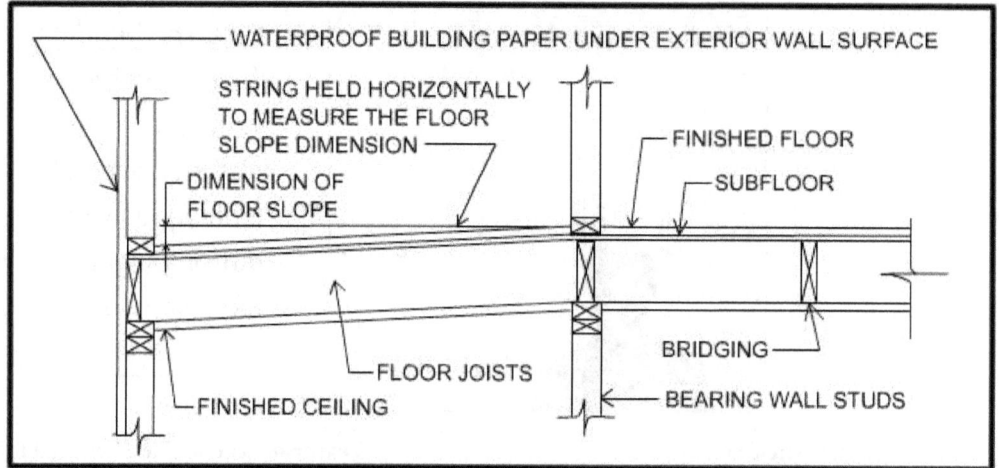

WATERPROOF BUILDING PAPER UNDER EXTERIOR WALL SURFACE
STRING HELD HORIZONTALLY TO MEASURE THE FLOOR SLOPE DIMENSION
FINISHED FLOOR
SUBFLOOR
DIMENSION OF FLOOR SLOPE
FLOOR JOISTS
FINISHED CEILING
BRIDGING
BEARING WALL STUDS

Some sloping and humped floors could be caused by the fashion in which they were built.

□ **patch, paint and monitor cracking** noted in the following locations:
   □ _____
   □ _____
□ **creaking sound heard** while walking on raised wood floor

FINISH FLOOR
SUBFLOOR BOARDS
WOOD BLOCKING
FLOOR JOISTS
'CREAK'
'CREAK'

Creaking sounds heard while walking a raised wood floor is likely due to the loosening of the nails which hold the subfloor down to the floor joists. The sound could also be created when one floor board is rubbed against another while weight is being applied and then removed.

□ **small fine cracks and creaks** (throughout house) (on _____) none were deemed structurally significant

☐ **brace** in (north - south) (east - west) **to increase lateral rigidity**

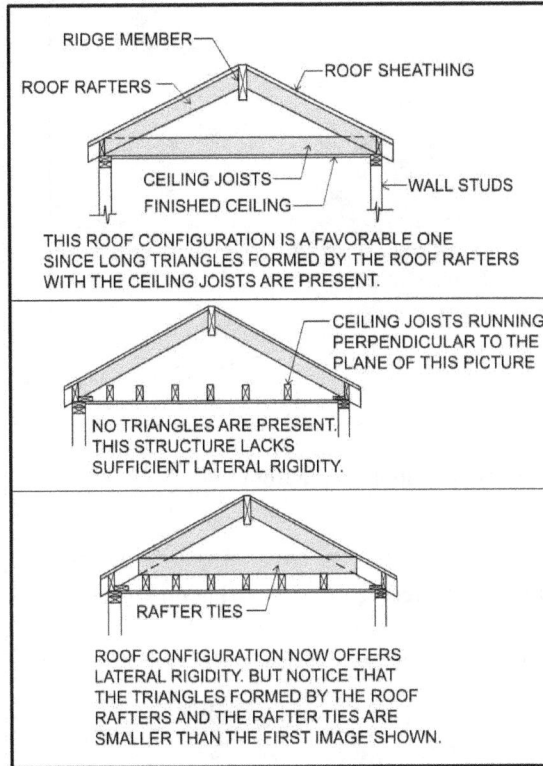

RIDGE MEMBER

ROOF RAFTERS

ROOF SHEATHING

CEILING JOISTS

FINISHED CEILING

WALL STUDS

THIS ROOF CONFIGURATION IS A FAVORABLE ONE SINCE LONG TRIANGLES FORMED BY THE ROOF RAFTERS WITH THE CEILING JOISTS ARE PRESENT.

CEILING JOISTS RUNNING PERPENDICULAR TO THE PLANE OF THIS PICTURE

NO TRIANGLES ARE PRESENT. THIS STRUCTURE LACKS SUFFICIENT LATERAL RIGIDITY.

RAFTER TIES

ROOF CONFIGURATION NOW OFFERS LATERAL RIGIDITY. BUT NOTICE THAT THE TRIANGLES FORMED BY THE ROOF RAFTERS AND THE RAFTER TIES ARE SMALLER THAN THE FIRST IMAGE SHOWN.

> The triangles formed by roof rafters and the ceiling joists help to make the house roof structure laterally rigid.

☐ **repair separated connections in attic**

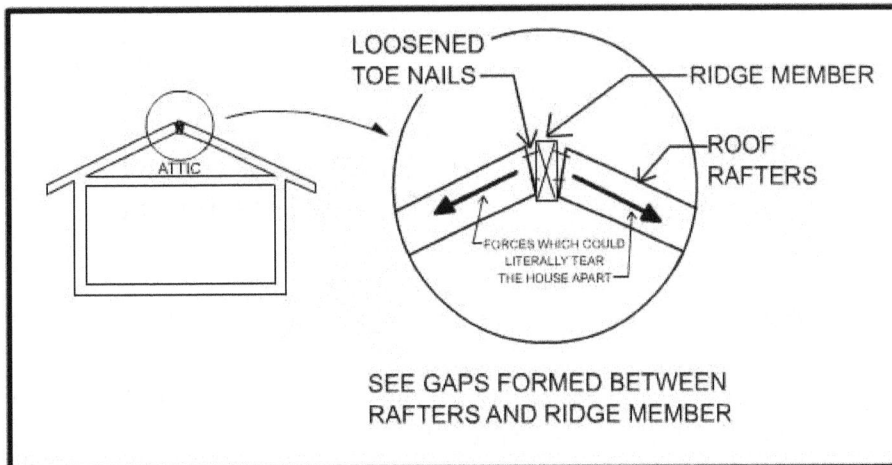

LOOSENED TOE NAILS

RIDGE MEMBER

ROOF RAFTERS

ATTIC

FORCES WHICH COULD LITERALLY TEAR THE HOUSE APART

SEE GAPS FORMED BETWEEN RAFTERS AND RIDGE MEMBER

> Problems with structural connections are leaders in the cause of structural failure.

□ **roof sags**

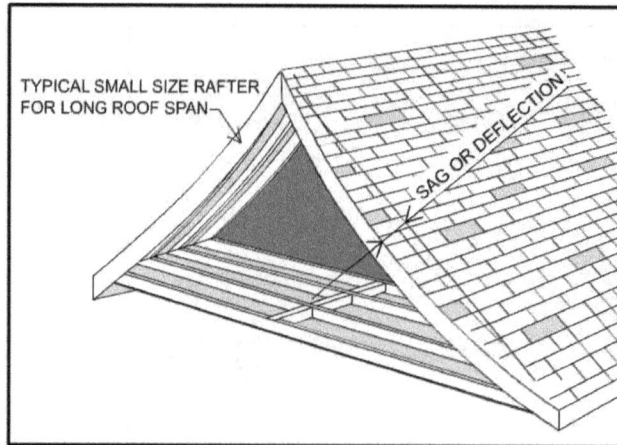

TYPICAL SMALL SIZE RAFTER FOR LONG ROOF SPAN

SAG OR DEFLECTION

Roof deflection is often due to the long span of undersized roof rafters.

□ **other source(s) of structural damage** from _____

Termites

□ evidence of **termites detected at** _____ - but **no structurally significant damage**

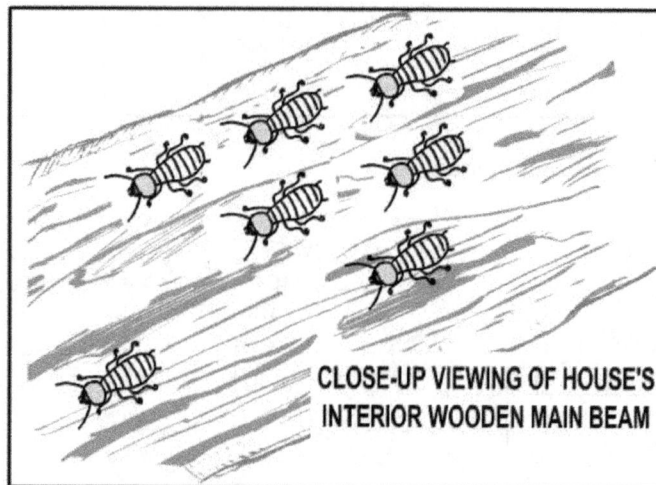

CLOSE-UP VIEWING OF HOUSE'S INTERIOR WOODEN MAIN BEAM

□ evidence of **termites detected at** _____ - **with some structural damage**

Serious structural damage can occur to a house because of a termite infestation problem. Entire replacement of affected wood members would be in order.

□ **recommend termite control work** as matter of prudent precaution

Trees/Vegetation

□ **(trim back) (crop) (tree[s]) (vegetative growth)** which (closely) brush (house) (utility lines)

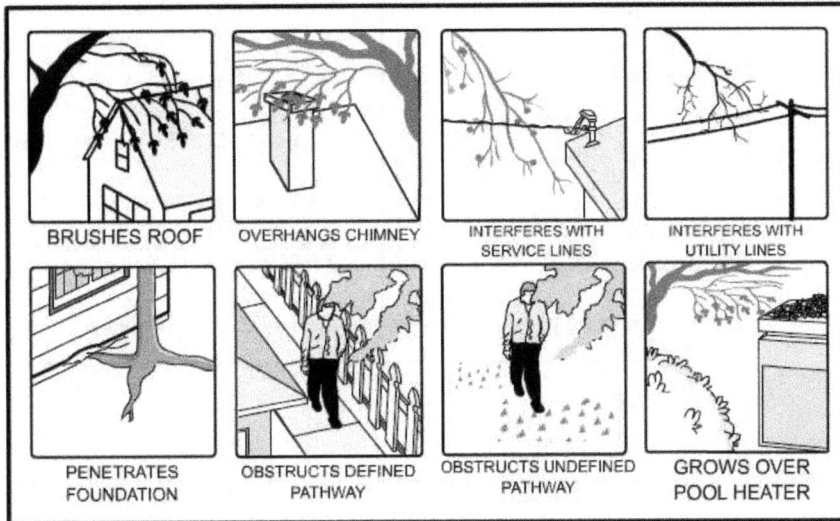

BRUSHES ROOF | OVERHANGS CHIMNEY | INTERFERES WITH SERVICE LINES | INTERFERES WITH UTILITY LINES

PENETRATES FOUNDATION | OBSTRUCTS DEFINED PATHWAY | OBSTRUCTS UNDEFINED PATHWAY | GROWS OVER POOL HEATER

Maintaining trim vegetative growth provides for a good margin of fire safety.

Ventilation

□ **add low screen vents to garage** lacking them

THIS GARAGE HAS BEEN EQUIPPED WITH TWO LOUVERED LOW-HEIGHT VENT SCREENS.

Toxic fumes emanating from car exhaust have little chance to escape from the garage and can kill! And that's the reason why low-height screened wall vent openings are needed for the garage.

□ **underfloor lacks adequate ventilation**

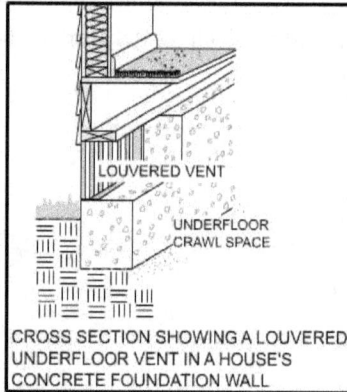

LOUVERED VENT

UNDERFLOOR CRAWL SPACE

CROSS SECTION SHOWING A LOUVERED UNDERFLOOR VENT IN A HOUSE'S CONCRETE FOUNDATION WALL

THIS HOUSE, BEING ON A RAISED FOUNDATION, HAS BEEN EQUIPPED WITH UNDERFLOOR VENTS ON ALL FOUR OF ITS SIDES. NOTICE THAT THE VENTS ARE SCREENED ONES AND EXIST JUST ABOVE THE HOUSE'S FOUNDATION WALL.

□ **ventilation can be provided to** (bathroom) (toilet compartment)

BATHROOM WITH A WINDOW

BATHROOM WITHOUT A WINDOW (BUT WITH AN EXHAUST FAN)

□ to prevent overheating of (air plenum) **(attic), ventilation needs to be provided**

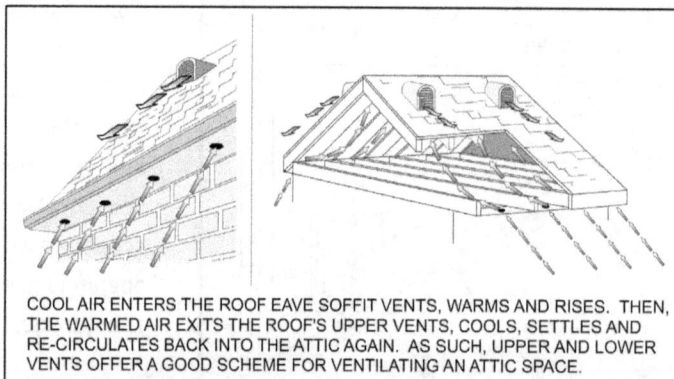

COOL AIR ENTERS THE ROOF EAVE SOFFIT VENTS, WARMS AND RISES. THEN, THE WARMED AIR EXITS THE ROOF'S UPPER VENTS, COOLS, SETTLES AND RE-CIRCULATES BACK INTO THE ATTIC AGAIN. AS SUCH, UPPER AND LOWER VENTS OFFER A GOOD SCHEME FOR VENTILATING AN ATTIC SPACE.

Without adequate attic ventilation, there could be the occurrence of overheating during hot days and the formation of condensation of wood attic members during cool summer nights. Consequently, rot damage can eventually result.

□ **vent flue** of (clothes dryer) (bathroom) _____ **exhausts to wrong place**

Waterproofing

☐ **evidence of chronic water seepage problems** had been observed by the following:
  - ☐ deterioration of some foundation wall length(s)
  - ☐ efflorescence found on various concrete foundation walls within the underfloor location
  - ☐ soil shrinkage cracks noted within the crawlspace
  - ☐ (rust) (staining) on bottom of furnace legs
  - ☐ dry water stains on bottom of some _____
  - ☐ damp odor detected in the _____

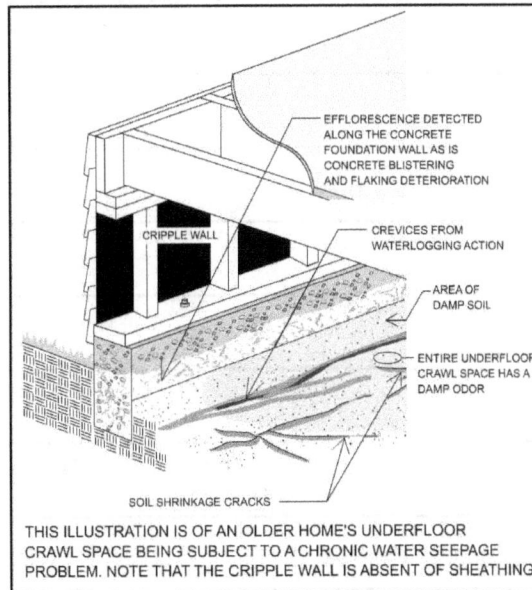

EFFLORESCENCE DETECTED ALONG THE CONCRETE FOUNDATION WALL AS IS CONCRETE BLISTERING AND FLAKING DETERIORATION

CRIPPLE WALL

CREVICES FROM WATERLOGGING ACTION

AREA OF DAMP SOIL

ENTIRE UNDERFLOOR CRAWL SPACE HAS A DAMP ODOR

SOIL SHRINKAGE CRACKS

THIS ILLUSTRATION IS OF AN OLDER HOME'S UNDERFLOOR CRAWL SPACE BEING SUBJECT TO A CHRONIC WATER SEEPAGE PROBLEM. NOTE THAT THE CRIPPLE WALL IS ABSENT OF SHEATHING.

☐ **some** white stains / **(efflorescence)** noted on house's foundation wall **is type of evidence** one finds **when water problems exist to a limited extent**

Window Problems

☐ the **following window problems** need attention:
  - ☐ _____
  - ☐ _____

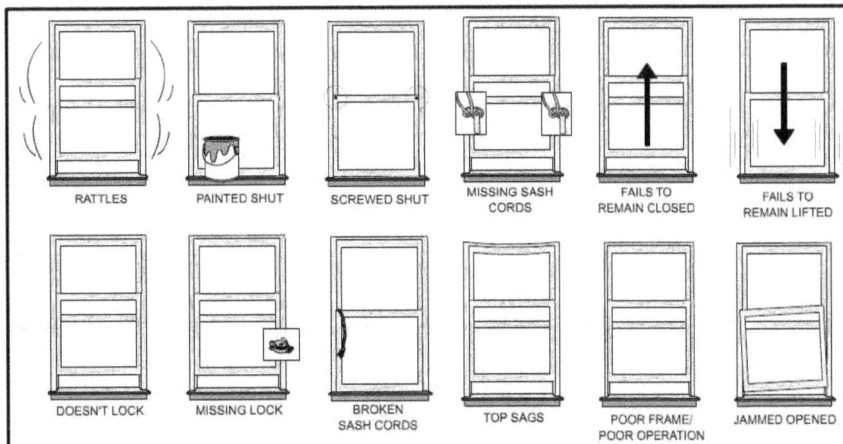

RATTLES   PAINTED SHUT   SCREWED SHUT   MISSING SASH CORDS   FAILS TO REMAIN CLOSED   FAILS TO REMAIN LIFTED

DOESN'T LOCK   MISSING LOCK   BROKEN SASH CORDS   TOP SAGS   POOR FRAME/ POOR OPERATION   JAMMED OPENED

Item Number   _Description of Condition, Issue or Problem_

_____. _____

_____. _____

_____. _____

_____. _____

_____. _____

_____. _____

_____. _____

_____. _____

_____. _____

_____. _____

_____. _____

_____. _____

_____. _____

_____. _____

_____. _____

_____. _____

_____. _____

_____. _____

Highlights of Home Inspection

Item Number	*Description of Condition, Issue or Problem*
_____.	_____
_____.	_____
_____.	_____
_____.	_____
_____.	_____
_____.	_____
_____.	_____
_____.	_____
_____.	_____
_____.	_____
_____.	_____
_____.	_____
_____.	_____
_____.	_____
_____.	_____
_____.	_____
_____.	_____

Item Number   _Description of Condition, Issue or Problem_

——. _____

——. _____

——. _____

——. _____

——. _____

——. _____

——. _____

——. _____

——. _____

——. _____

——. _____

——. _____

——. _____

——. _____

——. _____

——. _____

——. _____

——. _____

Highlights of Home Inspection

Item Number   _Description of Condition, Issue or Problem_

_____.   _____

_____.   _____

_____.   _____

_____.   _____

_____.   _____

_____.   _____

_____.   _____

_____.   _____

_____.   _____

_____.   _____

_____.   _____

_____.   _____

_____.   _____

_____.   _____

_____.   _____

_____.   _____

_____.   _____

_____.   _____

Presented here is needed data to be collected to help one determine the condition of the 5 key elements of the building.

Electrical System

- **overhead or underground:** (overhead) (underground) electrical service
- **number of wires:** (2-) (3-)
- **voltage:** (110) (220) volt
- **amperage:** (30) (60) (100) (125) (150) (200) (400) (_____) amps
- **electrical service for this home's electrical requirements:** (sufficient) (marginally sufficient) (insufficient)
- **type of electrical panel:** (circuit breaker panel) (electrical standup service panel) (fuse box)
- **condition of electrical panel:** (good) (satisfactory) (poor) (except as otherwise noted)
- **existence of electrical ground connection(s):** to a (water pipe) (and to a) (main stake)
  - □ but no electrical ground connection could be found to a (water pipe) (main stake)
  - □ an electrician should be engaged to locate the house electrical ground connections
- **condition of electrical ground connection(s):** (good) (satisfactory) (poor) (except as otherwise noted)
- **wiring type:** (romex) (bx) (flex conduit) (EMT) (knob and tube)
- **material of wiring:** (copper) (aluminum)
- **wiring condition:** (good) (satisfactory) (poor) (except as otherwise noted)

Heating System

- **number of zones:** (1-zone) (2-zone) (together these _____)
- **brand of heating plants:** (Carrier) (Lennox) (York) (Payne) (_____)
- **fuel type:** (gas-fired) (electric) (oil-fired)
- **type of heating:** (forced warm air furnace) (gravity) (electric radiant) (steam boiler) (hot water boiler)
- **B.T.U. per hour rating:** _____ (input) (output)
- **heat production requirement for this size home:** (sufficient) (marginally sufficient) (insufficient)
- **operation of unit(s) during inspection:** (it was operating) (they were operating)
- **and functioned:**
  - □ normally or within normal limits
  - □ within normal limits, except as noted
- **inoperation of units(s) during inspection:** (it was not operating) (they were not operating)
  - □ be certain that the heating plant is demonstrated to your satisfaction before closing
  - □ be certain that the heating plants are demonstrated to your satisfaction before closing
- **ventilation of fuel-fired heating plant(s):** (satisfactory) (restricted)
- **note comments regarding:** (the age of the heating plant[s]) (the condition of the firebox) (_____)

Plumbing System

- **type of water lines:** (copper) (&) (galvanized iron) (plastic)
- **observed condition of water lines:** (acceptable - with no water leaks detected) (acceptable, except as noted) (poor)
- **type of gas lines:** (black iron) (galvanized) (_____)
- **condition of gas lines:** (no odors detected) (no odors detected, except as noted) (poor)
- **type of drain lines:** (cast iron) (&) (galvanized iron) (plastic)
- **observed condition of drain lines:** (acceptable - with no leaks detected) (acceptable, except as noted) (poor)
- **waste drainage tests during the inspection:** (suggests satisfactory performance) (suggests satisfactory performance, except as noted)
- **reported type of waste drainage system:** (sewers) (an independent waste drainage system consisting of _____)
- **water pressure tested at outside hose bibb:** (_____) pounds per square inch
- **water pressure inside building:** (high) (normal) (generally somewhat low) (generally low)
- **number of plumbing fixtures:**
  - ☐ _____ sinks
  - ☐ _____ bathtub(s)
  - ☐ _____ toilet(s)
  - ☐ _____ stall shower(s)
  - ☐ _____ bidet(s)
- **operation of plumbing fixtures:** (okay) (okay, except as noted)

Structural System

In consideration of the age of the building, the size and construction type of the building, the

- **floors were level:** (within normal tolerance) (within normal tolerance, except as noted) (but some sloped beyond tolerance) (_____)
- **walls were plumb** (within normal tolerance) (within normal tolerance, except as noted) (but [one] [some] [leans] [bowed] [bulges])

The following **observable structural members were** (satisfactory) (satisfactory, except as noted):

- ☐ the concrete pier/footings
- ☐ the poured (concrete) (concrete block) foundation walls
- ☐ the wooden posts
- ☐ the (steel lally) (wood) column(s)
- ☐ the (steel) (wooden) main beams or girders
- ☐ the floor joists
- ☐ the ceiling joists
- ☐ the purlins
- ☐ the rafters
- ☐ the ridge member(s)

An **indirect examination** of the balance of the structural members reflected no (other) noteworthy problems.

126 Systems: Water Heating to Additional Items

Water Heating

- **brand(s) of heating unit(s):** (American) (A.O. Smith) (_____)
- **fuel type:** (gas-fired) (electric) (oil-fired)
- **number of tank(s):** (1) (2) (3) (4) (__)
- **tank capacity size:** (30) (40) (50) (75) (80) (100) gallons
- **recovery rate:** _____ gallons per hour
- **input rating:** _____ B.T.U.'s per hour
- **operation of unit during the inspection:** (it was operating) (it wasn't operating)
- **temperature of hot water produced:** _____ degree hot water
- **hot water production requirement for this home in consideration of the amount of hot water outlets there are available:** (sufficient) (marginally sufficient) (insufficient)

Additional Items to Check

- ☐ **rodent evidence:**
  - ☐ no evidence of rodent evidence for damage against the structure was detected
  - ☐ have the premises checked by a licensed pest control company
- ☐ **termite evidence:**
  - ☐ we couldn't locate any outward evidence of termite infestation in accessible and observable areas - although termites can exist in inaccessible and unobservable areas
  - ☐ have a separate termite inspection by a licensed treatment company
- ☐ **main floor water penetration evidence:**
  - ☐ there was no considerable evidence of flooding, seepage or leakage observed in the accessible and observable areas
  - ☐ there was no considerable evidence of flooding, seepage or leakage observed in the accessible and observable areas - but this doesn't mean to say that water problems will not develop after the inspection or this does not assume that water problems don't exist in the inaccessible and unobservable areas at the present time.
- ☐ **electrical remote disconnect(s) for the central air conditioning condenser(s):**
  - ☐ present
  - ☐ present at each unit
  - ☐ (is) (are) absent and should be provided
- ☐ **seismic straps around hot water heater:**
  - ☐ two heavy duty straps anchored this tank to a wall
  - ☐ only one strap anchored the tank
  - ☐ seismic straps need to be provided
- ☐ **temperature / pressure relief valve:**
  - ☐ was present
  - ☐ none exists
- ☐ **water pressure regulator:**
  - ☐ the reducing valve was present
  - ☐ none exists
- ☐ **fire-rated door between house and garage:**
  - ☐ present
  - ☐ does not exist
- ☐ **overhead garage door springs:**
  - ☐ safety springs were present for both sides of the garage's overhead door
  - ☐ one or more was broken
  - ☐ are not of the safety spring variety

□ **interior** (wooden) (wrought iron) (metal) **(banister[s]) (railing[s]):**
    □ sturdy
    □ need corrective work, including _____

□ **sampled operation of windows** in consideration of the age of the house:
    □ generally good
    □ generally fair
    □ generally sticky
    □ generally poor

□ **sampled operation of doors** in consideration of the age of the house:
    □ generally good
    □ generally fair
    □ generally sticky
    □ generally poor

□ (fiberglass) (loose fill) (_____) **insulation in attic space:**
    □ suitable
    □ suitable but is minimal by today's standards
    □ insulation is missing at _____

Check and find these items to be in working order, except as may be mentioned earlier and/or what is noted after them:

- ☐ well pump _____
- ☐ water pump _____
- ☐ sump pump _____
- ☐ electric strike - gate opener _____
- ☐ driveway's automatic (roll) (swing) gating _____
- ☐ _____ single overhead (lift) garage door(s) _____
- ☐ _____ single sectional garage door(s) _____
- ☐ _____ double overhead (lift) garage door(s) _____
- ☐ _____ double sectional garage door(s) _____
- ☐ side-by-side garage doors _____
- ☐ track garage doors _____
- ☐ _____ automatic garage door opener(s) _____
- ☐ exterior fire pit _____
- ☐ _____ gas barbecue _____
- ☐ underground lawn sprinkler system
  - ☐ but be sure all water spray action from those sprinkler heads that are located nearby the house are diverted away from the building structure
  - ☐ _____
- ☐ swimming pool pump and _____ motor _____
- ☐ swimming pool water fill _____
- ☐ _____ pool filter _____
- ☐ _____ (swimming pool) (spa) heater _____
- ☐ swimming pool light _____
- ☐ _____ pool sweep _____
- ☐ (spa) (hot tub) jets - bubbler _____
- ☐ (spa) (hot tub) filter _____
- ☐ sauna _____
- ☐ front door knocker _____
- ☐ (front) (side) doorbell(s) _____
- ☐ (electric) (gas) _____ cooktop _____
- ☐ (electric) (gas) _____ built-in range _____
- ☐ _____ (double) (self-cleaning) (electric) (gas) wall oven(s) _____
- ☐ _____ microwave oven _____
- ☐ _____ range hood / light / fan _____
- ☐ _____ kitchen exhaust fan _____
- ☐ _____ refrigerator _____
- ☐ _____ freezer _____
- ☐ _____ dishwasher _____
- ☐ kitchen sink water spray _____
- ☐ _____ kitchen sink faucet water spray _____
- ☐ _____ horsepower sink garbage disposal unit _____

☐ _____ trash compactor _____

☐ _____ instant hot water sink dispenser _____
       ☐ was producing _____ hot water

☐ _____ washer _____

☐ _____ (vented) (unvented) (gas) (electric) clothes dryer _____

☐ _____ light dimmer(s) _____

☐ _____ fireplace _____ damper _____

☐ _____ fireplace _____ damper _____

☐ _____ fireplace _____ damper _____

☐ _____ sliding glass door _____

☐ _____ (110 volt) (220 volt) room air conditioner _____

☐ _____ (110 volt) (220 volt) room air conditioner _____

☐ _____ (110 volt) (220 volt) room air conditioner _____

☐ furnace humidifier _____

☐ _____ central air conditioning system _____

☐ _____ central air conditioning system _____

☐ roof-mounted evaporative cooler _____

☐ hot water circulating pump _____

☐ _____ intercom _____

☐ _____ radio / intercom _____

☐ _____ security alarm system _____

☐ (battery) (hard-wired) (hard-wired with battery backup) smoke detector of the
_____

☐ (battery) (hard-wired) (hard-wired with battery backup) smoke detector of the
_____

☐ _____ carbon monoxide detector of the _____

☐ _____ carbon monoxide detector of the _____

☐ _____ central vacuum cleaning system _____

☐ _____ bathroom (exhaust) (/) (heater) fan _____

☐ _____ bathroom (exhaust) (/) (heater) fan _____

☐ _____ bathroom (exhaust) (/) (heater) fan _____

☐ _____ bathroom heat lamp _____

☐ _____ electric strip heater of the _____ bathroom _____

☐ _____ electric strip heater of the _____ bathroom _____

☐ _____ electric strip heater of the _____ bathroom _____

☐ pull-down ladder to the attic _____

☐ _____ attic fan _____

☐ _____ roof turbine ventilator(s) _____

☐ _____

☐ *Note that because some presently operating equipment is subject to failure before the time of closing, it is recommended that these items be once again demonstrated a day before escrow closes.*

Look at the premise in the following five aspects:

The (home) (building) was in:
For Cleanliness
- ☐ an unclean
- ☐ a relatively clean   state.
- ☐ a clean

The (home) (building) was:
For Maintenance
- ☐ not fit for occupancy.
- ☐ in a run-down
- ☐ in a worn
- ☐ in a reasonably maintained   condition.
- ☐ in a reasonably well maintained
- ☐ in a well maintained
- ☐ in a normal condition for new construction.

Nonetheless,
Detection of Problems
- ☐ many serious problems were found.
- ☐ some serious problems were found.
- ☐ few serious problems were found - most were moderate and minor problems.

The building is rated to be in a
From a structural engineer's standpoint
- ☐ structurally unsound
- ☐ potentially sound
- ☐ marginally sound   condition.
- ☐ fundamentally sound
- ☐ structurally sound

The building and premises are rated to be in
Taking all things into consideration
- ☐ unacceptable
- ☐ poor
- ☐ poor-to-fair
- ☐ fair   condition.*
- ☐ fair-to-good
- ☐ good
- ☐ good to excellent
- ☐ excellent

presuming, of course, for example, that
- ☐ *the grounds are deemed to be geologically sound;*
- ☐ *there are no hazardous wastes to be found;*
- ☐ *and the premises are deemed to be environmentally safe.*

Note that the condition of the building
- ☐ *might change after the inspection;*
- ☐ *that the building should be reinspected before escrow closes, preferably after the furnishings have been removed;*
- ☐ *and, that it is recommended that the seller certify that there are no additional problems above these inspection findings.*

PART III.

Report Form

Starter Information

Date(s) of Inspection _____

Street Address of Property _____

Town or City _____

Purchaser(s) _____

Age of Home or Building _____

Style of Home or Building _____

Building shall be considered to be **located** (on) (off) (a corner lot)

   Side of Street ☐ northerly ☐ southerly ☐ easterly ☐ westerly

Lot Size _____ front feet by _____ feet or _____ acre(s) in size

   Shape of Lot ☐ regular or rectangular ☐ irregular ☐ pie-shaped

Exterior Improvements

(concrete) (_____) **sidewalk**:
- ☐ partially uprooted
- ☐ cracked
- ☐ lacks the use of expansion joints
- ☐ poorly pitched
- ☐ in good condition
- ☐ _____

(concrete) (_____) **street curb**:
- ☐ juts outwardly
- ☐ cracked
- ☐ curves
- ☐ tall
- ☐ in good condition
- ☐ _____

(blacktop) (concrete) (concrete paver) (brick) **driveway**:
- ☐ poorly pitched
- ☐ cracked
- ☐ narrow
- ☐ in good condition
- ☐ _____

(attached) (detached) ____ **-car garage**:
- ☐ fundamentally sound
- ☐ okay, except as noted
- ☐ in good condition
- ☐ _____

(brick) (wood) (stone) (wrought iron) (_____) **mailbox post**:
- ☐ leans
- ☐ in good condition
- ☐ _____

wooden (_____) **decorative shutters:**
- ☐ old
- ☐ worn
- ☐ need painting
- ☐ in good condition
- ☐ _____

(concrete) (brick) (_____) **pathway** to (front) (main) (stoop) (porch):
- ☐ worn
- ☐ cracked
- ☐ in good condition
- ☐ _____

(front) (main) (concrete) (_____) **stoop**:
- ☐ poorly pitched
- ☐ need painting
- ☐ in good condition
- ☐ _____

(front) (main) (concrete) (_____) **porch**:
- ☐ poorly pitched
- ☐ need painting
- ☐ in good condition
- ☐ _____

(wooden) (_____) **raised back porch**:
- ☐ worn
- ☐ needs painting
- ☐ in good condition
- ☐ _____

(concrete) (brick) (wooden) (_____) **steps**:
- ☐ worn
- ☐ poorly pitched
- ☐ cracked
- ☐ in good condition
- ☐ _____

(wooden) (_____) **stairs**:
- ☐ needs reinforcement
- ☐ worn
- ☐ cracked
- ☐ in good condition
- ☐ _____

(concrete) (brick) (_____) **patio**:
- ☐ poorly pitched
- ☐ cracked
- ☐ in good condition
- ☐ _____

(wooden) (_____) **patio cover**:
- ☐ leans
- ☐ worn
- ☐ needs painting
- ☐ in good condition
- ☐ _____

(above-ground) (in-ground) **swimming pool**:

       □ no visible problems detected from the outside
       □ no evidence of significant differential settlement observed
       □ in good condition
       □ _____

spa: _____

(concrete) (brick) (_____) **decking surrounding pool**: _____

(concrete) (brick) (_____) **decking surrounding spa**: _____

additionally, the

_____

_____

_____

_____

_____

_____

_____

_____

_____

_____

_____

_____

Building Envelope

outdoor grading:

☐ allows water to pond next to (N) (S) (E) (W) side of the structure
☐ acceptable
☐ _____

landscaping:

☐ sparse
☐ mixes with other neighborhood landscaping
☐ _____

underfloor areaway wells:

☐ short
☐ normal
☐ _____

screened wall vent openings at underfloor area:

☐ missing
☐ torn
☐ missing
☐ are in good condition
☐ _____

hose bibbs:

☐ _____ didn't work
☐ _____ were counted
☐ _____

outdoor electrical outlets:

☐ none
☐ _____ were counted
☐ _____ is / are not of the ground fault interrupter variety
☐ are in good condition
☐ _____

caulking/sealing work:

☐ for example, around window and door frames, between the interfaces of the siding/trim, where needed, including sealing off any exterior areas of the house or building open to the elements should be routinely attended to
☐ in satisfactory condition
☐ _____

wood trim:

☐ weathered
☐ distressed in areas
☐ requires painting work
☐ does not need immediate painting
☐ is in generally good condition
☐ _____

(brick) (stucco) (stone) (wood) (_____) **exterior siding**:

☐ worn
☐ cracked in areas
☐ brick needs pointing work
☐ is in generally good condition
☐ _____

Note: there could be the possibility of damprotted wood inside building walls which does not display outward evidence of any structural damage. Until the development of such a sign, or if the walls are probed or removed, dryrot will remain undetected (should dryrot, in fact, exist).

broken or cracked windowpanes:

☐ (1) (2) (__) window panes were detected broken
☐ (1) (2) (__) window panes were detected cracked
☐ none were detected

window screens:

☐ not present
☐ _____ missing
☐ those that were present appear to be in _____ condition

rain gutters and downspouts (gutters and leaders):

☐ the building lacks their use
☐ old, could soon stand replacement
☐ holes were detected in the _____
☐ no holes detected
☐ in good condition
☐ _____

(asphaltic shingle) (_____ tile) (wood shingle) (wood shake)
(built-up gravel membrane) (mineral roll) (_____) **roof**:

☐ old, could soon stand replacement
☐ leaks at _____
☐ no evidence of leakage noted
☐ in generally good condition
☐ _____

roof flashing:

- ☐ in poor condition
- ☐ some flashing was lifted and is in need of attention
- ☐ was partly patched
- ☐ in good condition
- ☐ _____

observed metal flues above roof line:

- ☐ generally old and rusted
- ☐ aging
- ☐ in good condition
- ☐ _____

(brick) (stuccoed-over) (_____) chimney:

- ☐ leans
- ☐ separated from building
- ☐ fundamentally sound
- ☐ _____

Note: realize that the stack may not be safe during some periods of seismic activity.

attic ventilation:

- ☐ attic ventilation is absent
- ☐ attic ventilation is restricted
- ☐ acceptable

strange odors:

- ☐ an odor was detected in the _____
- ☐ no odors detected

ventilation of garage:

- ☐ low vents are absent
- ☐ the garage's low vent(s) were closed
- ☐ the garage's low vent(s) were blocked
- ☐ acceptable

(concrete) (blacktop) garage floor:

- ☐ incorrectly pitched
- ☐ poorly pitched
- ☐ is badly cracked and poses tripping hazards
- ☐ is cracked, but is functional
- ☐ minor cracking was noted
- ☐ is in good condition

Levels

SLAB-ON-GRADE (or slab-on-ground) **HOUSE**:
- □ has only one level
- □ has two principal levels
- □ contains three principal levels
- □ _____

RAISED FOUNDATION HOUSE:
- □ has only two principal levels
- □ has three principal levels
- □ _____

There are three types of low levels defined in this form. These are as follows:

1. The CRAWL SPACE level consists of (one) (two) or (__) **crawl space(s).
     It runs beneath**:
- □ the entire building.
- □ the majority of the building.
- □ a large portion of the building.
- □ a portion of the building.

The crawl space is accessible:
- □ through (_____) hatch opening(s) on the (N) (S) (E) (W) side(s) of the building.
- □ through (_____) hatch opening(s) in the (N) (S) (E) (W) foundation wall(s).

**2. The BASEMENT [and CRAWL SPACE] level.
     The basement is located**:
- □ off the _____.
- □ through a hatch in the _____ floor.

[Access to the crawl space can be obtained:
- □ through _____ hatch opening(s) in the (N) (S) (E) (W) foundational wall(s).]
- □ from off the basement location.]

3. The LOWER level which has been partitioned into:
- □ a _____,
- □ a _____,
- □ _____,
- □ and the crawl space. The crawl space is accessible:
  - □ through (_) hatch opening(s) on the (N) (S) (E) (W) side(s) of the building.
  - □ through (_) hatch opening(s) in the (N) (S) (E) (W) foundation wall(s).

On this level are located

- □ the _____ furnace(s),
- □ the _____ boiler(s),
- □ the gas main,
- □ the water main,
- □ the circuit breaker panel(s),
- □ the fuse box(es),
- □ the electric meter(s),
- □ the main plumbing lines and drain lines,
- □ _____ hot water heater(s),
- □ a water pump,
- □ a sump pump,
- □ a washing machine and a clothes dryer,
- □ the slop sink,
- □ a refrigerator,
- □ a freezer,
- □ a bathroom sink,
- □ toilet,
- □ stall shower,
- □ _____,

- □ _____,

- □ _____,

- □ _____,

- □ and a fire safety detector.

Realize that

- □ the water meter,
- □ the electric meter and circuit breaker panel,
- □ the electric meter and fuse box,
- □ the electric meter and electrical service panel,
- □ and the gas meter

are situated outside the house [as well as (is) (are)

- □ the (covered) hot water heater and
- □ the _____ central air conditioning condenser unit(s)].

The MAIN FLOOR (or the AT-GRADE LEVEL) contains:

_____

_____

_____

_____

_____

_____

_____

_____.

The SECOND FLOOR (or the UPPER LEVEL) comprises:

_____

_____

_____

_____

_____

_____

_____

_____.

[The THIRD FLOOR (or the UPPERMOST LEVEL) has been partitioned into:

_____

_____

_____

_____

_____

_____

_____.]

The ATTIC LEVEL (or the AIR PLENA LEVEL).

☐ **The (crawl) (standup) attic level was not accessible during our inspection.**

☐ **The (crawl) (standup) attic wasn't readily accessible during our inspection.**

☐ **Access to the (crawl) (stand-up) attic can be gained**
      ☐ through a hatch in the ceiling of the bedroom connecting hallway.
      ☐ through a hatch in the master bedroom closet ceiling.
      ☐ through a hatch in the _____ bedroom closet ceiling.
      ☐ via a pull-down ladder in the ceiling of the bedroom connecting hall.
      ☐ via a pull-down ladder in the ceiling of the _____.
      ☐ via a flight of steps leading from the (_____) floor connecting hall.
      ☐ via a flight of steps that are located in the _____.
      ☐_____.

It is (fully) (partially) (uninsulated) insulated:
      ☐ but has no catwalk or subfloor.
      ☐ and contains some planking across the ceiling joists.
      ☐ and contains a temporary catwalk.
      ☐ and contains a partial catwalk.
      ☐ and partially subfloored.
      ☐ (and) (but) fully subfloored.

Advisory Concepts

1. Learn whether a **Certificate of Occupancy** (or **Final Approval**) exists for:
   - ☐ for the entire home as it is comprised at the present time;
   - ☐ for the building's present usage;
   - ☐ for the home or building following a significant fire;
   - ☐ for the home or building following an explosion;
   - ☐ for a revised interior layout;
   - ☐ for added rooms;
   - ☐ for extended room(s);
   - ☐ for a structurally remodeled (kitchen) (bathroom);
   - ☐ for an enclosed porch
   - ☐ for the new construction
   - ☐ for _____.

2. Check if **Grading Permits and Approvals** are in order for:
   - ☐ the (later) significant movement of soil material;
   - ☐ the (later) significant retaining work done;
   - ☐ the (later) drainage work done.

3. Learn whether **Building Permits and Approvals** exist for:
   - ☐ the building or the re-building of the (_____) chimney;
   - ☐ the building of a raised deck;
   - ☐ the construction of a patio cover;
   - ☐ the later roofing cover installation;
   - ☐ perhaps the later aperture work;
   - ☐ the swimming pool;
   - ☐ the spa;
   - ☐ and the newer structural/addition work done.

4. **Electrical Permits** should have been provided for:
   - ☐ the newer electrical wiring;
   - ☐ the 220 volt (electrical service) (circuit breaker) panel installation;
   - ☐ the 220 volt room air conditioner hookup(s);
   - ☐ the central air conditioning hookup;
   - ☐ the electric range hookup;
   - ☐ the 220 volt outlet provided for the electric dryer;
   - ☐ the hookup(s) of the _____;
   - ☐ as well as for (the) (some) newer construction.

5. **Plumbing Permits and Approvals** are required for:
   - □ the installation of the exterior underground lawn sprinkler system;
   - □ the installation of the (later) hot water heater(s);
   - □ the relocation of the new water heater;
   - □ the new water main;
   - □ the addition of copper piping;
   - □ the dishwasher hookup;
   - □ the hookup of the laundry equipment;
   - □ the later plumbing fixture work;
   - □ as well as for some later construction.

6. **Mechanical Permits and Approvals** are required for:
   - □ the installation of the new (furnace) (boiler);
   - □ the installation of the central air conditioning system;
   - □ the (later) climate ducting work done.

7. Check whether there are any unsettled **building violations** or **citations** against the property.

8. Check whether there are any unsettled **fire department** **violations** or **citations** against the property.

9. Learn from the **building department**:
   - □ whether there has been any known occurrence of neighborhood area flooding;
   - □ the flood levels of any nearby streams and waterways;
   - □ and if there is any known active landslides, falling rock zones or other pertinent geological conditions which exist in the neighborhood.

10. Call the local **fire department** to learn if there ever was a fire in this building.

11. **Fire evidence** was observed _____.

12. Determine the **exact property size** and the **boundary** locations.

13. Learn of any **special zoning restrictions** in the event that future construction additions or changes be desired.

14. Ask the seller for a complete **approved set of plans** in addition to **building specifications**.

15. Determine your **legal rights** and your **obligations** relative to the following conditions:

      □ any possible **utility company** or other (company) **easements** which might exist for the right of way along this site;
      □ **water drainage run-off** conditions with respect to prospective neighboring properties;
      □ **utility lines** which **cross** this site to service the (_____) neighboring house;
      □ the **community alley** that is located behind the site;
      □ the **tree branch** and **root growth** that cross neighboring sites;
      □ the **common driveway**, including learning who is responsible to clean, repair, or repave it;
      □ the **lack of** the existence of a **front sidewalk**;
      □ the presence of **utility pole(s)** being in the _____ ;
      □ the existence of **utility lines** which appear to **run** (a) (an) (N)(S)(E)(W) direction (partially) above the _____ most section of this site ;
      □ the possibility that the _____ **driveway entrance apron** partly encroaches the neighbor's property;
      □ **light encroachment(s)** from neighboring site(s);
      □ any **other** possible **encroachment(s)**;
      □ the **setback distance(s)** of the _____ with respect to the _____ property line;
      □ **other setback distances**;
      □ and _____ .

16. Ask who owns all the **perimeter fences (or walls)** in the event that maintenance is needed in the future:

      □ (N) (S) (E) (W) _____
      □ (N) (S) (E) (W) _____
      □ (N) (S) (E) (W) _____
      □ (N) (S) (E) (W) _____ .

17. Determine whether a **town's boundary line** crosses this property

18. **Survey** the **surrounding area** to learn whether the property is located within sound range **of** any outstanding **noises** such as from:
    ☐ a schoolyard where children play
    ☐ a major thoroughfare
    ☐ a closeby railroad (which could produce vibrational effects from a passing train as well)
    ☐ a mixed use street
    ☐ _____

19. **Survey** the **surrounding area** to learn whether the property is located closeby an airport or below a flight pattern of low flying aircraft having disturbing sounds.

20. The **street lacks** adequate **lighting provision** which is not favorable by many from the standpoint of security.

21. Request the **termite control guarantee** for a posted sign exists in the _____ indicating that a control job has been recently conducted.

22. Obtain all **home service contracts** which the seller might have such as from
    ☐ a heating & air conditioning contractor
    ☐ appliance retailer(s)
    ☐ a pest control service
    ☐ a homeowner's warranty program

23. Examine the past **(gas) (oil) (electric) heating bills** because:
    ☐ the attic space is not insulated
    ☐ the attic has only minimal insulation
    ☐ in this old house the exterior walls have not been insulated
    ☐ the house doesn't utilize storm windows
    ☐ the house utilizes generally drafty old casement windows
    ☐ the house utilizes old drafty jalousie windows
    ☐ electric heat can be expensive

24. Recognize that this home uses **(aluminum) (steel) windows** which transmit heat through them more than wood windows.

25. Ask for a list of all **window screens** which are being **stored** in the _____ and have the owner provide you with a **directory** indicating their placement locations on the house.

26. Find out where all **stored door(s)** being stored in the _____ come from.

27. Realize that the house is in a **limited state of renovation**. Because problems with completing a renovation project are many, consider:
    - □ the use of on-site general contracting management supervision;
    - □ _____.

28. Ask the seller to **remove** all **debris and material** either being stored or observed to be lying about in such locations as:
    - □ outside the building
    - □ in the garage
    - □ in the attic

29. Have all **automatic garage door transmitters conveyed** to you.

30. Request that all **built-in blender or food center attachment(s)** be **conveyed** to you at the time of close.

31. Determine where the **closest fire hydrant** is located in relationship to this property for none was viewed in the immediate sight.

32. Realize that the **closest fire hydrant** observed is located _____.

33. Realize that all the **vegetative growth** on this premise should be **maintained cropped** as necessary to provide for a good margin of fire safety.

34. Recognize that there (is) (are) (one) (some) **tall tree(s)** nearby the house.

35. All **exterior drainage devices,** including the (leaders and gutters of the roof drainage system) (the _____ area drain) (the street curb drainage opening) (the concrete swale) (_____) should be **maintained free** of leaves, gravel, snow, ice, dirt and debris to prevent flooding or water backup action taking place at them.

36. Recognize that this home's **driveway** is a (comparatively **steep**) (steep) and, as such, driving along it can be both difficult and dangerous.

37. Recognize that the **building uses exterior plaster cement** for (section[s] of) its siding which can be a maintenance headache.

38. Request to **review** which **rooms** each **thermostat control activates** heating or air conditioning to.

39. Recognize that the _____ **room(s)** (is) (are) **unheated**. And recognize that this home's central **air conditioning** system **cools only** _____.

40. Realize that there is **no air conditioning** associated with this home.

41. Recognize that this home, having one central heating plant and which is activated and controlled by one thermostat, is considered to be a **'one-zone' heated home**.

42. Recognize that the forced **hot-air ducts** in the _____ have been installed **close to** or at the **ceilings** which is an ineffective scheme for heat because hot air rises.

43. Realize that the central **air conditioning duct registers** in the _____ have been installed at or **near the floors** which is not an efficient arrangement for cooling.

44. Realize that the house utilizes
  □ electrical resistance heat cables contained inside the ceilings
  □ warmed water through copper tube coils buried in the concrete floor slab
  □ warmed water circulating through tube coils which run in the ceilings
  for **radiant heat** as the source of heating system of this home.

45. Realize that the house utilizes an **electric heat pump** as the source of heating system of this home.

46. Recognize that
  □ every convenience electrical outlet
  □ most electrical outlets
  □ only some electrical outlets
  throughout the house don't have the third hole or **U-ground** that is normally found in today's **outlets** and, as such, should a 3-prong plug be used, one will need an adapter.

47. Recognize that there are **fewer electrical** convenience **outlets**
  □ throughout the building
  □ in some rooms of the building
  than are typically encountered in homes of today.

48. Recognize that the building still (wholly) (partially) utilizes some old **knob and tube wiring**.

49. Have the (balcony) (_____) **tested for its strength**, especially at its connections because you might have to budget for weak or adjustment connection repair.

50. Request that a viewing be made of the top of the chimney for **spark arrester** provision.

51. Recognize that the _____ **room(s)** (is) (are) exist **over** the **unheated garage**.

52. Recognize that there is **no direct access** to the
         □ basement
         □ garage
from the interior of the home.

53. Recognize that there is **little headroom clearance**
         □ at the foot of the steps that lead to the basement
         □ along the steps to the basement
         □ in the basement
         □ in the attic.
Watch your head when
         □ ascending this location.
         □ descending this location.
         □ traversing this location.

54. Recognize that the **steps** which lead to the
         □ basement are built (**steep**) (**narrow**).
         □ attic are built (steep) (narrow).
Exercise care while ascending or descending them.

55. Request verification of the fact that the house **is tied into** the **sewer lines**.
The _____ assured us that the house was indeed hooked up to sewers; but
         □ the drain line exited the back of the house.
         □ _____ .

56. Recognize that we noted the **presence of a sump pump** in the basement. This might reflect that the home's underfloor location suffers from a chronic water penetration problem; but the pump could also have been provided to control occasional basement flooding.
   - ☐ Even though it was working, one takes a risk of basement flooding should the electricity go out during stormy weather.
   - ☐ The sump pump should be demonstrated to your satisfaction before closing to see that it works well

57. Recognize that the **kitchen** has been **situated**
   - ☐ at a higher elevation than the garage and the home's entry poses an added chore for shoppers to bring bags of grocery items up to the kitchen.
   - ☐ at a lower elevation than the garage and the home's entry poses an added chore for shoppers to bring bags of grocery items down to the kitchen.

58. Recognize that
   - ☐ one of
   - ☐ some of
   - ☐ all of the

   appliances which stay(s) with the house (is) (are)
      - ☐ **old** appliance(s).
      - ☐ (a) comparatively old appliance(s).

59. Understand that the following **appliances do not come** with the sale of the house:
   - ☐ the washer
   - ☐ the dryer
   - ☐ the refrigerator
   - ☐ the freezer
   - ☐ the range
   - ☐ the microwave oven
   - ☐ the room air conditioner
   - ☐ the barbeque
   - ☐ _____.

The (owner) (real estate agent) informed us of this during our inspection. As such, these appliances were not (wholly) checked during our inspection.

60. We recommend that you **determine** exactly which **appliances, equipment and furnishings** are **part of** the seller's **property** and included along with the property sale. For example, do the
   - ☐ fireplace firescreen(s)
   - ☐ fireplace andirons
   - ☐ the exterior potted plants
   - ☐ _____

remain with the house?

61. Recognize that the main level of the **building** has been **built on a concrete slab** and that it is normal to find some fine cracking in the slab.

62. Be sure that all **food center attachment(s)**
    (is) (are) surrendered to you at the time of
    closing since the replacement of such attachments are pricey.

63. Realize that the _____ **bedroom(s)** lack(s) window(s), but instead have been provided **with sliding glass door**(s). When fresh air is desired, the sliding glass door(s) must be opened.

64. Make sure to **keep** the **house burglar-safe**. Remember, an intruder could easily enter the house through the
    ☐ underfloor crawl space hatch opening.
    ☐ pet door opening.
    ☐ _____.

65. Realize that there is **no security alarm system** associated with this home.

66. Realize that there is **no intercom system** associated with this home.

67. Determine **if** the **fireplace is** designed and capable to be **used only as a gas-burning fireplace** or also, as a wood burning fireplace. We observed the presence of a gas main here, but suspectfully the fireplace is capable of being utilized for both.

68. Understand that the **water heater is an electric unit** which has a lower recovery rate than oil or gas-fired water tanks. As such, once the water in the tank has been used up, one will have to wait a considerable lengthy time for more hot water.

69. Understand that the _____ has **no hookup** at the present time.

70. Understand that the _____ is **disconnected** at the present and, thus, inoperative.

71. Realize that the _____ is an **ineffective** one for the _____.

72. Understand that the _____ we were told is presently **no longer used**.

73. Recognize that the seller reported that the
    - ☐ dishwasher
    - ☐ freezer.
    - ☐ microwave oven
    - ☐ _____

    is **inoperative and** makes **no representations** regarding it. Consider getting a separate estimate of repair from a reputable appliance repairperson.

74. Request the **bill(s) of sale** for the following newer items:
    - ☐ _____
    - ☐ _____
    - ☐ _____
    - ☐ _____
    - ☐ _____
    - ☐ _____

75. Learn whether the **security sign** placed in the
    - ☐ front yard
    - ☐ front window
    - ☐ _____

    indicates the presence of a working security alarm system or is just being used as a deterrent to discourage would-be intruders from illegally entering the house.

76. Realize that there is an **incinerator** in the _____ yard.

77. Do not use the **heater** in the _____ since it is **unvented** and is no longer permitted.

78. *For buyers of new homes:*

    Request guarantees against defective **workmanship and defects** in materials on roofing, plumbing, electrical work, heating, ventilating and air conditioning work.

79. *For buyers of new homes:*

    Get the **names of** the material **suppliers and subcontracting firms** that were involved with the construction of the house. Ask for their telephone numbers, email addresses and their physical addresses as well.

80. *For buyers of new homes:*

    Ask the **builder to supply** you with the **manufacturers' guarantees for** the **appliances**, the appliance instruction manuals and any instructional videos which are associated with the appliances.

81. *For buyers of new homes:*
Request that the builder accordingly furnish you with **samples of** roofing cover **material**, tiling, some wood and masonry, wallpaper, paint, stain and carpeting.

82. *For buyers of new homes:*
Recognize that on account of an **agreed allowance** with the builder, the **purchaser provides** the following for this home:
        ☐ the installation of all finish flooring
        ☐ _____
        ☐ _____
We learned of this by the _____ during our inspection.

83. *For buyers of new homes:*
Recognize that we were told that the **builder does not provide** the following:
        ☐ a furnace humidifier;
        ☐ a mailbox;
        ☐ storms and window screens;
        ☐ perimeter fencing;
        ☐ a back patio;
        ☐ an underground lawn sprinkler system;
        ☐ a lawn, shrubbery and other landscaping;
        ☐ a washer and dryer;
        ☐ and _____.

84. *For buyers of new homes:*
Request that the **builder** additionally **provide guarantees** (if any) in connection with the following:
        ☐ paint and cabinet touch-ups;
        ☐ _____.

85. *Limitations on your inspection:*
Ask the seller for permission to **move back area rugs and view** the **floors under the carpets**. Doing this will allow you to see the type of floors being covered over and to discover possible existing floor problems.

86. *Limitations on your inspection:*
Ask that the **security alarm system be** completely **demonstrated** to your satisfaction before closing (for the owner did not fully demonstrate the entire system to us). If need be, request that the seller or the security alarm company itself demonstrate the system to you.

87. *Limitations on your inspection:*

Since the electricity was off during our inspection, we could not determine general electrical problems and demonstrate

- ☐ the outlet and fixture performances;
- ☐ the air conditioning system(s);
- ☐ the automatic overhead garage door opener;
- ☐ the doorbell(s);
- ☐ the electric _____ heating system;
- ☐ the electric hot water heater;
- ☐ the _____ exhaust fan(s) of the _____;
- ☐ the furnace(s)/fan(s);
- ☐ the heat lamp(s);
- ☐ the intercom;
- ☐ the dishwasher (and other remaining appliances);
- ☐ the electric range oven;
- ☐ the range hood;
- ☐ the trash compactor;
- ☐ _____;
- ☐ _____;
- ☐ _____;

Moreover, request a demonstration of...; etc..

Lastly, request an examination of the following:

- ☐ the remainder of the garage (after the material removal);
- ☐ some venting/flue work out to the exterior including for the _____;
- ☐ the attic space(s) which (was) (were) inaccessible during our inspection. We usually look for evidence of past fires, evidence of roof leaks, any condensation damage, the structural integrity of the rest of the framing members, and any evidences of rodent and termite infestation;
- ☐ the remainder of the attic space(s). We usually look for evidence of past fires, evidence of roof leaks, any condensation damage, the structural integrity of the rest of the framing members, and any evidences of rodent and termite infestation;
- ☐ _____;
- ☐ _____;
- ☐ _____.

Unless all these items can be checked and demonstrated to your expectations before closing, we feel you take a big risk in this regard. This is why it is so important to have everything demonstrated and be satisfied that all is in working order.

88. *Limitations on your inspection:*

Since the gas was off during our inspection, we could not demonstrate
- ☐ the furnace(s) and heating (including the thermostat(s) for heating);
- ☐ the furnace's hot water heating capability;
- ☐ the gas-fired hot water heater;
- ☐ the _____ fireplace gas main(s)/loglighter(s);
- ☐ the gas cooktop/range and oven;
- ☐ the gas dryer;
- ☐ the barbeque;
- ☐ the heating capability of the (pool) / (spa heater);
- ☐ the heater in the _____;
- ☐ _____;
- ☐ and determine the hot water temperature(s) nor whether gas odors exist.

Moreover, request a demonstration of...; etc..

Lastly, request an examination of the following:

- ☐ the remainder of the garage (after the material removal);
- ☐ some venting/flue work out to the exterior including for the _____;
- ☐ the attic space(s) which (was) (were) inaccessible during our inspection. We usually look for evidence of past fires, evidence of roof leaks, any condensation damage, the structural integrity of the rest of the framing members, and any evidences of rodent and termite infestation;
- ☐ the remainder of the attic space(s). We usually look for evidence of past fires, evidence of roof leaks, any condensation damage, the structural integrity of the rest of the framing members, and any evidences of rodent and termite infestation;

- ☐ *see item 92 for continuation* _____;
- ☐ _____;
- ☐ _____;
- ☐ _____;
- ☐ _____;
- ☐ _____;
- ☐ _____;
- ☐ _____.

Unless all these items can be checked and demonstrated to your expectations before closing, we feel you take a big risk in this regard. This is why it is so important to have everything demonstrated and be satisfied that all is in working order.

89. *Limitations on your inspection:*

Since the gas and electricity were off during our inspection, we
- □ could not determine whether gas odors exist;
- □ determine the hot water temperature(s);
- □ demonstrate the furnace(s) and heating (including [the] [their] thermostat[s]);
- □ the gas-fired hot water heater;

- □ *see 88 for continuation*;
- □ also, we could not demonstrate the outlet and fixture performances;

- □ *see 87 for continuation;*
- □ nor determine (other) general electrical problems, etc...

Moreover, request a demonstration of...; etc..

Lastly, request an examination of the following:

- □ the remainder of the garage (after the material removal);
- □ some venting/flue work out to the exterior including for the _____;
- □ the attic space that was not accessible during our inspection. We usually look for evidence of past fires, evidence of roof leaks, any condensation damage, the structural integrity of the rest of the framing members, and any evidences of rodent and termite infestation;
- □ the remainder of the attic space. We usually look for evidence of past fires, evidence of roof leaks, any condensation damage, the structural integrity of the rest of the framing members, and any evidences of rodent and termite infestation;
- □ *see item 92 for continuation* _____;
- □ _____;
- □ _____;
- □ _____;
- □ _____;
- □ _____;
- □ _____;
- □ _____.

Unless all these items can be checked and demonstrated to your expectations before closing, we feel you take a big risk in this regard. This is why it is so important to have everything demonstrated and be satisfied that all is in working order.

90. *Limitations on your inspection:*
> **Since there was no water to the house** during the inspection, we could not observe the water pressure, nor could we demonstrate the following:
>> □ the operation of the plumbing fixtures;
>> □ the hot water heating capability;
>> □ the dishwasher;
>> □ the washing machine;
>> □ the laundry drain;
>> □ the swimming pool equipment;
>> □ the underground lawn sprinkler system;
>> □ the well;
>> □ and the _____.

> Moreover, request a demonstration of...; etc..

> Lastly, request an examination of the following:...

91. *Limitations **in time** on your inspection:*
> □ Understand that **we were limited in our inspection**.
> □ Recognize that we were granted little time in our inspection.
> □ Recognize that we were granted little time in our inspection.
>> The (seller) (real estate agent) had to leave and requested that we 'wrap up' our inspection.

> Request a demonstration of: *see item 92 for continuation*; etc..

> Moreover, request an examination of the following:
>> □ the remainder of the garage (after the material removal);
>> □ some venting/flue work out to the exterior including for the _____;
>> □ the attic space that was not accessible during our inspection. We usually look for evidence of past fires, evidence of roof leaks, any condensation damage, the structural integrity of the rest of the framing members, and any evidences of rodent and termite infestation;
>> □ the remainder of the attic space. We usually look for evidence of past fires, evidence of roof leaks, any condensation damage, the structural integrity of the rest of the framing members, and any evidences of rodent and termite infestation;
>> □ *see item 92 for continuation* _____;
>> □ _____.

> Unless all these items can be checked and demonstrated to your expectations before closing, we feel you take a big risk in this regard. This is why it is so important to have everything demonstrated and be satisfied that all is in working order.

92. *Limitations on your inspection:*

Request a demonstration of:

- □ some windows (and door[s]) which were not sampled by us;
- □ the _____ furnace(s) and (its) (their) heating capability(ies), including the operation of (the) (their) thermostat[s])
  - □ since the gas pilot(s) (was) (were) off during our inspection;
  - □ since (it) (they) (was) (were) off for the summer;
  - □ _____ ;
- □ the balance of the (furnace's) (furnaces') heating capability(ies), including the balance of the operation of (its) (their) thermostat(s);
- □ the heating and cooling capabilities of the climate control unit(s), including the operation of their thermostat(s);
- □ the balance of the climate control (unit's) (units') heating and cooling capabilities, including the balance of the operation of (the) (their) thermostat(s);
- □ the balance of the operation of the radiant ceiling healing (in the _____) to reach (its) (their) ultimate temperature (for [it] [they] felt only slightly warm to the touch moments after the thermostat(s) [has] [have] been activated);
- □ the dishwasher;
- □ the other cycles of the dishwasher;
- □ the self-cleaning operation(s) of the oven(s) (since it takes longer for a self-cleaning 'pyrolytic' oven to clean itself than is the duration of a normal inspection);
- □ other central vacuum cleaning outlets;
- □ the _____ fireplace gas main;
  - □ because its line have been found capped;
  - □ because _____ ;
- □ the (fire safety detector[s]) (smoke detector[s]) of the _____ ;
- □ other intercom outlets;
- □ the overhead garage door(s) by the use of (its) (their) transmitter(s) (which were not available);
- □ the exterior area (drain's) (drains') water acceptance ability;
- □ the _____ gate to the _____ (because it was locked);
- □ the heating capability(ies) of the (swimming pool) (spa) heater (and their Ortega valve)
  - □ for (its) (their) gas pilot (was) (were) off (for the winter) (during our inspection);
  - □ for _____ ;
- □ the pool heater's water warming capability;
- □ the (balance of the) operation of the exterior underground lawn sprinkler system (and its [Rainbird] [_____] panel);
- □ all the timer(s);
- □ the performance of some electrical receptacles;
- □ and the lights of the _____ which didn't go on;
- □ etc..

Moreover, request an examination of the following:

- □ the remainder of the garage (after the material removal);
- □ some venting/flue work out to the exterior including for the _____;
- □ the attic space(s) which (was) (were) inaccessible during our inspection. We usually look for evidence of past fires, evidence of roof leaks, any condensation damage, the structural integrity of the rest of the framing members, and any evidences of rodent and termite infestation;
- □ the remainder of the attic space(s). We usually look for evidence of past fires, evidence of roof leaks, any condensation damage, the structural integrity of the rest of the framing members, and any evidences of rodent and termite infestation;
- □ the access for the water and waste connections of the _____ tub(s) (if [this access] [one] [they], in fact exist[s]);
- □ viewing the water and waste connections within the plumbing access(es) provided for the ____ bathtub(s) (since [the] [their] cover(s) were ____ shut);
- □ the underfloor crawl space;
- □ the balance of the crawl space
  - □ (although [part of] [the majority of] the crawl space had been viewed, some plumbing lines and drain lines, [ductwork] as well as some structural members prevented our complete access to view all areas);
  - □ (the access opening[s] [was] [were] [too] [quite] small for entrance);
- □ some rooms that were quickly walked through;
- □ locating the central air conditioning condensate line location(s);
- □ locating (the) (some) climate air return register(s);
- □ some roof and chimney areas;
- □ other (lengths) (areas) of the _____ exterior _____ wall(s) where (it was) (they were) largely covered by vegetative [over]growth [and other lengths (such as on the neighboring side(s))] ;
- □ the _____ (since one would have to go onto the neighboring property to examine it fully);
- □ some (hillside) property which had not been (walked) (climbed);
- □ locating any waste drainage cleanouts;
- □ the independent sewage disposal system including
  - □ verifying the reported septic tank size capacity(ies), whether a drainage field does actually exist as reported (instead of seepage pit[s]) and viewing within its cleanout or inspection opening. What would be helpful in this investigation would be to obtain the (possible) layout plans for this matter, the possible permit(s) and other (possible) prepared documentation, including the bill of sale for this work;
  - □ requesting verification of the reported fact that this system consists of _____ septic tank(s) which are connected to _____ (leach field[s]) (seepage pit[s]) in the _____ yard, viewing within (its) (their) cleanout or inspection opening(s), and determining the tank capacity size(s). What would be helpful in this investigation would be to obtain the (possible) layout plans for this matter, the possible permit(s) and other (possible) prepared documentation, including the bill of sale for this work;
  - □ determining what the system actually consists of: for example, is there more than one septic tank and is the septic tank connected to a leach field or to a seepage pit? The owner could not answer this question. Also, determine the tank capacity size(s) and (its) (their) location. If possible, view within (its) (their) cleanout or inspection opening(s). [Lastly], verify whether or not the house and (garage) (_____) utilize the same septic system.] What would be helpful in this investigation would be to obtain the (possible) layout plans for this matter, the possible permit(s) and other (possible) prepared documentation, including the bill of sale for this work;
  - □ _____;
- □ etc..

Unless all these items can be checked and demonstrated to your expectations before closing, we feel you take a big risk in this regard. This is why it is so important to have everything demonstrated and be satisfied that all is in working order.

93. *Limitations on your inspection:*

Because it snowed heavily, details of the roof, the sidewalk, the driveway and other exterior improvements could not be directly examined. When the snow melts, the following would have to be **carefully look**ed at:

☐ the roof;
☐ the grounds;
☐ the sidewalk;

☐ _____ :

☐ _____ :

☐ _____ :

☐ _____ :

☐ _____ :

☐ _____ :

☐ _____ :

☐ _____ :

☐ _____ :

☐ and other exterior improvements.

94. **Locate** the **utility meters**.

95. Have the **well water checked**.

Air Conditioning

- ☐ old central **air conditioning compressor** unit(s)
  - ☐ approaching trouble-free life expectancy
  - ☐ at trouble-free life expectancy
  - ☐ beyond trouble-free life expectancy
- ☐ old central **air conditioning condensing** unit(s)
  - ☐ approaching trouble-free life expectancy
  - ☐ at trouble-free life expectancy
  - ☐ beyond trouble-free life expectancy
- ☐ **condensing unit**(s) **miss**(es) seismic **straps**
- ☐ **secure** condensing **unit**(s)
- ☐ **bottom of condensing unit** is **short of 3 inches** above gradework
- ☐ big house has **small** air conditioning **system**

Appliances

- ☐ realize **no garbage disposal** unit
- ☐ **no dishwasher hookup**
- ☐ **no gas dryer hookup**
- ☐ **no electric dryer hookup**
- ☐ **no dishwasher and gas dryer**
- ☐ **no dishwasher and electric dryer**
- ☐ _____ **bathroom exhaust fan** needs **reconnecting**
- ☐ _____ **bathroom exhaust fan** is **noisy**
- ☐ _____ is **inoperative**. Request a repair estimate.

Banisters and Railings

- ☐ **no railing** at _____ **steps**
- ☐ **no railing** on _____ **stoop**
- ☐ **resecure shaky** _____ **railing**

Bathroom

- ☐ **bathroom** could stand **modernization**
- ☐ **chipped** _____ **sink**
- ☐ cultured marble **sink counter was burned**
- ☐ **cracked** _____ **sink**

Carpentry

- ☐ **close off** partially **opened** _____ **wall**
- ☐ **door**(s) **stuck closed** at _____
- ☐ **window**(s) **stuck closed** at _____
- ☐ **no attic hatch cover**

Caulking

- ☐ **caulking/sealing work needed** at
  - ☐ around window and door frames
  - ☐ between the interfaces of the house's siding/fascia
  - ☐ between the house structure and the chimney
  - ☐ where needed, including sealing off exterior areas of the house open to the elements

Chimney and Fireplace

- ☐ **check chimney**
  - ☐ masonry **chimney** stack **leans** or is **bending**
  - ☐ masonry **chimney** stack **walls** are built too **thin**
  - ☐ **walls of** the **chimney** feel **hot**
  - ☐ newer **chimney** on exterior wall is **not equipped with an air intake** opening
  - ☐ **chimney lacks an ashpit** cleanout
- ☐ **chimney needs proper height**
- ☐ **add spark arrestor**
- ☐ **relocate log lighter valve outside chamber**
- ☐ masonry **repair** is **needed to** _____ fireplace **chamber**
- ☐ **small outer** fireplace **hearth**
- ☐ **outer hearth** is **cracked**
- ☐ **no damper door**
- ☐ **damper** door **needs adjustment**
- ☐ **clean** _____ **fireplace**
- ☐ **clean** _____ **fireplace** and **adjust damper**
- ☐ **equip fireplace with firescreening**
- ☐ **smoke stains** seen **over** the **fireplace opening**
- ☐ **wood finish** too **close above** the **fireplace opening**

Doorbells

- ☐ **no doorbells** or **door knockers**
- ☐ **doorbell inoperative**
- ☐ **doorbell** has been **located inside** the storm **door**

Doors

- ☐ **missing door** at _____
- ☐ **door scratches** floor upon extension at _____
- ☐ **jammed door** at _____
- ☐ **door can't fully close** at _____
- ☐ **door failed to remain** in a **closed** position at _____
- ☐ **door didn't close properly** at _____
- ☐ **sliding door** was **off track** at _____
- ☐ **door between house and garage** (is not a fire-rated door) (lacks a fire barrier)
- ☐ the **following door problems** need attention:
  - ☐ _____
  - ☐ _____

Drainage

- ☐ possible **poor grading** at_____
- ☐ **add drain at driveway**
- ☐ possibly **add weepholes at** _____ **retaining wall**

Electrical

- ☐ **bury uncovered** electrical **wiring** at _____
- ☐ _____ **utility pole leans**
- ☐ **frayed** overhead **service lines**
- ☐ **low clearance of** overhead electrical **service lines**
- ☐ if **house electrical ground connections** do not exist
- ☐ **small electrical service:** _____ wire _____ volt ____ amp service. ____ amp service recommended
- ☐ **electric service marginal** ____ wire ___ volt ___ amp service. ___ amp service recommended
- ☐ **electrical service** is **sufficient** but if you add:
  - ☐ significant or central air conditioning
  - ☐ major electrical appliances (like a self-cleaning range)
  - _____ amp service is then recommended
- ☐ home utilizes (some) (all) **aluminum wiring**
- ☐ **know your size and type of wiring**: (12 gage) (14 gage) (Copper) (Copper-clad)
  - (_____)
- ☐ **secure** electrical **conduit** at _____
- ☐ **electrician** should be engaged **to check** and make corrective work measures to the following:
  - ☐ _____
  - ☐ _____
  - ☐ _____
- ☐ close off **open J-boxes** at _____
- ☐ **extension cord(s) (outlet[s])** used
- ☐ **ground fault interrupter(s)** recommended
  - ☐ at _____ sink(s)
  - ☐ at _____ outdoor outlet(s)
  - ☐ inside the garage
  - ☐ as part of a swimming pool or spa light circuit breaker
  - ☐ to control an inside tub spa motor
- ☐ **no backyard outlet** for general convenience
- ☐ **no** _____ **bathroom outlet**
- ☐ **could not cause** _____ **outlet to work**
- ☐ **tighten** internal screws of **old outlets** for some of these screws tend to loosen up with time
- ☐ _____ outlet(s) have **reversed polarity**
- ☐ _____ outlet(s) have **open ground connection**
- ☐ **dangerously located receptacle** at:
  - ☐ behind a kitchen cooktop
  - ☐ within arms reach of a bathtub
  - ☐ low hanging light fixture directly over a bathtub
  - ☐ _____

☐ _____ **exterior outlet(s)** and **switch(es) lack protection** from the elements
☐ **flickering light** in _____
☐ **light** was (**hanging** by its wiring) **(loose)**
☐ **light inside small closet** poses a **fire hazard**
☐ further **specific items of electrical repair** include:

     ☐ _____
     ☐ _____
     ☐ _____
     ☐ _____

Exterior Improvements

☐ **uprooted sidewalk**
☐ **patching concrete cracks** noted in:
     ☐ front sidewalk
     ☐ driveway
     ☐ pathway to the front porch
     ☐ _____
     ☐ _____
☐ corrective **masonry repair** is needed to:
     ☐ _____
     ☐ _____
     ☐ _____
☐ **replace** sections of **stone and mortar** _____ when this **improvement** reaches this state of deterioration for:
     ☐ it possessed numerous cracked joints
     ☐ it was settled
     ☐ it was uprooted
☐ **provide access route** to _____ yard
☐ **recommend retaining wall** at _____
☐ **increase** height and length of **retaining wall**
☐ _____ **outdoor wall leans**
☐ **discount** _____ that is in poor condition
☐ **(repave) (resurface) (seal) blacktop driveway** that was (cracked) (quite worn)
☐ **seal blacktop driveway** that shows signs of wear
☐ **repave** (areas of) distressed **concrete driveway** that was (severely cracked) (in poor condition)
☐ **oil stains** mark driveway
☐ differential **settlement of** swimming **pool**
☐ **rusted diving board bolts**
☐ **low height patio cover**

Exterior Siding

☐ recommend **corrective wooden siding** / weatherproofing work which includes:
     ☐ closing up / sealing off sections open to weather and insect exposure;
     ☐ replacing damaged siding members;
     ☐ securing looser wood siding members
     ☐ and caulking/sealing around window and door frames, at the interfaces of the siding and fascia, etc. (where needed) so as to protect against the elements.

☐ **crawl space access cover** was _____

☐ **replace** affected **damprotted post** base

☐ **replace** the following **exterior woodwork** which was damprotted:

     ☐ _____

     ☐ _____

     ☐ _____

☐ some **cracks in** the exterior **stucco walls**

☐ **monitor stucco cracks**

☐ **reparge** fallen/missing exterior **plaster cement fascia**

☐ **re-point** the _____

☐ **install fence** where none exists at

     ☐ alongside the foot edge of the hillside slope for a fall down this embankment could be dangerous

     ☐ _____

☐ **fence off** the swimming **pool**

☐ **discount** _____ **fence** in state of disrepair

☐ the _____ **fence** is in **worn** condition and needs attention:

     ☐ several lengths of which _____

     ☐ we saw its damaged sections as well

     ☐ _____

☐ **repair** sections of **leaning fence** in the _____ yard

Garage

☐ due to **garage's poor condition** and/or the fashion of its construction, the following corrective work measures will be needed:

     ☐ structural retrofitting work, including _____

     ☐ _____

     ☐ _____

☐ repair **dented/knocked-in section of rear garage wall** noted by car impact damage

☐ **add concrete carstops** to (garage) (carport)

☐ **garage floor incorrectly pitched**

☐ **no overhead garage door**

☐ **side-by-side garage doors** noted

☐ no automatic **garage door opener**

☐ overhead **garage door springs in way of pathway**

☐ **broken** overhead **garage door spring**

Glazing

☐ **replace cracked panes** detected at _____

☐ **cracked glazing** detected at the (_____ bathroom tub) (_____ bathroom stall shower)

☐ **reputty around** _____ **panes** of window glass due to their:

     ☐ cracked glazing compound

     ☐ loosened glazing compound

     ☐ fallen glazing compound

☐ **check whether there is safety tempered glass** at the following:
- ☐ the _____ sliding glass door(s)
- ☐ all other exterior glass door(s)
- ☐ the transom window(s)
- ☐ the sidelights
- ☐ the _____ stall shower door(s) and enclosure(s)
- ☐ the _____ bathtub sliding doors
- ☐ the _____

☐ **low-to-floor windows** of the _____ **need safety tempered glazing**

Heating

- ☐ realize _____ **room** is **absent of** direct **heating**
- ☐ **heat failed to emanate** from _____
- ☐ **furnace ventilation** is **restricted**
- ☐ **furnace** has _____ problem while in operation - seller should have his contractor check this out and repair as deemed necessary
- ☐ **firebox cracked (and crumbling)** - recommend replacing it
- ☐ **old gravity furnace** - budget for a modern forced air furnace replacement in the years ahead
- ☐ **old furnace** - because of its age, budget for a replacement in the years ahead
  - ☐ nearing its rated life
  - ☐ at its rated life
  - ☐ past its rated life
- ☐ **skimpy furnace** - we would have expected a heating plant of more B.T.U.s
- ☐ **separated** heating plant **exhaust flue** - notify the owner to have this condition corrected at once
- ☐ **soot streaks** noted off _____
- ☐ **asbestos duct** thermal **wrapping possible**
- ☐ **long flat run of** fuel-fired furnace's **exhaust duct**
- ☐ **dented ducting** at _____
- ☐ **no humidifier** on the furnace

Hot Water Heating

- ☐ **water heater works inefficiently**
- ☐ **old hot water heater**
  - ☐ nearing its rated life
  - ☐ at its rated life
  - ☐ past its rated life
- ☐ **small hot water heater**: existing capacity _____ proposed capacity _____
- ☐ **small and old hot water heater**: existing capacity _____ proposed capacity _____
- ☐ **popping sounds** from **hot water heater**
- ☐ **dented hot water heater**
- ☐ **stained hot water heater**
- ☐ hot **water heater's vent flue** found **separated**
- ☐ **equip water heating system with temperature/pressure relieve valve**
- ☐ **pressure relief valve leaks**
- ☐ **water heater's cleanout drain drips**
- ☐ **water heater is not anchored**

Insulation

- ☐ **uninsulated attic**
- ☐ **minimal insulation** found **in attic**
- ☐ **re-lay attic insulation**

Kitchen

- ☐ **kitchen** could stand **modernization**
- ☐ **kitchen and bathroom** need **modernization**

Irrigation Sprinklers

- ☐ **no sprinkler system in** (front) (side) (back) **yard(s)**
- ☐ **divert** sprinkler **spray from** the building **structure** at _____
- ☐ **sprinkler line leaks** at _____
- ☐ old **sprinkler system lacks anti-syphon valves**
- ☐ **several problems with irrigation system** include:
  - ☐ _____
  - ☐ _____
  - ☐ _____

Leaders and Rain Gutters

- ☐ (no) (some areas lack) **leaders and gutters**
- ☐ **add extension leader(s)** to _____
- ☐ **leaders and gutters aging**
- ☐ some **items of** corrective **roof drainage system work** include:
  - ☐ _____
  - ☐ _____
  - ☐ _____
- ☐ **poor pitch of** rain **gutters**
- ☐ **clear leaders and gutters**

Legal (Items of Conformance)

- ☐ **low ceiling height in** _____
- ☐ **narrow width of room in** _____
- ☐ **small room** area in _____
- ☐ **bathroom opens to kitchen**
- ☐ what looks to be a **bedroom is not a bedroom**
- ☐ realize **bedroom has no closet**
- ☐ **improper clearance in** underfloor **crawl space**
- ☐ **doorway at** _____ **fails to meet minimum size** dimensions
- ☐ hinged **shower door opens inwardly**
- ☐ **garage door does not lead to a "bedroom"**
- ☐ **fire-rated door between house and garage**
- ☐ **improper** dimensions of **stairway run and riser**
- ☐ **step** risers **vary in height**

- ☐ **small clearance** height **along stairway**
- ☐ **baluster** stairway **spacing** is **too wide**
- ☐ **incorrect** stair **handrail's** wall **projection**
- ☐ **window too small in** _____
- ☐ **window sill too high** over _____ bedroom floor
- ☐ _____ **bedroom window security bars** are **absent of interior release** handle
- ☐ **wall between house and** attached **garage** isn't of adequate fire resistive construction
- ☐ **no attic access**
- ☐ exterior wood **siding** starts too **low-to-grade** along _____
- ☐ separate electrical **service lines cross** a later added non-permitted **swimming pool**
- ☐ **fuel heating plants** are located **under stairs**
- ☐ **garage size is too small**
- ☐ **room entry** is **absent of a light switch** or a switch controlling an electrical outlet
- ☐ **wonder whether approvals are in order** for the following:
  - ☐ _____
  - ☐ _____
  - ☐ _____

Lighting

- ☐ **exterior lighting** is **recommended outside** the _____ yard
- ☐ **replace missing light fixture at** _____
- ☐ hanging **light fixture at** _____ **may sway against** _____
- ☐ hanging **light fixture at** _____ **hangs too low**
- ☐ **light** fixture **hangs low over** _____ **bathtub**
- ☐ **clearance** is **needed around light canister** in attic

Locks

- ☐ **provide lock at** _____
- ☐ realize (master bedroom) (smaller bedroom) **entry door(s) did not contain locks**
- ☐ recommend an **emergency key release** for operating the garage door manually in the event of an electrical power failure
- ☐ **provide** a **lock at the** _____ **bathroom door for privacy**

Painting

- ☐ **paint** a marking **to make** the existence of the **elevation differential obvious** at _____
- ☐ **exterior of (house) (building) could stand a paint job** for aesthetic reasons
- ☐ **exterior trim needs painting**
- ☐ **touch up trim** where some peeling paint
- ☐ exterior **metal trim needs painting**
- ☐ **repair fine cracking** during painting at _____

Patchwork

☐ **patched** _____ **ceiling from** reported former **leak** above
☐ **patched** _____ **ceiling from** lighting **fixture removal**
☐ **patched** _____ **ceiling - ask the owner** and get any guarantees regarding this work
☐ **ask** the **owner about the patchwork / or staining** that was noted at the following
example locations:
   ☐ _____
   ☐ _____

Peeling Paint

☐ **peeling paint** noted **on** _____ **wall - hoping no rot**
☐ **peeling paint** noted **on** _____ **wall - likely from poor bonding**

Pest Control

☐ **presence of** _____, a **monthly service** with a licensed pest
control contractor is recommended for at least a year
☐ **presence of numerous bees** noted in the _____, **call** an **exterminator**
☐ **call exterminator to remove** an active _____ **nest** at _____
☐ **presence of the following pests**, we recommend a monthly service with a
licensed pest control contractor for at least a year
   ☐ _____
   ☐ _____
   ☐ _____

Plumbing

☐ standing **water inside water meter pit**
☐ **plumber to check** the following:
   ☐ _____
   ☐ _____
   ☐ _____
☐ **wet** area along the _____ **yard** probably caused **by damaged pipe**
☐ **lower water pressure:**
   ☐ (hot) (cold) water (low) (somewhat low) at _____ sink faucet
   ☐ (hot) (cold) water (low) (somewhat low) at _____ sink faucet
   ☐ (hot) (cold) water (low) (somewhat low) at _____ sink faucet
☐ **clogged aerator(s)** detected at:
   ☐ _____ sink faucet
   ☐ _____ sink faucet
   ☐ _____ sink faucet
☐ **high water pressure**
☐ **rusty water** likely reflects rusty galvanized piping:
   ☐ (hot) (cold) water at ___ sink faucet - but (cleared) (did not clear) after a moment of running water
   ☐ (hot) (cold) water at ___ sink faucet - but (cleared) (did not clear) after a moment of running water
   ☐ (hot) (cold) water at ___ sink faucet - but (cleared) (did not clear) after a moment of running water

- □ because of (some) (most) (all) **old galvanized plumbing** (with pressure loss) (with rusting), **budget** for new copper piping
- □ **galvanized plumbing with no pressure loss and rusting** - believe it doesn't pose a serious problem in the immediate future
- □ **ask extent of copper piping** installation
- □ **active leakage** at _____
- □ **corrosion of pipe** at _____
- □ **corrosion of pipe atop water heater** from electrolysis
- □ length(s) of **water line(s) rest on soil**
- □ **piping touches wood** member(s)
- □ **banging water hammer noise** at _____ faucet when water turned off
- □ **chattering noise** when _____ faucet is turned on
- □ **gas odor** at (meter) (_____)
- □ **waste backup** at _____
- □ **old sewer lines**
- □ **septic system (aging)**(at its rated life)(beyond its rated life expectancy)
- □ later **added bedrooms, but** private **waste system wasn't increased**
- □ **examine private sewage disposal system and have periodically cleaned**
- □ **no air gap**
- □ **water empties through air gap**
- □ (_____ sink) (_____bathtub) **water was slow to drain**
- □ **cracked** _____ **sink**
- □ **leak** at _____ **under** _____ **sink**
- □ **taped elbow** under _____ sink
- □ **water drips from** _____ **faucet**
- □ _____ sink's left and right **faucets are reversed**
- □ _____ **faucet turns clockwise**
- □ replace **missing pop-up drain plug** at _____ sink
- □ _____ sink's **drain plug didn't hold** its basin **water**
- □ possible need for **replacement of stall shower pan**
- □ **small size stall shower**
- □ **wrong finish of stall shower**
- □ **back water siphonage** at old _____ tub
- □ **no tub plumbing access** for _____ tub
- □ **leakage** at _____ **diverter valve**
- □ **drain mechanism didn't work** - stopper used at _____
- □ **rubber stopper used** at _____ tub
- □ _____ **tub's plug didn't hold water**
- □ **cramped clearance**(s) offered **at** _____ **toilet**
- □ eventually replace _____ **toilet finely cracked** - but no leakage
- □ _____ **toilet tank cover broken**
- □ _____ **toilet leaks at its base**
- □ _____ **toilet moves**
- □ **water trickles into** _____ **toilet bowl**
- □ **dripping water after** _____ **toilet** was **flushed**
- □ _____ **toilet runs**
- □ _____ **toilet flushed weakly**
- □ **hold lever** at _____ **toilet**
- □ some **plumbing fixture problems noted:**
  - □ _____

Pool

- ☐ differential **settlement of** swimming **pool**
- ☐ **worn pool** needs attention
- ☐ **pool needs resurfacing**
- ☐ **re-seal coping joint**
- ☐ **unheated** swimming **pool**
- ☐ **pool's water heater aging**
- ☐ **old pool filter**
- ☐ **old pool pump**/motor
- ☐ **pool** was **not fenced off**
- ☐ **diving board bolts rusted**

Regrout

- ☐ **regrout** _____ **sink**
- ☐ **regrout** _____ **bathtub**
- ☐ **regrout** _____ **stall shower**

Removal

- ☐ **clear underfloor** crawl space free of debris
- ☐ **remove** stored **material near (furnace)** (water heater)
- ☐ **remove rodent droppings** from (attic) (_____)
- ☐ **clean roof** free of leaves and debris
- ☐ **remove** _____ **resting on roof**

Roof

- ☐ **replace** _____ **roof** (at) (beyond) **rated life:**
  - ☐ evidence of leakage on _____
  - ☐ some roofing repairs already made of late
  - ☐ _____ causes us to believe that replacement time is now
- ☐ **replace soon** _____ **roof** (at) (beyond) rated life:
  - ☐ evidence of leakage on _____
  - ☐ brace for periodic patching
  - ☐ immediate roofing repair should be instituted
- ☐ **replace soon** _____ **roof rapidly aging:**
  - ☐ no significance evidence of leakage could be found
  - ☐ brace for periodic patching
  - ☐ immediate roofing repair should be instituted
- ☐ **repair** _____ **roof** which appears to be **in generally** _____ **condition:**
  - ☐ no significance evidence of leakage could be found
  - ☐ some _____ (was) (were) noted
  - ☐ some _____ (was) (were) noted

Screens

- ☐ **re-screen** _____ **underfloor vent screens** that were (torn) (damaged) (missing)
- ☐ **no screen door** at _____ entrance to the house
- ☐ **missing** _____ **sliding screen door**
- ☐ **no window screens** provided on house
- ☐ **window screens missing** at _____
- ☐ **ripped screen** found at _____
- ☐ **vent openings** at _____ **need re-screening** work
- ☐ **add screening to attic vents**

Seek Information

It is recommended that you further inquire about the following:

- ☐ determining whether mineral rights come along with the sale of the property;
- ☐ learning whether there are any underground utilities and plumbing supply and waste lines which cross the home site to any of the neighboring properties;
- ☐ more about the history and use of the site and additional information about the site's subdivision. For instance, was the property part of a fruit grove?
- ☐ determining whether the house has been later equipped with a new water main;
- ☐ additional information about the adequacy of street drainage in the neighborhood, especially in front of the house;
- ☐ the cost of fire insurance for the house and learning whether it would be difficult to obtain. Ask if there has been any known fire to have occurred in the locality of the home. For instance, the known "Malibu Fire" burned the neighbor's house down. You may also wish to learn more about the extent of water spray action from the irrigation sprinklers present;
- ☐ more about the neighboring parcels of land, including what they have been zoned for and who owns them. For instance, the seller spoke of zoning for 2-family homes across the street from this house. Ask if there are any neighboring land parcels which are presently landlocked;
- ☐ more about the environmental locality of this dwelling. This includes, for example, determining with certainty whether the nearby electrical transformer vault, the not-too-distant utility pole and wiring pose any possible harmful health effects to the residents of the house such as during seismic activity or by means of possible radiation;
- ☐ additional information about the nearby water channel. For example, learn who cleans and maintains this channel. Ask, too, if water which runs along it attracts insects or emits odors;
- ☐ determining whether gnats or other flying insects frequent the home's yards where a multitude of such insects are noted to hover about the property;
- ☐ determining whether a vehicle has ever run into the home and, if so, learn exactly what damage did it do;
- ☐ determining whether the street storm drain in front of the house poses a safety hazard to small children for it has a wide unprotected opening. Learn, too, whether foul odors are emitted from this storm drain or whether it attracts insects at times;
- ☐ more about the lot size relative to the minimum size zoned lot permitted in the locality
- ☐ determining whether cable television is now possible in the neighborhood or, perhaps, will be possible in the near future;
- ☐ learning whether the exterior tiles have been recently sealed;

☐ determining that sewage which exits the house is done by gravity flow and does not require pumping through the waste lines. If this is so, is there a hermetically sealed pump to do this work?

☐ determining whether it is required for the house to be connected to city sewers when they are installed along the street in front of the house;

☐ determining the exact route of the home's sewer lines in exiting the home site

☐ why the street curb in front of the house has been marked with painted numerals

☐ learning of any possible encroachments;

☐ how the perimeter fences, walls and curbing run relative to the property lines. For example, one fence doesn't run straight, but juts to one side at its mid-length;

☐ what remedy(ies) (if any) does the seller intend to correct before closing;

☐ where the collected water from the outside area drains exit. Could it be to the drainage outlet in the street curb?

☐ determining whether the swimming pool has been equipped with overflow drains

☐ determining whether the planter along the outside wall of the house has been waterproofed;

☐ learning whether the close-to-grade wood used in the construction of this home utilizes pressure-treated wood with an approved preservative, or is of a durable variety;

☐ determining whether anchor bolts have been used along mud sillplates to help secure the house framing (called the superstructure) to its respective foundation in the event of seismic activities. The finished walls prohibit examination of this condition;

☐ learning for what kind of pests does the extermination service treat against;

☐ learning the age of the house's tile roof, including learning whether it has a new underlayment (since many homeowners of tile roofs merely replace the old underlayment and any damaged tiles);

☐ determining whether tub, door and shower glazing as well as low-to-floor window and transom window glazing consist of safety tempered glazing which is appropriate for these glass sections;

☐ how well secure is the climate control unit mounted upon the roof;

☐ how well the mirrored panels have been fastened to the wall. Are they glue-adhesive fastened?

☐ verifying the existence of vinyl asbestos tile finish flooring in this home. A laboratory can make a positive identification of it;

☐ learning whether the mineral asbestos is present in all acoustical ceiling spray material. Again, a laboratory can make a positive identification of it;

☐ learning whether acoustical ceiling spray, which was reportedly recently removed from the house, was performed by a certified or licensed asbestos abatement contractor (if asbestos was, in fact, found to be present in that acoustical spray material);

☐ additional information about the community's shared well water supply system that the house is connected onto. This was provided by a private company with each homeowner having been granted transferable shares of well usage. The home's private well was disconnected and is not in use;

☐ determining whether the efflorescence which was seen in the fireplace chamber reflects a chimney water penetration problem possibly because of faulty flashing. A chimney contractor/or a roofer will have to check this out;

☐ determining whether the self-cleaning oven requires exterior venting and, if this is so, learn whether it has been so equipped;

- ☐ determining if there is pre-wiring already installed underground to serve an outside post lamp. If so, ask then if all that would be required is the post lamp itself
- ☐ what the timer controls;
- ☐ determining whether or not the firm which architecturally designed the home or the home's remodeling work is a duly licensed architectural firm and, further, had been engaged to oversee the construction;
- ☐ and whether or not the installation of fire sprinklers are (or have been) required in the building;
- ☐ determining whether belonging to the local homeowners association is mandatory or not;
- ☐ (new home) determining whether any possible design changes conform to the issued plans (which should, of course, be approved plans). If not, then request to see possible final amended documentation or addenda for any possible changes. For instance, the builder spoke of a shared connecting bathroom to serve two bedrooms but, instead, it was later decided after the plans were building department -approved that each bedroom was to have its own bathroom and was so accordingly built that way. The building department inspector red-lined in and signed off this change at the job site
- ☐ (new home) for what length of time is the structural integrity of the house guaranteed for;
- ☐ (new home) determining if the builder offers guarantees relative to paint and cabinet touch-ups;
- ☐ (condominium) learning whether the homeowners of the building are involved in any possible existing litigation matters or other possible action taken with respect to possible building defects and deficiencies;
- ☐ (condominium) requesting verification of the fact that the common walls which separate the apartment units are of the correct fire-rated wall variety;
- ☐ (condominium) and determining whether guarantees exist for the building's fire sprinkler system and elevators, or possibly whether there are service contracts to maintain them.

Soils/Geological

- ☐ **poor grading** on _____ side(s)
- ☐ **geologist to examine** the premise grounds before commitment including for:
    - ☐ hillside sloughing / debris or rock slides
    - ☐ slump slippage
    - ☐ subsidence
    - ☐ lateral creep
    - ☐ soil erosion
    - ☐ the building's close proximity to the hillside slope
    - ☐ _____ geological condition
- ☐ **distress** at _____ **probably** resulted **from settlement** - but verify with geologist
- ☐ **provide ground cover** at bare _____ slope

Staining

- ☐ **old** dry **stains on underfloor members** likely by past plumbing leakage-but ask owner
- ☐ **old** water **stains on** _____ **ceiling probably** from a **past** plumbing **leak**
- ☐ **old** water **stains on** _____ **ceiling reported** from a **past** plumbing **leak**
- ☐ **water stains mark** _____ **but** appear **old and inactive** at the present time
- ☐ **old** water **staining marks** _____ but **ask the seller** about this and obtain any guarantees
- ☐ **old**, dry water **stains** seen **at** the following **example locations** and hopefully corrected:

☐ old staining exists on _____ ;
☐ _____ ;
☐ _____ .

☐ **old stains in attic - antedate latest roofing** installation work
☐ **old,** dry water **staining / blister damage / patchwork** were seen **at** the following **example locations** and hopefully the problems which caused the conditions have been corrected:

    ☐ old staining exists on _____ ;
    ☐ blister damage exists along _____ ;
    ☐ patchwork detected at _____ .

Stairs

☐ **reinforce** _____ **weak steps**

Structural

☐ **re-point and patch** (vertical) (horizontal) **crack in** ____ **foundation wall** and monitor
☐ **following crawl space structural work is required:**
    ☐ _____
    ☐ _____
☐ **recommend** house **framing be secured to** its **foundation**
☐ **deteriorated foundation wall(s) at** _____
☐ **structural damage** detected **from termites at** _____
☐ **off-center post loading**
☐ **temporary shoring under house** at _____
☐ **main beams** at _____ are **in poor condition**
☐ concrete **slab-on-grade cracked at** _____
☐ **add** (bracing) (reinforcement support work) for **bouncy** _____ **floor**
☐ **out-of-plumb** _____ **wall(s)**
☐ **crack in** _____ **exterior wall** at line of new addition
☐ **cracks radiating out over** _____ **window(s)** and _____ **door(s)**
☐ **crack at** _____ **ceiling and wall juncture** in the _____
☐ **area of** _____ **floor slopes**
☐ **area of** _____ **floor slopes - get access** to see whether there are supportive problems
☐ **patch, paint and monitor cracking** noted in the following locations:
    ☐ _____
    ☐ _____
☐ **creaking sound heard** while walking on raised wood floor
☐ **small fine cracks and creaks** (throughout house) (on _____) none were deemed structurally significant
☐ **brace in** (north - south) (east - west) **to increase lateral rigidity**
☐ **repair separated connections in attic**
☐ **roof sags**
☐ **other source(s) of structural damage** from _____

Termites

☐ evidence of **termites detected at** _____ - but **no structurally significant damage**
☐ evidence of **termites detected at** _____ - **with some structural damage**
☐ **recommend termite control work** as matter of prudent precaution

Trees/Vegetation

□ **(trim back) (crop) (tree[s]) (vegetative growth)** which (closely) brush (house) (utility lines)

Ventilation

□ **add low screen vents to garage** lacking them
□ **underfloor lacks adequate ventilation**
□ **ventilation can be provided to** (bathroom) (toilet compartment)
□ to prevent overheating of (air plenum) **(attic), ventilation needs to be provided**
□ **vent flue** of (clothes dryer) (bathroom) _____ **exhausts to wrong place**

Waterproofing

□ **evidence of chronic water seepage problems** had been observed by the following:
  □ deterioration of some foundation wall length(s)
  □ efflorescence found on various concrete foundation walls within the underfloor location
  □ soil shrinkage cracks noted within the crawlspace
  □ (rust) (staining) on bottom of furnace legs
  □ dry water stains on bottom of some _____
  □ damp odor detected in the _____
□ **some** white stains / **(efflorescence)** noted on house's foundation wall **is type of evidence** one finds **when water problems exist to a limited extent**

Window Problems

□ the **following window problems** need attention:
  □ _____
  □ _____

Item Number   _Description of Condition, Issue or Problem_

_____. _____

_____. _____

_____. _____

_____. _____

_____. _____

_____. _____

_____. _____

_____. _____

_____. _____

_____. _____

_____. _____

_____. _____

_____. _____

_____. _____

_____. _____

_____. _____

_____. _____

_____. _____

_____. _____

_____. _____

_____. _____

_____. _____

_____. _____

_____. _____

_____. _____

_____. _____

_____. _____

_____. _____

_____. _____

_____. _____

_____. _____

_____. _____

_____. _____

_____. _____

_____. _____

_____. _____

_____. _____

_____. _____

_____. _____

_____. _____

_____. _____

_____. _____

_____. _____

Systems

Electrical System

- **overhead or underground:** (overhead) (underground) electrical service
- **number of wires:** (2-) (3-)
- **voltage:** (110) (220) volt
- **amperage:** (30) (60) (100) (125) (150) (200) (400) (_____) amps
- **electrical service for this home's electrical requirements:** (sufficient) (marginally sufficient) (insufficient)
- **type of electrical panel:** (circuit breaker panel) (electrical standup service panel) (fuse box)
- **condition of electrical panel:** (good) (satisfactory) (poor) (except as otherwise noted)
- **existence of electrical ground connection(s):** to a (water pipe) (and to a) (main stake)
  - □ but no electrical ground connection could be found to a (water pipe) (main stake)
  - □ an electrician should be engaged to locate the house electrical ground connections
- **condition of electrical ground connection(s):** (good) (satisfactory) (poor) (except as otherwise noted)
- **wiring type:** (romex) (bx) (flex conduit) (EMT) (knob and tube)
- **material of wiring:** (copper) (aluminum)
- **wiring condition:** (good) (satisfactory) (poor) (except as otherwise noted)

Heating System

- **number of zones:** (1-zone) (2-zone) (together these _____)
- **brand of heating plants:** (Carrier) (Lennox) (York) (Payne) (_____)
- **fuel type:** (gas-fired) (electric) (oil-fired)
- **type of heating:** (forced warm air furnace) (gravity) (electric radiant) (steam boiler) (hot water boiler)
- **B.T.U. per hour rating:** _____(input) (output)
- **heat production requirement for this size home:** (sufficient) (marginally sufficient) (insufficient)
- **operation of unit(s) during inspection:** (it was operating) (they were operating)
- **and functioned:**
  - □ normally or within normal limits
  - □ within normal limits, except as noted
- **inoperation of units(s) during inspection:** (it was not operating) (they were not operating)
  - □ be certain that the heating plant is demonstrated to your satisfaction before closing
  - □ be certain that the heating plants are demonstrated to your satisfaction before closing
- **ventilation of fuel-fired heating plant(s):** (satisfactory) (restricted)
- **note comments regarding:** (the age of the heating plant[s]) (the condition of the firebox) (_____)

Plumbing System

- **type of water lines:** (copper) (&) (galvanized iron) (plastic)
- **observed condition of water lines:** (acceptable - with no water leaks detected) (acceptable, except as noted) (poor)
- **type of gas lines:** (black iron) (galvanized) (_____)
- **condition of gas lines:** (no odors detected) (no odors detected, except as noted) (poor)
- **type of drain lines:** (cast iron) (&) (galvanized iron) (plastic)
- **observed condition of drain lines:** (acceptable - with no leaks detected) (acceptable, except as noted) (poor)
- **waste drainage tests during the inspection:** (suggests satisfactory performance) (suggests satisfactory performance, except as noted)
- **reported type of waste drainage system:** (sewers) (an independent waste drainage system consisting of _____)
- **water pressure tested at outside hose bibb:** (_____) pounds per square inch
- **water pressure inside building:** (high) (normal) (generally somewhat low) (generally low)
- **number of plumbing fixtures:**
  - ☐ _____ sinks
  - ☐ _____ bathtub(s)
  - ☐ _____ toilet(s)
  - ☐ _____ stall shower(s)
  - ☐ _____ bidet(s)
- **operation of plumbing fixtures:** (okay) (okay, except as noted)

Structural System

In consideration of the age of the building, the size and construction type of the building, the
- **floors were level:** (within normal tolerance) (within normal tolerance, except as noted) (but some sloped beyond tolerance) (_____)
- **walls were plumb** (within normal tolerance) (within normal tolerance, except as noted) (but [one] [some] [leans] [bowed] [bulges])

The following **observable structural members were** (satisfactory) (satisfactory, except as noted):
- ☐ the concrete pier/footings
- ☐ the poured (concrete) (concrete block) foundation walls
- ☐ the wooden posts
- ☐ the (steel lally) (wood) column(s)
- ☐ the (steel) (wooden) main beams or girders
- ☐ the floor joists
- ☐ the ceiling joists
- ☐ the purlins
- ☐ the rafters
- ☐ the ridge member(s)

An **indirect examination** of the balance of the structural members reflected no (other) noteworthy problems.

Water Heating

- **brand(s) of heating unit(s):** (American) (A.O. Smith) (_____)
- **fuel type:** (gas-fired) (electric) (oil-fired)
- **number of tank(s):** (1) (2) (3) (4) (__)
- **tank capacity size:** (30) (40) (50) (75) (80) (100) gallons
- **recovery rate:** _____ gallons per hour
- **input rating:** _____ B.T.U.'s per hour
- **operation of unit during the inspection:** (it was operating) (it wasn't operating)
- **temperature of hot water produced:** _____ degree hot water
- **hot water production requirement for this home in consideration of the amount of hot water outlets there are available:** (sufficient) (marginally sufficient) (insufficient)

Additional Items to Check

☐ **rodent evidence:**

    ☐ no evidence of rodent evidence for damage against the structure was detected

    ☐ have the premises checked by a licensed pest control company

☐ **termite evidence:**

    ☐ we couldn't locate any outward evidence of termite infestation in accessible and observable areas - although termites can exist in inaccessible and unobservable areas

    ☐ have a separate termite inspection by a licensed treatment company

☐ **main floor water penetration evidence:**

    ☐ there was no considerable evidence of flooding, seepage or leakage observed in the accessible and observable areas

    ☐ there was no considerable evidence of flooding, seepage or leakage observed in the accessible and observable areas - but this doesn't mean to say that water problems will not develop after the inspection or this does not assume that water problems don't exist in the inaccessible and unobservable areas at the present time.

☐ **electrical remote disconnect(s) for the central air conditioning condenser(s):**

    ☐ present

    ☐ present at each unit

    ☐ (is) (are) absent and should be provided

☐ **seismic straps around hot water heater:**

    ☐ two heavy duty straps anchored this tank to a wall

    ☐ only one strap anchored the tank

    ☐ seismic straps need to be provided

☐ **temperature / pressure relief valve:**

    ☐ was present

    ☐ none exists

☐ **water pressure regulator:**

    ☐ the reducing valve was present

    ☐ none exists

☐ **fire-rated door between house and garage:**

    ☐ present

    ☐ does not exist

☐ **overhead garage door springs:**

    ☐ safety springs were present for both sides of the garage's overhead door

    ☐ one or more was broken

    ☐ are not of the safety spring variety

☐ **interior** (wooden) (wrought iron) (metal) **(banister[s]) (railing[s]):**

    ☐ sturdy

    ☐ need corrective work, including _____

☐ **sampled operation of windows** in consideration of the age of the house:

    ☐ generally good

    ☐ generally fair

    ☐ generally sticky

    ☐ generally poor

☐ **sampled operation of doors** in consideration of the age of the house:

    ☐ generally good

    ☐ generally fair

    ☐ generally sticky

    ☐ generally poor

☐ (fiberglass) (loose fill) (_____) **insulation in attic space:**

    ☐ suitable

    ☐ suitable but is minimal by today's standards

    ☐ insulation is missing at _____

Items in Working Order

☐ well pump _____

☐ water pump _____

☐ sump pump _____

☐ electric strike - gate opener _____

☐ driveway's automatic (roll) (swing) gating _____

☐ _____ single overhead (lift) garage door(s) _____

☐ _____ single sectional garage door(s) _____

☐ _____ double overhead (lift) garage door(s) _____

☐ _____ double sectional garage door(s) _____

☐ side-by-side garage doors _____

☐ track garage doors _____

☐ _____ automatic garage door opener(s) _____

☐ exterior fire pit _____

☐ _____ gas barbecue _____

☐ underground lawn sprinkler system
       ☐ but be sure all water spray action
         from those sprinkler heads that are
         located nearby the house are diverted
         away from the building structure
       ☐ _____

☐ swimming pool pump and _____ motor _____

☐ swimming pool water fill _____

☐ _____ pool filter _____

☐ _____ (swimming pool) (spa) heater _____

☐ swimming pool light _____

☐ _____ pool sweep _____

☐ (spa) (hot tub) jets - bubbler _____

☐ (spa) (hot tub) filter _____

☐ sauna _____

☐ front door knocker _____

☐ (front) (side) doorbell(s) _____

☐ (electric) (gas) _____ cooktop _____

☐ (electric) (gas) _____ built-in range _____

☐ _____ (double) (self-cleaning) (electric) (gas) wall oven(s) _____

☐ _____ microwave oven _____

☐ _____ range hood / light / fan _____

☐ _____ kitchen exhaust fan _____

☐ _____ refrigerator _____

☐ _____ freezer _____

☐ _____ dishwasher _____

☐ kitchen sink water spray _____

☐ _____ kitchen sink faucet water spray _____

☐ _____ horsepower sink garbage disposal unit _____

☐ _____ trash compactor _____

☐ _____ instant hot water sink dispenser _____
           ☐ was producing _____ hot water

☐ _____ washer _____

☐ _____ (vented) (unvented) (gas) (electric) clothes dryer _____

☐ _____ light dimmer(s) _____

☐ _____ fireplace _____ damper _____

☐ _____ fireplace _____ damper _____

☐ _____ fireplace _____ damper _____

☐ _____ sliding glass door _____

☐ _____ (110 volt) (220 volt) room air conditioner _____

☐ _____ (110 volt) (220 volt) room air conditioner _____

☐ _____ (110 volt) (220 volt) room air conditioner _____

☐ furnace humidifier _____

☐ _____ central air conditioning system _____

☐ _____ central air conditioning system _____

☐ roof-mounted evaporative cooler _____

☐ hot water circulating pump _____

☐ _____ intercom _____

☐ _____ radio / intercom _____

☐ _____ security alarm system _____

☐ (battery) (hard-wired) (hard-wired with battery backup) smoke detector of the

_____

☐ (battery) (hard-wired) (hard-wired with battery backup) smoke detector of the

_____

☐ _____ carbon monoxide detector of the _____

☐ _____ carbon monoxide detector of the _____

☐ _____ central vacuum cleaning system _____

☐ _____ bathroom (exhaust) (/) (heater) fan _____

☐ _____ bathroom (exhaust) (/) (heater) fan _____

☐ _____ bathroom (exhaust) (/) (heater) fan _____

☐ _____ bathroom heat lamp _____

☐ _____ electric strip heater of the _____ bathroom _____

☐ _____ electric strip heater of the _____ bathroom _____

☐ _____ electric strip heater of the _____ bathroom _____

☐ pull-down ladder to the attic _____

☐ _____ attic fan _____

☐ _____ roof turbine ventilator(s) _____

☐ _____

☐ *Note that because some presently operating equipment is subject to failing before the time of closing, it is recommended that these items be once again demonstrated a day before escrow closes.*

Ratings

The (home) (building) was in:

For Cleanliness
- ☐ an unclean
- ☐ a relatively clean   state.
- ☐ a clean

The (home) (building) was:

For Maintenance
- ☐ not fit for occupancy.
- ☐ in a run-down
- ☐ in a worn
- ☐ in a reasonably maintained   condition.
- ☐ in a reasonably well maintained
- ☐ in a well maintained
- ☐ in a normal condition for new construction.

Nonetheless,

Detection of Problems
- ☐ many serious problems were found.
- ☐ some serious problems were found.
- ☐ few serious problems were found - most were moderate and minor problems.

The building is rated to be in a

From a structural engineer's standpoint
- ☐ structurally unsound
- ☐ potentially sound
- ☐ marginally sound   condition.
- ☐ fundamentally sound
- ☐ structurally sound

The building and premises are rated to be in

Taking all things into consideration
- ☐ unacceptable
- ☐ poor
- ☐ poor-to-fair
- ☐ fair   condition.*
- ☐ fair-to-good
- ☐ good
- ☐ good to excellent
- ☐ excellent

presuming, of course, for example, that
- ☐ *the grounds are deemed to be geologically sound;*
- ☐ *there are no hazardous wastes to be found;*
- ☐ *and the premises are deemed to be environmentally safe.*

Note that the condition of the building
- ☐ *might change after the inspection;*
- ☐ *that the building should be reinspected before escrow closes, preferably after the furnishings have been removed;*
- ☐ *and, that it is recommended that the seller certify that there are no additional problems above these inspection findings.*

www.ingramcontent.com/pod-product-compliance
Lightning Source LLC
LaVergne TN
LVHW061259060426
835509LV00013B/1487